KUT
The Death of an Army

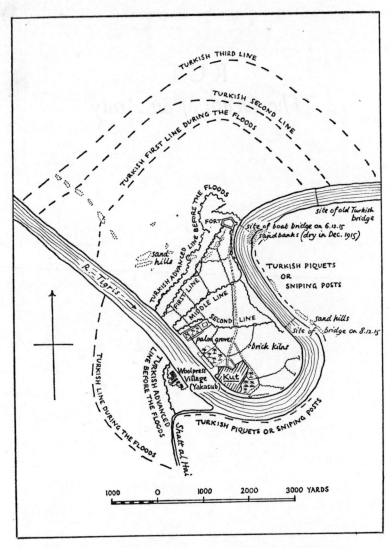

The Defence of Kut al Amara December 1915—April 1916

KUT

The Death of an Army

RONALD MILLAR

LONDON

SECKER & WARBURG

First published in Great Britain 1969 by
Martin Secker & Warburg Limited
14 Carlisle Street, Soho Square, London WIV 6NN

Copyright © 1969 by Ronald Millar

SBN: 436 27990 8

Printed in Great Britain by
The Camelot Press Ltd., London and Southampton

CONTENTS

ILLUSTRATIONS

All illustrations are contemporary. The author and publishers would like to thank the Imperial War Museum for permission to use illustrations 1–11, 13; and Lt. Col. A. J. Barker for illustration 12.

MAPS

'No man goes as far as he who knows not whither he goes.'

Oliver Cromwell

I

THE ROAD TO NOWHERE

It was late in the afternoon of one day in mid-May 1916. The remains of the Palace and Audience Hall of Chosros 1, plundered and destroyed by the Arabs under Omah 300 years before, reared high above the parched, brown country on the left bank of the Tigris.

Ctesiphon was no stranger to violence and bloodshed. For centuries it had been the battlefield of the Middle East. Assyrians, Persians, Greeks, Arabs and Justinian's Romans had fought and died at this tumulus-bubbled and desolate spot. Now the brazen sun of Mesopotamia was once more to be the accomplice in the death of another army. Approaching the white-stone ruins was a long, straggling column of some 2,000 British soldiers. Some still wore the remains of khaki drill tropical uniform; others were almost naked. They had stumbled and staggered for nearly fifteen miles that day without water or food. The suffocating heat had reduced the men to the point where brains were numb and eyes had taken on the blank stare of the hopeless. The wake of the column was strewn with human litter, the dead, the dying and others, unable to march any further, waiting for death from the rifle-butts of their Arab guards.

These Kurdish guards had gone on the rampage soon after the troops had marched out of the temporary Turkish prisoner-of-war camp at Shumran, now some eighty miles behind. At first they had stolen the prisoners' food rations, then their water-bottles and even their boots. Those who had managed to retain their footwear had tried to help their less fortunate comrades whose blood- and dirt-caked feet had refused to carry them any further, but it had been too much. Now those who fell behind were never seen again. Earlier these men had fought back at the

savagery of their guards but now almost senseless with sun-
stroke and exhaustion they were resigned to their fate. Some
were even impatient for death and an end to their misery.

A party of British officer prisoners-of-war, separated from
their men at Shumran a week before and now being taken upstream by steamer, saw just a part of the tragedy. The men were
frequently attacked by the mounted guards for no discernible
reason. As the column drew near the halted steamer the blistered
faces of the men could be clearly seen. As they straggled by they
held their hands out hopelessly to the officers. Some fell and
were beaten with cudgels and by what appeared to be whips.
Many were desperately ill with cholera and a green ooze issued
from their lips. One private chose death in his own time. He
halted and fumbled inside the remains of his tunic for a cigarette
end. Lighting it, he drew deeply, and then with his arms about his
head as if to shield the hateful column from sight, he threw himself face downwards in the hot dust. He puffed steadily as the
first rifle blow struck his body then the cigarette, still smoulder-
ing, rolled from him. Where the man had obtained the cigarette
was difficult for the officers to guess, for all tobacco had been
exhausted many weeks before. It was thought that the man
must have been saving the cigarette for a special occasion.

Thus the pitiful trail into captivity spread its dry bones from
Shumran, through Aziziya, Baghdad, Tikrit, Mosul, Nisibin,
Ras al 'Ain, Mamourra and Aran. The ambassador of the then
neutral United States of America, Mr. Bissell and his country's
consuls in many parts of the Turkish Empire, saw the results of
the terrible march and protested with all the means at their disposal. In a number of cases they were able to ease the plight of
the British and Indian troops. In others they could do nothing.
Some of the troops survived; the majority marched on for ever.

At the end of the war a British parliamentary report deplored
what it described as the indifference and apathy of the Turkish
authorities. But the events that led up to this tragic affair
clearly displayed that the Ottomans did not have the sole mono-
poly of these shortcomings. Just six months before these men of
the 6th Poona Division had been considered invincible. British
newspapers had feted their victories and there had been many.

But they had been urged on to reap the harvest of too much optimism and too little foresight. 'Baghdad by Christmas' had been the call. The strategy had almost succeeded but the advance, like so many others down the centuries, had foundered at Ctesiphon.

The Mesopotamian theatre of World War 1, dubbed a sideshow because it lacked the emphasis of the numbers of the Western Front, in actuality wanted for nothing in the way of calamity and horror. In fact it generated its own kind of nightmare.

The original expedition to Mesopotamia had quite modest objectives. For some years prior to the outbreak of war Great Britain had exercised a protectorate over the sheikdoms of Kuwait and Mohammera. This influence became vital as the British Navy began to rely increasingly on oil for its motive power as the junction of the pipeline which ran down from the Persian oilfields was on Aberdan Island in the Shatt al Arab at the confluence of the Tigris and Euphrates rivers. Britain had also purchased a controlling interest in the Anglo-Persian Oil Company which owned the pipeline. To protect the 150 miles of pipeline was beyond the resources of the British military at the time but it was considered that if Basra was captured this would encourage the Arabs in the area to throw off the cruel oppression of their Turkish masters and join the victors. This would be the first stone in an avalanche that would sweep the Turks out of Mesopotamia altogether.

On 22 November 1914, within three weeks of the commencement of hostilities against Turkey, Basra was occupied without difficulty by two Indian Army brigades under the command of Lieutenant-General Sir A. Barrat. The Turks fled northwards but the Arabs, far from supporting or even remaining indifferent to the British occupation, were drawn to the side of the enemy. The Arabs had succumbed to the brilliance of German and Turkish agents who had preached a *Jehad* or Holy War wherein the forces of Islam would unite against their Christian oppressors. These agents had also been at work in Egypt, Arabia, Persia, Afghanistan and within India itself. Basra, however, had been captured by little more than a rattle of sabres and nobody was concerned overmuch by the disaffection of the Arabs. It was now that the heady wine of victory began to flow too well and the party began to get out of hand.

The expedition—designated 'Indian Expeditionary Force "D" '—was in no condition for a prolonged overseas campaign. A non-aggression treaty with Imperial Russia and economies over the preceding years had reduced the Indian Army to a standard commensurate with that of the South African War. These reductions had been made on the assumption that India need not contemplate a war against a modern army and its army's equipment was restricted to the requirements of a frontier war against fractious tribesmen. The shortage of artillery was acute; there were no heavy guns; although a plan to form an air corps had been approved shortly before the outbreak of war nothing had yet been done about it. Other deficiencies included such items as wire-cutters, telephones, transport for drinking water, Very lights, signal rockets, tents, mosquito nets, sun-helmets, periscopes, telescopic sights, loophole plates, flares, hand-grenades and even blankets and clothing. It was in medical arrangements, however, that the shortages were the most acute in every department. There was a lack of drugs, dressings, and splints for broken limbs. There was not one hospital ship available for service in Mesopotamia. These shortages were amplified by the extremely enervating and unhealthy climate. Within a matter of weeks temperatures fluctuated between 20 and 122 degrees Fahrenheit and almost every noxious disease was endemic.

Such considerations, however, were engulfed in the wave of optimism which succeeded the rout of some 4,000 Turkish irregulars at Basra. Sir Percy Cox, formerly adviser on the area to the Viceroy of India, Lord Hardinge, and now with the expedition as political agent, threw his considerable authority on the side of those who were in favour of further conquests, even of Baghdad itself. Cox was of the opinion that such an advance would meet with slight opposition from the enemy which must now be badly demoralised. The capture of Baghdad would almost equal in importance that of Constantinople.

The Indian Government, however, although impressed, would have none of it. After the despatch of another brigade to complete the 6th Poona Division under Major-General Townshend no further troops were available for such an ambitious plan. In fact this and the other expeditions to France, Egypt and East Africa had already reduced that country's military state to a level which gave rise to grave concern. The territorial troops which had replaced the regular units were fit neither in training nor in equipment for such a role. Already there was trouble on the North West Frontier (the merest mention of this quarter was enough traditionally to rush a viceroy into the thicket of near hysteria) and the political unrest in the Punjab threatened daily to deteriorate into something worse.

The Baghdad faction, however, refused to be entirely put off. If an advance to Baghdad was temporarily out of the question, why not one of a more modest nature to Qurna which was only another fifty miles further inland? The advantages of such a move were listed as 1. its commanding military value; 2. possession of the town would mean the control of the whole Shatt al Arab; 3. it would have an advantageous effect on the morale of the local Arabs; and 4. it would gain the entire rich cultivated area from Qurna to the sea. The then Secretary of State for India, Lord Crewe, objected but he was overruled and the operation was successfully concluded on 9 December with the surrender of the town and the capture of 1,200 prisoners. It was at Qurna in February 1915 that the viceroy inspected his troops and returned to India entirely satisfied with their state and with high hopes of future conquests.

On 9 April Sir John Nixon arrived in Mesopotamia with sufficient troops to make up an incomplete army corps and instructions to occupy the whole of the Basra vilayet (province). It was confidently expected that the imminent landings in Gallipoli (1 May) and an expected Russian advance in Armenia would prevent any Turkish reinforcements from arriving in Mesopotamia. Although the force was now doubled its medical equipment had not been increased and the two divisions (6th and 12th) had only enough field ambulances for one. There was also a serious shortage of trained officers for at the outbreak of war all the Indian Army officers who had been on leave in the British Isles had been impressed for service in France.

The arrival of Nixon in Mesopatamia has been described as a landmark—it was more like the trump of doom. To comply with his orders meant the advance of some sixty miles further inland and the capture of Amara on the Tigris and Nasiriya on the Euphrates. These towns were approximately 100 miles apart. Here another deficiency began to assert itself. Mesopotamia, which consists of the lower basins of those two great rivers, presents some unique problems to an occupying force. Practically the whole of lower Mesopotamia is below the level of these rivers in the flood season. At one time, the rivers had been kept in check by low mud walls called 'bunds' but due to Turkish neglect and mismanagement, along with native indolence, the 'bunds' had fallen into disrepair. Because of its low-lying nature just one break was enough to flood many square miles of surrounding country.

The rivers are lined with marshes which are not contiguous with the waterways but are sometimes as much as four miles away from the banks. The land in between is bare and flat and criss-crossed with numerous creeks and ancient and modern irrigation channels. These marshes wander at the behest of the prevailing winds. A strong northerly wind, for example, causes them to migrate for a mile or even two in a southerly direction, edging silently forward, some twelve to fifteen yards in a minute. The annual rainfall is only six and a half inches but five-sixths of this falls between October and April. A slow, steady fall seldom occurs and sudden violent downpours deliver the average rainfall *en bloc*. The effect of this is to turn the sandy loam soil into a thick, tenacious mud and all movement is brought to a slithering, sticky halt. A tented military encampment on raised ground would suddenly find itself entirely surrounded by quagmires. The building of mud 'bunds' around encampments and trenches to prevent inundation became the normal occupation of the troops.

The rainfall, however, has little to do with the two annual floods which occur in March and in April. These major floods are caused when the rivers are overloaded by the seasonal melting of the ice and snow at their sources in the Armenian and Caucasus mountains. Unfortunately, these inundations occur when the ferocity of the winter rainstorms is beginning to abate and when a reasonable temperature prevails which would permit comfortable military manœuvre. In April, when the waters start to recede, the temperature soars into the hundreds, not just for days but for weeks at a time. Mesopotamia changes from a freezing, waterlogged, wilderness into a parched oven. The floods evaporate or crawl back into the rivers which shrink for a great deal of their length to a depth of little more than four feet.

River transport was, therefore, essential for the movement of troops and supplies but because of Mesopotamia's extreme climatic fads, the craft had to be of a shallow draught. If the depth below the waterline was much more than thirty-six inches they would be useless for a greater part of the year.

Before Nixon had left for Mesopotamia he had been instructed to forward to India details of his transport requirements as soon as he was able to assess them. On 10 July 1915, he complied. Nixon thought that six paddle steamers, three stern-wheel steamers, eight tugs, and forty-three barges would answer his immediate needs.

He warned the authorities at army headquarters in Simla:

> The inadequacy of the light-draught fleet has, nevertheless, been a constant source of delay, uncertainty and anxiety. Now it is clear that time and experience will not mend matters, but that wear and tear and the course of events must inevitably tend to steady diminution of the shipping for military operations on these rivers.[1]

Nixon enclosed a full and complete appraisal by his chief of staff, General Kemball, who concluded:

> In short, more powerful light-draught river steamers and plenty of them, and not only ships, but personnel and material for their maintenance, are regarded by the general staff of this force as our principal need. It is also thought necessary to add the warning that if steps are not taken in good time

to meet these requirements there are grave risks of a breakdown at possibly a serious moment. At the present time we
cannot make the most effective use of the troops available
owing to the want of ships, and in any crisis, insufficiency
of river transport would limit the scope of reinforcements,
while a breakdown of shipping might have still more serious
consequences. A properly equipped river fleet would double
and treble the effective value of the Army in occupation of
Mesopotamia at the present moment, and would continue
to be an important military asset, even if a broad gauge
railway to Baghdad were built. The formation of this fleet is
considered therefore as our special and most important need
at the present time.[2]

Eventually, after considerable delay because of divided
responsibility, the request for river transport was forwarded to
London. It was considered, quite correctly, that it would be
quicker to have the river-craft built in Britain rather than in
India, which lacked the necessary materials and skilled labour.

The India Office in London then proceeded to enact a master-
piece of bureaucratic cheese-paring. It approached the London
firm of Lynch Brothers who, having held the transport con-
cession for the Tigris for more than half a century, had more than
a fair idea of the type of craft required. Lynch Brothers offered
to place the necessary instructions with the shipbuilders,
arrange for the shipment of parts and supervise the erection on
arrival at Basra. The firm would bring an expert from Mesopotamia to see that all went smoothly and that there were no
delays. They would do this, the firm said, for ten per cent of the
value of the order, which was estimated to come to a total of
£600,000. The India Office reacted sharply. The officials said
that they thought the fee was far too high but they were prepared to make a payment of 1,500 guineas. The firm answered
that they considered this figure inadequate but, purely for
patriotic reasons, would provide the service mentioned for a
nominal 2,000 guineas. The offer was refused.

Acting on the advice of its part-time consultant naval
architect, Sir John Biles, the India Office borrowed the necessary

drawings from Lynch Brothers and approached a firm of shipbuilders themselves. The result was chaos. Certain 'improvements' were incorporated in the designs of the craft which made them almost useless for the purpose for which they were required. For example, larger engines were thought necessary so that the tugs could navigate the rivers with greater ease. This decision was made without thought that more powerful engines would increase the weight of the craft and increase their draught over the maximum governed by the drought depth of the rivers. The parts were despatched to Basra in crates that were neither numbered nor did they contain the necessary erection instructions or plans. Unskilled personnel, without mechanical means of lifting the heavy metal sections or the knowledge to put them together, floundered in mud and bewilderment. Such was the ignorance of such operations that the first bottom sections to arrive were placed in the river without superstructure. The would-be erectors watched amazed as they sank from view. Once Nixon had submitted the required report on the transport situation he dismissed the matter from his mind. Although he complained privately of the inhibiting nature of the shortage he never did so to India. He completely ignored the inevitable consequences of this neglect.

Nixon first defeated a determined Turkish counter-attack, supported by a large number of Arabs, which was launched almost at the gates of Basra (11–13 April). He then despatched two infantry and one cavalry brigades up the Karun river to punish some Arabs who had seized the pipeline at Ahwaz. Having thus secured his base and lines of communication the Army Commander turned his attention to the pursuit of glory—the capture of Amara and Nasiriya.

Townshend, with his 6th Division, improvised a mock fleet from the few available river steamers and disguised *mahailas* (small river dhows). So successful was this subterfuge that the Turkish commander of Amara surrendered his 700-strong garrison to a party of twenty-four British soldiers and sailors in the mistaken impression he was heavily outnumbered.

Nasiriya presented little difficulty to Major-General Gorringe's 12th Division but the harrowing experiences of the 400 British

and Indian wounded should have served as a warning to Nixon
as to what could—and did—happen later on a much larger
scale. Needless to say it was not heeded.

This succession of victories stimulated the authorities in
India to agree to a further advance. On 17 July Hardinge
telegrammed Austen Chamberlain, who had now succeeded
Crewe at the India Office, that the occupation of Kut al Amara
was a strategic necessity. After several communications
Chamberlain's caution was overcome and he assented to the
advance. By 14 September Townshend had taken Sheikh Saad
and the following day the fortified Turkish positions at Es
Sinn were overrun. On the 29th he out-thought and outfought
the Turks at Kut and, of his own accord, pursued the enemy
out of Aziziya, a further fifty miles to the north and almost
half-way to Baghdad. The British newspapers reported that if a
mirage had not got in the way the entire Turkish force would
have been annihilated. The age-old magic of Sinbad's city was
beginning to have a powerful pull. As it was the Turks escaped.
The British casualties were 1,000 but it was estimated that the
Turks lost over twice that number. Before the battle both sides
had been roughly equal in strength at about 11,000. Another
150 miles of river had been opened up and Nixon now moved his
headquarters to Aziziya (4 October). Those who were for an
advance to Baghdad began to champ at the bit again.

Sir Beauchamp Duff, the elderly commander-in-chief of the
Indian Army at Simla, had asked Nixon to prepare a plan for a
subsequent advance to Baghdad when he had sent him to
Mesopotamia. This was not forwarded until mid-August and
although it did not refer to any river transport difficulties
which by then had become apparent it did set out the advantages of following the fleeing Turks. Nixon's plan was endorsed
by the Chief of General Staff, Sir Percy Lake, but this officer
also said that the plan was not possible unless troops were
returned from France and elsewhere. Nixon, now safely en-
sconced at Aziziya, announced that the enemy was no longer
in retreat but had occupied Ctesiphon. He was of the opinion
that this offered a first-class opportunity of smashing them.
Meanwhile, the War Cabinet had decided to appoint a committee,

with delegates from the Foreign Office, General Staff, Admiralty and India Office, to consider the possibilities of an advance to Baghdad. Nixon informed Simla that he had overcome his navigational troubles by marching his troops, thus lightening his vessels. Stores and equipment would be offloaded into barges which would then be towed by the steamers. Whitehall turned a receptive ear.

On 8 October Chamberlain asked Nixon what additions to his present force would be required to occupy and hold Baghdad. Nixon said that no additions would be necessary to beat Nur-ud-Din and to occupy Baghdad but a further division would be required if the occupation was to be a permanent one.

Meanwhile, the Secretary of State for India had wired Hardinge, informing him that the War Cabinet was impressed with the military and political advantages of taking Baghdad and every effort would be made to provide the necessary troops. On 21 October the interdepartmental committee issued its report. The committee was of the opinion that only 9,000 enemy troops plus some Arab irregulars were in front of Nixon and no Turkish reinforcements need be expected for the next two months. By the end of January, however, the Turks might be able to concentrate about 60,000 troops at Baghdad but it was considered that by this time Nixon would have been reinforced by two extra Indian divisions from France. The committee recommended the occupation of Baghdad but as it feared that this move might upset the Mesopotamian Arabs it was suggested that their leaders should be assured that an independent Arab state would be created later.

One of the faint voices crying in the Mesopotamian wilderness was that of Townshend himself. His point of view differed markedly from that of Nixon. The commander of the 6th Division said that he considered that at least two divisions would be required to take Baghdad; he only had one which was tired and suffering heavily through sickness. He estimated that 20,000 Turks were waiting for him at Ctesiphon and he was also acutely aware of the river transport problem. Nixon did not agree there was one; anyway he thought that enough transport would be captured at Baghdad to bring up future reinforcements.

No hospital ships would be immediately required as the 400 casualties (Nixon's estimate) that would probably be incurred at Ctesiphon could be accommodated in Baghdad. Other factors began to obtrude into the argument which at best had never been much more than one-sided. The Indian Government wanted the war in Mesopotamia concluded as soon as possible as the situation in the Punjab was deteriorating, Afghanistan was wobbling and Persia, which also appeared to have succumbed to the overtures of the German and Turkish *Jehad* promoters, looked about to enter the war against the Allies. At home there was the imminent failure of the expedition to Gallipoli, Bulgaria seemed about to enter the war on the side of the Central Powers and crush Serbia, and the Franco-British offensive in Champagne and Loos had ground to a bloody halt.

So on 24 October 1915, the final sanction for the capture of Baghdad was given despite a dissenting vote by the Secretary of State for War, Earl Kitchener of Khartoum. Two more divisions were promised 'as soon as possible', although even the optimistic Nixon had once said that a division would be required to combat any Turkish counter-attack within two months. The Indian Government, however, did undertake to rake up another two brigades or so if things went awry in the interim.

On 20 November, Townshend, lacking confidence, with his 6th Division lacking in equipment, wanting in morale and wearied by the intolerable climate, began his fatal advance to Ctesiphon and one of the biggest tragedies in British military history.

II

CTESIPHON

The cold air of the Mesopotamian winter huddled Major H. L. Reilly, Royal Flying Corps, into the cockpit of his B.E.2c biplane. Below, to the right the dun-brown plain stretched unbroken and treeless to the snow-capped Pusht-i-Kuh mountain range which divided Mesopotamia from Persia. Over his shoulder to the left rolled the yellow Tigris, the height of the river banks showing clearly that it was the low-water season. Reilly could see a straggling flotilla of *mahailas* sailing slowly upstream, barely making progress against the current. He watched the crews haul on ropes and the single, great, patchwork, lateen sails swing as the craft tacked in turn round a bend.

A small convoy of modern river steamers, moored against the left bank near a huddle of mud huts at Lajh, next caught Reilly's eye. This would be Townshend's river transport and escort. Here the tented encampment of the British 6th Division, seemingly quite enormous, stretched away from the river bank. Tiny khaki figures waved and Reilly waggled his wings in acknowledgement.

It would be dark in about two hours but it was necessary to make reconnaissance flights either in the early morning or late afternoon as at any other times the mirage made accurate observation difficult. Reilly's mission was to make such a flight towards Baghdad to detect if the Turks were moving reinforcements towards Ctesiphon.

Ahead of him, and about four miles to his left, was the hundred-foot high Arch of Ctesiphon and Reilly pulled his stick back and began to climb to avoid passing too low over the Turkish camp. At 6,000 feet he levelled off. A tent-counting reconnaissance flight over Ctesiphon that morning had revealed that the Turks had not received any reinforcements. Reilly, as flight commander, had checked the other pilot's sketches and maps himself and had counted the groups of tents but there had been no further addition since the last reconnaissance flight on 13 November, ten days ago. At the northern Turkish camp, gesticulating Arabs and soldiery pointed their rifles up at him, but Reilly heard and felt nothing. He had seen something of far greater interest, and banking the B.E.2c into a tight turn, made his way closer to the encampment. Rifle and machine-gun bullets began to cut into the fabric of his lower wing but Reilly knew he must verify what he had seen. There were dozens of new tents, hundreds in fact. Reilly abandoned his trip to Baghdad and reversed his course. Despite earlier reports large reinforcements had arrived. As his aircraft was not fitted with wireless he scribbled a note on the map and marked the position of the reinforcements. To save time he decided to drop his clip-board, with the message, from the aircraft when he flew over the British camp. Reilly calculated that at least another 7,000 enemy troops had lately joined Nur-ud-Din's force.

There was a whine and a sharp crack. A belch of black smoke came from the engine and a fine spray of oil clouded Reilly's goggles. The engine cut. It had been struck by a bullet. Reilly eased the aeroplane into a long shallow glide. He saw a smooth strip of ground, unbroken by irrigation ditches, and bumped into a safe landing. Reilly had been walking for almost three hours when the Arabs captured him.

At his headquarters at Lajh on the left bank of the Tigris Major-General Charles Vere Townshend studied the map before him. He could be reasonably confident that it was accurate. The aerial reconnaissance of Ctesiphon that morning had shown him that nothing had changed. He had asked for a further flight to be made towards Baghdad to see how the land lay, and to make sure that no Turkish reinforcements were on their way. He had heard nothing from the pilot so far, but his plan of attack for the following day could be easily modified, or abandoned, if required.

Townshend had been advised by Nixon's staff that 13,000 Turkish troops with thirty-eight guns had dug themselves in at

Ctesiphon. This had been more or less confirmed by that morning's aerial reconnaissance. Where were Townshend's 20,000 enemy troops now? Almost convinced, Townshend decided that it would be advisable to tell his troops that there were only between 10,000 and 11,000 Turks at Ctesiphon. His own force amounted to about 12,000 infantry, thirty guns, forty-six machine guns and 1,000 cavalry. Townshend considered that if he announced that he had a numerical advantage over the enemy it would bolster the morale of his troops, especially that of the large number of Mohammedans amongst them from the north of India.

The Turks had been swift to take advantage of the fact that Ctesiphon was of special significance to all Mohammedans. Leaflets smuggled to the Indian troops told them that the tomb of Suliman Pak, one of the best-loved servants of the Prophet, was at Ctesiphon. The leaflets accused the Mohammedan troops of fighting for the infidel British against the Turks, their true religious brothers. If this was not serious enough, now they were intending to aggravate the offence by fighting at a spot that was of deep religious significance to Islam.

This propaganda was so effective that Townshend could no longer trust his Mohammedan troops. A private of the 20th Punjabis had shot a fellow sentry and his N.C.O. before deserting to the enemy. Townshend had sent the offending battalion back to Amara where it could do no harm. In its place Townshend had received the 66th Punjabis which arrived that morning. Townshend gave strict orders that the place must never again be referred to as Suliman Pak; henceforth the ancient Parthian name of Ctesiphon would be used exclusively and his battle maps were altered accordingly.

Townshend, as was the custom, had decided to launch his attack against the main Turkish positions on the left bank of the Tigris. Nur-ud-Din had not been idle while the British had debated the advance to Baghdad. He had prepared three defensive lines. The first and main line of defence, extending from the river bank for over six miles in a north-east direction, consisted of fifteen earthworks or redoubts, spaced at intervals of between 400 and 600 yards, connected by a continuous line of trench. The redoubts and the trench had been dug deep and would have been undetectable except for barbed wire entanglements some forty yards in front. Two redoubts on low mounds at the extreme right of the line were plainly visible, however. These imposing-looking earthworks were marked 'V.P.' (Vital Point) by Townshend. In the centre of the Turkish first line was a large and curious L-shaped earth mound, dating from antiquity. Each 'arm' of the mound, running south and east respectively, was about 500 yards long, forty or fifty feet high and about 250 feet wide at the base. This was labelled 'High Wall'. Just north of 'High Wall' was another ferocious looking redoubt on a mound. Because of a deep drainage ditch which protected its face this was called 'Water Redoubt'.

The part of the first line which lay on the right bank extended west along an old Tigris watercourse. The river had once continued for about eleven miles below Qusaiba before turning northwards towards Lajh. In 1912, however, because of the acute bend which gave endless navigational troubles to shipping, the Turks had dug through the narrowest part of the peninsula and altered the course of the river. Where the river curved in front of the Turkish first line lay a barrage of sunken native craft heavily seeded with mines.

Two miles to the rear of the first line, and roughly parallel with it, ran the Turkish second line. This was just to the rear of the Arch of Ctesiphon which dominated the battlefield. The line of deep trenches ran along a string of low sandhills for some four or five miles with its northern extremity curving away towards the rear. The third line, far behind, was along the bank of the Dyala River. The only Turkish communication across the Tigris, to the defences on the right bank, was by a bridge of boats to the rear of the second line and to the north-west of Ctesiphon village.

It should be mentioned here that Ctesiphon, Quasaiba, Bustan and Lajh, although described on battle maps as 'villages', were each nothing more than a collection of half a dozen or so derelict mud huts.

Although Townshend did not know it, his earlier estimate of the Turkish combatant strength had become remarkably accurate. With the newly arrived 51st Division, Nur-ud-Din's force now numbered 18,000 infantry, fifty-three guns and nineteen machine-guns with 400 Iraq Cavalry Brigade. In addition there were several thousand camel-mounted Arabs organised into two 'tribal' brigades under Turkish army officers who had been brought back from retirement. The regular infantry divisions were the 35th, 38th, 45th, and the 51st. It was the encampment of this latter division that Major Reilly had sighted from the air.

Nur-ud-Din felt far from confident about the outcome of the approaching battle. His 35th and 38th Divisions had been badly mauled by Townshend at Kut and, although these had now been completely made up to complement, their fighting spirit was in doubt. The 45th and 51st Divisions, especially the latter which had done particularly well against the Russians in the Caucasus, could be relied upon to put up a stiff resistance, but would this be enough? No accurate estimate of Townshend's force was available; Turkish intelligence was scarcely efficient. There was not one aeroplane available for aerial reconnaissance in the whole of Mesopotamia. Even telephonic communications with forward observers and outposts were frequently interrupted by the Arabs who, although they had yet to discover the significance of the copper telephone cable, were acutely aware of its market value and invariably stole it almost as fast as the Turkish engineers could unwind it. Nur-ud-Din had few maps; a surprising shortcoming as the Turks had been in occupation of Mesopotamia since 1638. In fact the maps captured with Major Reilly were the most accurate and up to date at the Turkish commander-in-chief's headquarters. Completely unaware of the paucity of the force that opposed him, this normally pessimistic man shuddered.

At 1.30 a.m. Townshend issued his orders for the next day's battle. He divided his force into four columns:

Column 'A'

Commander: Major-General W. S. Delamain:
16th Infantry Brigade   2/Dorsets
                         104th Rifles

30th Composite Brigade   24th Punjabis
                          2/7th Gurkhas
                          66th Punjabis
                          117th Mahrattas
82nd Battery, Royal Field Artillery (6 guns)
1/5 Hants Howitzer Battery (4 guns)
Half 22nd Company, Sapper and Miners

Column 'B'
Commander: Brigadier-General W. G. Hamilton:
18th Infantry Brigade   2/Norfolks
                         7th Rajputs
                         110 Mahrattas
                         120th Infantry
63rd Battery, Royal Field Artillery (6 guns)
Half 22nd Company, Sappers and Miners

Column 'C'
Commander: Brigadier-General F. A. Hoghton:
17th Infantry Brigade   1/Oxford & Buckinghamshire
                             Light Infantry
                         22nd Punjabis
                         103rd Mahrattas
                         119th Infantry
76th Battery, Royal Field Artillery (6 guns)
86th Heavy Battery, Royal Garrison Artillery (one section,
    i.e. 2 guns)
17th Company, Sappers and Miners
48th Pioneers
One Squadron of 23rd Cavalry

'Flying Column'
Commander: Major-General Sir Charles C. J. Melliss, V.C.:
6th Cavalry Brigade   'S' Battery, Royal Horse Artillery
                             (6 guns)
                         7th Lancers
                         16th Cavalry
                         33rd Cavalry

Maxim Machine Gun Battery
Motor Machine-Gun Battery (two armoured cars and two motor lorries)
7th Punjabis (these were to be equipped with sufficient mule-drawn transport carts to carry half the battalion at a time).

Townshend explained to his four column commanders that his plan for the next day's battle followed in principle Part 1, Section 102, paragraph 3 of 'Field Service Regulations (1914)', which stated:

Broadly speaking, success in battle may be sought by a converging movement of separated forces so turned as to strike the enemy's front and flank simultaneously, few, if any, reserves being retained by the Commander-in-Chief.

The attack would proceed accordingly. At dawn (about 6.30 a.m.) Hoghton's Column 'C' was to advance on the centre of the Turkish line so as to make the enemy deduce that this was where the main attack was being delivered and rush his reserves to this sector. At 7.30 a.m., when Hoghton's feint would be producing the required results, Hamilton's Column 'B' would make for the enemy's left and rear. At the same time Melliss's 'Flying Column', far to the right, was to move forward and attack the Turkish second line and the reserves at Qusaiba. As soon as the enemy had begun to react to Column 'B's' attack, Delamain's Column 'A' was to advance against the enemy's redoubts at 'V.P.'. Delamain's move was to be the signal for an all-out attack by all the columns on the enemy's line, flank and rear. Then every available gun was to switch on to 'V.P.'.

Townshend explained that the plan was similar to the one which had proved so successful at Es Sinn earlier in the year, but in order to confuse the enemy it would differ in one important detail. The principal blow would be dealt by Delamain's Column 'A' and not by Column 'B' as in the previous battle.

The naval flotilla comprising the gunboats, *Firefly, Comet, Shaitan* and *Sumana* in company with the *Shushan* and *Mahsoudi*, towing barges mounted with heavy guns, was to bombard all enemy positions to the south-west of 'High Wall'. The senior naval officer, Captain W. Nunn, R.N., was given a free hand as to the pursuit of the enemy.

The four columns were to move off out of Lajh under cover of darkness immediately and take up their positions. Each man was to carry one full day's rations and as much water as possible. The role of Townshend's two remaining aircraft, a converted Short seaplane and a Maurice Farman, was to keep the major-general informed as to the line of the enemy's retreat. These instructions were telegraphed to the air station at Aziziya.

Although Townshend ended his conference on this bright note he was also doubting whether the result of the battle on the morrow would be victorious. Even though he was completely unaware of the arrival of the Turkish 51st Division Townshend knew that he was outnumbered and would be attacking against an enemy which excelled in defensive fighting. All his knowledge of warfare warned him that there was, at least, an even chance that disaster was waiting for him at Ctesiphon. His knowledge of warfare, both theoretical and practical, was extensive indeed.

Although the fifty-four years old, London-born major-general was the son of a minor railway official, he was also the great-grandson of the first Marquis of Townshend who had taken command of the British force at Quebec when General James Wolfe fell in 1769. Born in reduced circumstances, young Charles' home life does not appear to have been a happy one. His relatives constantly tried to put him in the Royal Navy. Such an idea was anathema to Townshend who was convinced that his destiny lay with the army but he prevailed and after a few family wrangles he entered Sandhurst. He was gazetted to the Royal Marine Light Infantry in 1881.

Townshend was attached to the column which marched up the Nile Valley to relieve Gordon at Khartoum in 1885 and was involved in the subsequent retreat and battles when it fell. As a young captain he successfully defended Fort Gupis, near Chitral in Northern India, for forty-three days against hostile tribesmen. This was the sensation of the day and for this he received a brevet majority and was created a Companion of the Bath—a surprisingly high honour for such a young officer.

Townshend was with Kitchener in the Sudan and was promoted brevet colonel. He resigned his appointment in 1899 and returned to India, but longing for more activity he applied for, and obtained, a posting to the South African War. The surroundings, however, proved to be uncongenial and he returned to London in September 1900 and adjusted himself to life as a major in the Royal Fusiliers.

Very few of his colleagues had really forgotten that he was the hero of Chitral, a fact which may have been slightly resented by his superiors, who disliked some other peculiarities that he displayed. Townshend had developed a passion for theatrical society and possessed exceptional gifts as a drawing-room raconteur, banjo player and general entertainer. He was capable of an inspired flow of quotations and quips in excellent French and was also an expert mimic. (This talent was later to form the basis of a rumour, almost certainly unfounded, that Nixon on hearing that the general officer commanding the 6th Poona Division could imitate him with extraordinary precision, far from being flattered had regarded Townshend ever after with suspicion.) The senior officers of the Royal Fusiliers were somewhat taken aback. These traits, which could possibly be viewed with amused tolerance if detected in a junior officer, were somewhat out of place in a soldier of standing and distinction. He was, therefore, transferred to a battalion of the regiment then serving in India. Despite this setback, in 1904 he was again promoted brevet colonel and a year later appointed military attaché in Paris; thereafter he became military commander of the Orange River Colony in South Africa and remained in that province until promotion to major-general in 1911. After a short spell in England he again left for India to take command of two Indian brigades. His persistent efforts to obtain a command at the fighting front were rewarded in 1915 when he took over the 6th Poona Division in Mesopotamia. His blinding passion was, and had been for some time, French military science. He revered Foch and to some extent the training of his troops was somewhat coloured by that of St. Cyr. His officers, when temporarily out of favour, were known to remark that their commanding officer was acting at being Napoleon again. According to some of them Townshend had developed some of the quirks and mannerisms of the First Consul.

In the early hours of 23 November 1915, Nur-ud-Din began to receive the first reports that indicated the attack was imminent. These indicated that the enemy troops were carrying out a number of evolutions on his extreme left flank. At 5 a.m. the Turkish commander-in-chief was informed that an enemy force, estimated at a cavalry and infantry brigade, was making straight for his third line at Diyala. It was as much as the Turkish general's staff officers could do to restrain him from hauling his 51st Division out of Qusaiba where it was in reserve and sending it posthaste to Diyala. Still not entirely convinced that the British were not trying to encircle him, Nur-ud-Din sent his cavalry brigade instead. He was reassured only when he received a further report that the British column had now altered its direction of march and was moving towards Qusaiba.

Townshend's troops awoke cramped, cold and still tired. Although they had reached their attack positions some six hours before, a knife-edged wind had made sleep difficult. With heavy eyes they peered into the faint light of dawn. A dense mist enshrouded the enemy positions and the Tigris, and did not disperse when the sun rose at 6.30 a.m. Yelling sergeants brought the men to their senses and Hoghton's column spread itself out along a front of some 1,500 yards and began to advance. Unable to see ahead for any appreciable distance they cautiously felt their way forward in the direction of the Ctesiphon Arch.

Just before 7 a.m. the guns of the British naval flotilla opened fire on a stretch of river bank opposite Bustan where an earlier aerial reconnaissance had reported the enemy were preparing a new redoubt. Fifteen minutes later Hoghton's artillery began to pound the enemy positions in front of the slowly advancing column. There was no answering fire of any description.

At 7.40 a.m. the mist began to lift and Townshend's headquarters, located near Column 'C's' now vacated assembly point, was able to exchange heliograph messages with both Hamilton and Delamain. Hamilton was becoming agitated. Although he could hear artillery fire he had not heard a single rifle shot. Hamilton signalled Townshend: 'Cannot hear Hoghton's guns. Should I advance?'[2] The major-general was in roughly the same dilemma. Although he could both hear and see that Hoghton's artillery was at work he also had not heard any rifle fire from the advancing, but mist-obscured, infantry. He decided he could not delay his turning attack any longer so gave Hamilton, and Melliss on his far right, permission to advance.

At 8 a.m. the mist lifted completely and the Arch shoved its immense shoulders above the desert. Hoghton's advancing infantry could see its façades and recesses clearly against the cloudless blue sky, but even after closing within 2,000 yards of the enemy line they still had not drawn any response. So devoid of life did the Turkish positions seem that Hoghton began to doubt that they were occupied at all. At 8.30 a.m., just as Hamilton's and Melliss's columns were beginning their advance, Hoghton sent an officer and three men forward to take a closer look at the Turkish trenches.

Crouched low the four trotted forward. Fifty yards from the wire the scouts dropped to their hands and knees and crawled quietly forward across a belt of bare but broken ground, the scrub having been burnt away by the Turks to give a clear and unobstructed field of fire. All four were killed instantly as the enemy's machine-guns opened up. As Hoghton's orders were to attack the enemy's trenches in concert with Delamain's advance on 'V.P.' and not before, having now drawn the enemy's fire he ordered his column to dig in. His range finders placed him within 2,500 yards of the Arch.

What happened next has never been explained. A number of reliable witnesses, including Townshend and Delamain, thought they saw 'masses' of enemy troops falling back from the Turkish left flank. Later the Turks denied making any such retreat. Delamain signalled Townshend 'The enemy are in full retreat. May I advance on "V.P."?'[3] Townshend, thinking that this 'retreat' had been caused by the advancing columns of Hamilton and Melliss, gave his consent and Delamain's column began to move forward. The British artillery fire began to plough into the redoubts on the Turkish left.

Hoghton received the news that the Turks were in retreat with some surprise but nevertheless he ordered his troops out of their hastily scraped holes to continue their advance. For a thousand yards the advance progressed over ground criss-crossed by ditches, two or three feet in depth. Hoghton's troops had got to within 900 yards of the enemy positions when the Turkish artillery, machine-guns and rifles, opened up with terrible accuracy.

Hamilton's column, leaving their medical units and reserve ammunition behind, moved forward across a plain devoid of any cover. For some 12,000 to 15,000 yards they were unopposed but then ran into heavy rifle fire from some shallow pits concealed in low scrub. The enemy troops, estimated at some 200, were soon driven out and most of them killed. To their left Hamilton's men could see Delamain's column advancing against 'V.P.'. Hamilton's leading troops, the Norfolks and 110th Mahrattas, continued to press forward until they were brought to a stand-still by heavy machine-guns and rifle fire. The enemy, some 4,000 against Hamilton's 2,500, were in positions covered by the Turkish left flank. The casualties on the British side began to mount.

Far away to the right of Hamilton's troops, Melliss's 'Flying Column' was encountering some stiff resistance. Before the advance had proceeded very far, the Turkish Iraq Cavalry Brigade had approached the right flank of the column, threaten-ing to cut off its transport, field ambulance and signal section. The attack had been beaten off without too much difficulty but after advancing another 1,200 yards the 76th Punjabis in their transport carts had come under heavy fire from enemy infantry. There had been a fierce fight but the resistance proved too strong and they had been forced to dig in. Their losses had been severe, including their two senior British officers. The Cavalry Brigade, to the right, had also met with heavy artillery and rifle fire and, suffering considerably, had been forced to dismount and con-tinue their advance leading their terrified horses.

It had been a little before 9 a.m. when Delamain had received Townshend's agreement to his attack on 'V.P.'. His column commenced its advance on a front of about 600 yards. The

1   General Sir Charles Townshend, Commander of the 6th
Indian Poona Division

2 The Arch at Ctesiphon. The Battle of Ctesiphon, 22–24 November 1915, was followed by General Townshend's retirement to Kut al Amara

Gurkhas advanced on the northern corner of 'V.P.', while the 24th Punjabis moved towards the right. The distance to be covered by the attacking infantry was about 5,000 yards.

The advance rapidly covered two-thirds of the distance to 'V.P.' before coming under heavy artillery fire. Progress was then made in hundred-yard dashes by the men who flung themselves on the ground for a short breather after each spurt. Given covering fire from machine-guns posted to the left and right the Indian troops pressed forward despite rapidly mounting casualties until halted by the barbed wire forty yards to the front of the Turkish positions. There was a heavy burst of fire, a roar of cheers and Delamain's infantry burst through the wire and into the enemy redoubts. At 10 a.m. 'V.P.' was in British hands and was found to be full of enemy dead and wounded. The surviving Turks fled in wild disorder towards their second line.

On entering the Turkish position a number of the Gurkhas, Mahrattas and Punjabis, still full of fight, swung southwards and pushed against a redoubt which was pouring fire on them from the left. By the time Delamain had arrived at 'V.P.' this little band had vanished from view into the Turkish trenches. Because of this for the rest of the day Delamain was under the impression that the 30th Composite Brigade, led by Colonel S. H. Climo, was much stronger than it actually was. He did, however, see the fleeing Turks and, wishing to take advantage of this disorderly retreat, ordered Climo to continue the pursuit towards the second line. The 30th Composite Brigade pressed onwards, despite a large number of Turkish snipers who kept up a hot fire until the attackers came within 600 yards and then got up and bolted.

Meanwhile Hoghton's column, which had temporarily halted in its stride when it met with the heavy enemy fire, had pressed forward again although robbed of artillery support which had ceased to fire because of a mirage—the bane of accurate observation in Mesopotamia—and for fear of hitting its own troops. By 10.30 a.m. the 17th Brigade had got within 700 yards of the Turkish trenches and although the 119th Infantry had now begun to feel the enfilade fire from the enemy positions at 'High Wall' it had not suffered many casualties as yet.

B

Townshend, thinking that the Turkish flight caused by Delamain's attack might well presage an overall disorderly retirement by the enemy towards the third line at Diyala, decided to shift his headquarters to 'V.P.'. At 10.45 a.m. the major-general and his staff mounted their horses and galloped across the two miles of open country to 'V.P.'. The Turks seized this opportunity to mark their progress with a few well-aimed salvos of artillery.

Meanwhile, Climo's advancing troops had come under heavy fire. His primary object was the capture of eight Turkish field-guns which could be seen some way to the west of 'V.P.'. Climo's Indian troops, suffering heavily, had become somewhat demoralised and disheartened but the Gurkhas made a final rush which swept them over the Turkish reserve trenches, which were found later to be full of enemy dead and wounded. The troops then pressed on towards the guns, now abandoned, but they had hardly taken possession of them when a sharp artillery bombardment prompted a further forward movement to spoil the accuracy of the well-ranged Turkish guns. This advance continued for nearly another half-mile but the attackers were still some way short of the Turkish second line when they were checked.

On his arrival at 'V.P.' Townshend could see that the battle was by no means won and he decided to bring Hoghton's column closer to 'V.P.' so as to add more weight to Delamain. Townshend considered that the Turks to his left might retire of their own accord if they found themselves isolated by a heavy attack in the region of 'V.P.'. He ordered his senior staff officer, to use his own words, 'To send a message to Hoghton to bring up his left shoulder and move on "V.P."'.[4] The precise wording of this controversial order is not known for Hoghton was to die at Kut and all his staff officers, who saw the order, were killed at Ctesiphon. Townshend's order meant that Hoghton's column would have to move across in front of an entrenched enemy with its flank exposed to concentrated machine-gun and rifle fire at a thousand yards' range. Hoghton could but comply.

Leaving a few detachments and machine-gun sections to try to keep the enemy's heads down by rapid covering fire, Hogh-

ton's 17th Infantry Brigade began to move across a plain almost
completely devoid of natural cover, at right angles to the direction of the attack. The Turks responded as Hoghton feared.
Every kind of weapon opened up on the British troops as they
side-slipped across the front. Rifle, machine-gun fire and shrapnel inflicted very heavy casualties. Some who witnessed the
move were impressed by the calm way this catastrophic evolu-
tion was carried out, especially by the Oxfords. Others thought
it grotesque, the men moving as sleep-walkers. With their
numbers greatly reduced the brigade at last reached the meagre
cover of a ditch, some 200 yards to the east of 'Water Redoubt'.

Townshend and Delamain watched the decimation of the 17th
Infantry Brigade with dismay. It was obvious that the position
to the left was becoming serious. Hoghton's advance had been
checked and his troops scattered and strong lines of Turkish
reinforcements could be seen advancing to fill the unoccupied
trenches to the south of 'V.P.'. It became essential that 'Water
Redoubt', in fact any other redoubt in the Turkish first line still
in enemy hands, should be captured. Accordingly, Delamain
ordered his artillery to try to check the advancing enemy troops
and then despatched his last reserves, a half-battalion of the
Dorsets and of the 22nd Sapper Company, to help Hoghton
capture the remaining trenches and redoubts.

Given this temporary respite the Oxfords rose from their
shallow ditch and charging over the last hundred yards clambered through the wire and captured 'Water Redoubt' but not
without grievous losses. The Turkish troops caught in the
redoubt were either killed or captured.

Climo's advance and the capture of 'V.P.' seriously weakened
the resistance of the Turks in front of Hamilton and many of
them, seeing their comrades fleeing towards the second line,
decided to join them.

At about 11.30 a.m. the British Cavalry Brigade, far out on
the right, had tried to get round the enemy's flank but had
been so strongly counter-attacked by the Turkish 51st, which
had now moved up from Qusaiba, and the Iraq Cavalry Brigade,
that the British troops had been outflanked themselves and
forced to withdraw for a short distance. Heavy shell fire from

'S' Battery had made it possible for them to hold on for a while, but just before 1.30 p.m. the cavalry had fallen back even further, almost to their pre-dawn assembly point.

Just before midday, the news had reached Nur-ud-Din that his 45th Division, one of those in which he had high hopes, had been virtually destroyed. The arrival of this information had been delayed by a party of Arabs who had vanished into the sandhills with a length of telephone cable. Orders were at once despatched to Jevad Bey, commanding the Turkish reserve, to push forward to check the further decay of the division. Leaving an engineer company behind to check the increasing numbers of Turkish troops which were scurrying rearwards, Jevad Bey had advanced. It had been this movement that had checked Climo's progress when about 800 yards from the Turkish second line. Meanwhile, the badly shattered and discouraged Turkish 38th Division, which had been holding 'Water Redoubt', had retired in disorder to Ctesiphon village.

By 1.30 p.m. the whole Turkish front line was in British hands. The 76th Punjabis were still holding on to their positions but the Cavalry Brigade was being held at its assembly point by sheer press of enemy numbers. Hamilton was unable to progress any further and Climo's advance, although it had captured the eight Turkish guns, had now come to a standstill. To the south, Hoghton was trying to reform his brigade, which had become critically disorganised.

At about noon Nixon and his staff had made a surprise appearance at 'V.P.'. Townshend had told him that he thought all was going well but now he was beginning to realise that Jevad Bey's attack had been delivered by fresh troops. This could be the only reason for the prolonged and persistent Turkish defence. Townshend was still under the impression that only a slightly numerically superior force opposed him. The major-general was given a further jolt when he recognised Climo among the steady stream of wounded who were now being carried past him.

Just before 2 p.m. Climo's force had begun to give way before Jevad Bey's determined onslaught. At first the Indian troops had started to slip away with the wounded. The Dorsets had vainly tried to rally the disheartened Indians but it had been hopeless and they had been left on their own. So intense had become the British fire in trying to repel the attackers that grease started to bubble out of the woodwork of the rifles and the sights became too hot to touch. Because all the column's transport mules had been killed or maimed ammunition began to run short. Efforts were made to manhandle the heavy ammunition boxes forward, but the distance was too great and very little reached the fighting line.

Townshend watched developments through the smoke of action. He realised that something had to be done—and quickly. He ordered Delamain to collect together as many troops as he could and assault the Turkish second line. Delamain thereupon asked Hoghton for the troops, which he had lent him, to be returned and to advance with as many as he could collect to give him support in the coming attack. Signallers, orderlies, anyone who appeared to be unemployed, were dragooned into a makeshift force totalling about sixty in all. After ordering his guns up to 'V.P.' Delamain gave the word for the polyglot force to advance.

The Turkish rifle fire rose to a crescendo and although the force picked up small groups of men as it progressed these barely made up for the losses. But at last it came level with Hamilton's 7th Rajputs. There was a rapid consultation and the Rajput's commander, Colonel H. O. Parr, agreed to combine in an attack on the Turkish second line defences which were about 300 or 400 yards ahead. Some progress was made but several lines of Turkish infantry were seen advancing towards Delamain's guns and 'V.P.' and it was realised that any further forward movement was out of the question. Delamain ordered Parr and his Rajputs back to their former position. Hoghton moving up in support fared little better. He had only been able to collect about 250 men (from six different battalions). The intention was to advance to the left of Delamain's line so as to relieve the pressure. Hoghton's British troops led the advance across the open expanse of desert towards the enemy entrenched in some sandhills about 1200 yards from 'V.P.'. The movement was unmolested until it came within 300 yards of the enemy where

it encountered an extremely hot reception. Halting, the British
line returned the fire but it was well and truly checked. Casualties were thick on the ground and the troops began to look over
their shoulders for signs of approaching reinforcements, which
would make an assault on the Turkish second line practicable.
There were none. The sun sank lower in the sky. Hoghton held
on until it was dark and then he withdrew. Two out of his four
British officers had been killed and some sixty troops in his
small force either killed or wounded.

On the British right the 76th Punjabis were still stoutly
resisting attacks by part of the Turkish 51st Division. The
greater part of this division, together with the Iraq Cavalry
Brigade, were being held off by Melliss but at dusk Townshend
ordered the Cavalry Brigade to retire on 'V.P.'. At 5 p.m.
Hamilton's column, which had dug in during the afternoon as
far as the hard ground would permit, made a final attempt to
press forward but before this attack had had time to develop a
messenger from Townshend told him to break off the action and
retire to 'V.P.' for the night.

Shortly before sunset at 5 p.m. Townshend had reluctantly
come to the conclusion that he could make no further progress
that day. He decided to regroup his force and resume the offensive the following morning. He thought it very likely that the
Turks who, from the number of dead lying around, must have
lost heavily, would retire during the night to their third line at
Diyala. He ordered the British troops to consolidate their positions in the Turkish first line. Hoghton was to hold 'V.P.' and
one mile of trenches to the south; Delamain's troops were to
hold the line from this point to the river, and Hamilton's men
towards the right.

Although the concentration of the British troops on 'V.P.'
was unhindered by the Turks, who had now ceased firing and
withdrawn to their second line, Townshend began to realise that
his troops were in no condition to attack the following day. His
infantry losses were immense. Hoghton had lost 700 men, Delamain 1,000 and Hamilton between 800 and 900. The major-
general modified his orders. As soon as his force had regained a
semblance of order he proposed to take up a more modest posi-

tion near the river where it would be easier to obtain water and food, replenish his ammunition and evacuate his wounded.

Townshend then created a nightmare for himself. During the day's actions all the wounded had been carried to the rear. Now that it was dark, he decided to group them at 'V.P.'. When 'V.P.' had been captured by Delamain at 10 a.m. that morning it was already full of Turkish dead and wounded. To these were added the stricken British and Indian troops. The usual Indian Army method of carrying wounded, on litters, or in panniers slung across the backs of mules, had completely broken down because of the heavy slaughter of men and mules. All wounded unable to walk were brought to 'V.P.' in springless transport carts. The jolting of these carts produced intense suffering and the night was made hideous by the cries of the men. There was little food and water for the wounded, and the medical staff, barely adequate to cope with 400 men, was now faced with the problem of treating ten times that number.

Of 371 British officers, 130 had been killed or wounded. The 255 Indian officers had been reduced to 111. Of the 12,000-odd combatants, 4,200 had become casualties.

As the harvest of the day's reaping was being gathered at 'V.P.' a bitter night wind began to sigh over the flat country and probe its fingers into the trenches where the wounded were lying. They told some terrible stories. When 'Water Redoubt' had been assaulted those wounded but able to crawl into the irrigation ditch in front of the Turkish earthworks had been given a harrowing experience. The Turks, who seemed always able to produce one more card from their sleeves, had flooded this ditch with water. Many of the wounded men had the choice of either drowning or raising their heads above the level of the ditch and being shot down. Others, unconscious, would have drowned if they had not been held up for most of the day by their unwounded comrades. In the three hours that the wounded lay in the flooded ditch, before the capture of the Turkish first line, the water turned crimson. When the Turkish line was clear of the enemy, the wounded were lifted from the ditch and were left lying in their soaking uniforms until the overworked stretcher parties were able to collect them. Those still able to

walk wandered about looking for the few existing field dressing
stations which were crowded and hopelessly inadequate to deal
with the situation. All night parties searched the day's battlefield for wounded. It was standard procedure to have small
parties of men following in the wake of the advancing troops to
collect dropped rifles and other valuable war material. A subaltern of the Oxfords in charge of one party described his experiences:

> When the attack commenced I followed closely behind my
> brigade (17th), but the fire was so heavy and my carts such
> good aiming marks for the enemy artillery that for a consider-
> able time I could not get on with my work; and plenty of
> work there was to do. The whole area was strewn with dead
> and wounded, discarded equipment, rifles, and wounded
> ammunition mules, so that I did not know where to begin
> first. I detailed half my party to carry on with their own work
> of collecting what material they could in the 'Water Redoubt'
> while the other half I used to help the wounded who were so
> numerous that it was quite beyond the power of the ambu-
> lance staff to look after them.[5]

Nur-ud-Din, who during the day's action had lost some 9,500
killed or wounded and a further 1,200 taken prisoner, was profoundly gloomy. Shortly after 9 a.m., following consideration of
the reports which reached his headquarters, the Turkish commander-in-chief issued orders that if it was not possible to
reoccupy the front line without further fighting, the whole force
was to retire to the second line. He spent the night reorganising
his battered force into two army corps; the 38th and 35th
Divisions would be called the XIII Army Corps; the 51st
Division with the 45th the XVIII.

During the night Townshend fully appreciated that his force,
men and animals alike, was exhausted, suffering from cold and a
lack of food and water. His brigades were still disorganised and
troops wandered back and forth trying to find their comrades.
Townshend could see that all his transport carts would be
required to carry his wounded to Lajh, some twelve miles distant. As daylight broke, to further hamper the reorganisation of

his troops into an effective fighting force, high winds whipped up
dense dust storms which obscured the view in every direction.
Townshend could see that his plan to continue the offensive was
hopeless. His force required food, water, rest and reorganisation.
Townshend ordered that only the portion of Turkish line from
'Water Redoubt' to 'High Wall' was to be defended and his
troops were to concentrate in that area. His naval flotilla and
supply ships were told to come upstream to Bustan.

Townshend, however, had his hopes raised by a false report
from the pilot of a reconnaissance aircraft, which said that the
Turks had completely vacated their second line and retreated to
Diyala leaving only a small rearguard of some one or two battalions. The enemy, the airman added, had towed their bridge of
boats further upstream. Townshend now began to believe that
an offensive was still possible. He ordered his Cavalry Brigade
to advance and reconnoitre the watering facilities near the
Ctesiphon Arch. Hoghton's column was to remain at 'V.P.'
until all the wounded had been evacuated, while the infantry
were to leave Melliss's 'Flying Column' and join Hamilton. The
latter commander was to complete the reorganisation of the
18th Brigade at 'V.P.' and then move to 'High Wall', Delamain's 16th Brigade was to reorganise at 'Water Redoubt'. His
Gurkhas and 24th Punjabis were to advance from the first line
and take up a position near the Ctesiphon Arch.

The Cavalry Brigade advanced westwards towards the Arch
and arrived at the river bank and began to water its horses.
Soon after 10 a.m. the Gurkhas and Punjabis, numbering about
400, accompanied by the Maxim Battery and a section of the
82nd Field Artillery, discovered a small tumulus about 2,000
yards South of the Arch and took possession of it. This became
known subsequently as 'Gurkha Mound'. The small party had
not been in occupation long before the Turks opened fire on
them from their second line about 2,000 yards away. The
Cavalry Brigade, which also had been fired upon, was forced
away from the river bank and later returned to 'High Wall'.
They arrived to find a crowd of troops curiously examining two
enormous mortars. They were large brass weapons obviously
extremely ancient, with ornately decorated barrels. Thoughts of

towing the mortars away as prizes were rapidly abandoned when they were found to be far too heavy. Although these weapons were left at 'High Wall' the troops of the 6th Division were never able to quite forget them, as later events proved.

Quite a large number of wounded were still at 'V.P.' when, for some unaccountable reason, a near-by field battery started to pump shells into the Turkish second line. The retaliatory fire was instant and accurate and several shells exploded among the sufferers. The Turkish artillery along the river bank also became quite lively and as this prevented the British ships from reaching Bustan, Townshend was forced to realise that his base would have to remain at Lajh.

Turkish headquarters learned during the morning that the British had entirely evacuated the area to the north and west of 'V.P.' and Nur-ud-Din, realising for the first time that the British force had also suffered heavy casualties and was probably disorganised, ordered a counter-attack on his former first line of trenches. First signs of the attack were seen by the British force at about 4 p.m. At this time Hoghton's 17th Brigade was still at 'V.P.'. The evacuation of the wounded was still proceeding and although every available transport cart was employed in this task, the numbers were so great that only about half had been taken away by sunset. When news of the Turkish counter-attack reached Townshend he sent two battalions from the 18th Brigade to strengthen Delamain and returned the 76th Punjabis to Hoghton at 'V.P.'

At about 5 p.m. the field battery with the small force at 'Gurkha Mound' withdrew to 'High Wall'. This, and a glimpse of the retiring Cavalry Brigade, boosted the morale of the advancing Turkish 35th Division but they were checked by fire from 'Gurkha Mound'.

As soon as the Turkish attack appeared to be a serious one, Townshend passed word down his line that all wounded still waiting at 'V.P.' for transport who were capable of walking should make for Lajh as best they could. A stream of limping, hopping, bandaged men began to make the journey. The more seriously wounded were left lying at the bottom of the trenches.

The Turkish 35th and 38th Divisions moved forward slowly.

By dusk the 45th Division had advanced to within 600 yards of 'V.P.' but it was not until some two hours later that heavy rifle fire opened up all along the line of the Turkish attack. Hoghton's strength at 'V.P.' did not number more than 1,200 'effectives' and these were greatly hampered by the wounded lying around their feet. The Turkish 45th Division continued to attack 'V.P.' until about 2 a.m., but with the exception of a few men who remained within about 200 yards of the British trenches, they at last withdrew, badly discouraged. It is possible that this division had been waiting for the arrival of the Turkish 51st Division before pressing home a heavier and more determined attack but they waited in vain. The 51st had become completely lost. They continued to wander until 2.30 a.m. when they were found by a messenger from the XVIII Army Corps commander and ordered to return to the second line. Unfortunately the horseman did not wait to show them the way and the 51st, considerably exhausted and bewildered, did not arrive back at its appointed place until well after it had become light.

It was extremely fortunate for the British that the 51st did not arrive. Hoghton was running short of ammunition and the situation had become so critical that Townshend had been forced to despatch a column of waggons to fetch more from Lajh. Only by great exertions did it arrive back at the British line by 3 a.m.

Delamain, reinforced by the Norfolks and 120 of the 18th Brigade, was holding four redoubts and connecting trenches to the south of 'V.P.'. Jevad Bey's detachment of the 51st Division attacked the centre of this line, held by a major part of the 16th Brigade, with determination. Townshend, with Delamain, was in 'Water Redoubt' from about 9 p.m. onwards and it was only with difficulty that six vigorous attacks on this position were repulsed. Water for the cooling jackets of the overheated British guns ran short but they were kept in action by the time-honoured method of troops supplying liquid from their natural resources. One of the defenders said: 'They [the Turks] came back to the attack with a great gust of fire that swept down on us like a storm from the Himalayas. Above the din of artillery, rifles cracked like a thousand whips.'[6] At one point the enemy

actually forced their way into the British trenches only to be
bombed out again by the Dorsets.

Southward of 'Water Redoubt' the attack never got near the
British line. Turkish accounts of this action said that its 38th
Division scampered off as soon as they were fired upon. But
things were very different at 'Gurkha Mound'. The 400 defenders
were desperately beating off attack after attack. The 'Mound'
was now entirely surrounded by wildly cheering Turks of the
35th Division who were making frantic efforts to overwhelm the
Gurkhas and Punjabis. Muhammed Amin, one of Nur-ud-Din's
staff officers, wrote later:

> The 35th strove for hours in front of that brave and deter-
> minded little force and, though it lost many men, did not gain
> its end, and many did not succeed in drawing near. Early in
> June 1916, I met Captain C. H. Stockley [commanding the
> Maxim Battery], one of that brave band after his capture at
> Kut al Amara, on the deck of the *Khalifa*. He and some
> hundred of his companions were being taken to Baghdad.
> That officer, as we passed Ctesiphon, gave us many remini-
> scences of that night's fight between his detachment and the
> 35th Division. According to him, that detachment consisted
> of 100 men of the 24th Punjabis and 300 of 7th Gurkhas and a
> [Maxim] machine-gun company, under the command of the
> brave and daring Lieutenant-Colonel Powell—in all 400 men
> and a machine-gun company. Having listened with a forced
> politeness and disdain I was far from feeling in reality, to the
> relation of the secrets of that night by Mr. Stockley, I must
> confess to a deep hidden feeling of appreciation of the dead of
> that brave, self-sacrificing enemy detachment, which for
> hours, only 400 strong, opposed and finally drove back the
> thousands of riflemen of the 35th Division to the second line
> of defence.[7]

At 3.30 a.m. Nur-ud-Din received another of those reports
that seemed expressly designed to produce in him a feeling of
deep melancholy. It came this time from the commander of his
XVIII Army Corps. The report read:

51st Division has lost its direction and is in an unsupported situation. 45th Division, which till sunset continued its attack has retreated in the dark to the second line. I am neither in touch with the XIII Army Corps on the right or the 51st on the left. If reinforcements cannot be sent the divisonal commander [presumably of the 45th Division] considers it impossible to advance and reports the enemy's main body in the Diriyyer group ['V.P.']. At the present all the 45th Division's battalion and company commanders have been killed and the much reduced companies are commanded by N.C.O.'s. Thus we may say that the 45th Division does not exist. Under these circumstances there is no hope for success of the attack. I have ordered the 51st Division back to the second line. I suggest an attempt to defend this line.[8]

But before receiving this elegy, Nur-ud-Din had already issued orders for the withdrawal of his force to the second line. He told the Iraq Cavalry Brigade to cover his retirement and then withdraw itself. A squadron of cavalry was to remain on the look-out among the sandhills well to the left of the 51st Division.

Nur-ud-Din was not short of Job's comforters. His headquarters that night were described as being 'in the depth of despair and despondency. On every brow could be seen the moral and physical signs of discouragement and fatigue. Neither the situation, nor the defences of the second line, were such as to hold out hopes of prolonged resistance.'[9] The Turkish commander, completely unaware of the deplorable state of his enemy, decided that he had only two courses left open to him. Either to break contact with the enemy and retire to a safer position such as the Diyala line or to wait where he was in a state of readiness to retire and hope for the best. Nur-ud-Din chose the latter course.

No records of the British casualties which resulted from the night attack have survived, but they appear to have been comparatively light. The official returns for the 23rd and 24th said that eighty-two were killed or wounded, although a number of these undoubtedly occurred during daylight before the attack.

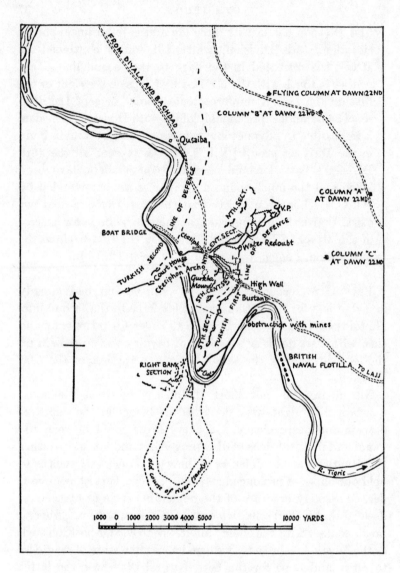

The Battle of Ctesiphon

All was quiet when dawn broke on 24 November. The condition of the wounded still lying at the bottom of the trenches was appalling. There was no water left at all, either for drinking or for bathing wounds. Because of the Turkish counter-attack the previous evening the transport carts, which had been on their way up from Lajh with rations, had been sent back. When food arrived eventually at 8 a.m. that morning, the troops, hale and wounded alike, had not eaten for sixty-three hours. The sound of the picks and shovels, as troops dug shallow graves for the dead, was heavy that morning.

The transport of the wounded to Lajh commenced again in the afternoon. Each with a load of three lying and three sitting, the mule-drawn springless transport carts started on their ten-mile journey to the river. The iron-shod wheels sent shock after shock through the bodies of the men. Although these were the serious cases with head or stomach wounds and broken limbs, no mattresses were available to protect them from the jolts. The carts bumped and clattered over the rough ground. Every few hundred yards a ditch had to be crossed and had to be taken at a rush to get up the other side. The iron floors of the carts rose up and struck the wounded jarring blows on the head. The mules, or in some cases ponies, drawing the carts, reduced to a state of terror by the cries of the men and the smell of blood, frequently broke into a bucketing canter. Some of the wounded, unable to stand the protracted torture, threw themselves out of the carts. All along the trail wounded men, in blood-soaked bandages, staggered and crawled, adding to the mounting congestion.

Shortly before noon of the 25th Townshend cabled Nixon:

The result of yesterday's afternoon and all night battle wherein the Turks, who have been largely reinforced, assumed [the] offensive, was that our wearied men hung on with utmost tenacity and repulsed the Turks at all points. The Turks fell back into their second line entrenchment where they are digging in still. I have concentrated my troops on river bank at 'High Wall'. Hoghton [is] still at 'V.P.' which he is holding on to in order to evacuate the wounded. He will

concentrate with me this afternoon after which I shall retire
to Lajh Reach where my ships are and wait events. Every
sound military reason points to necessity of retirement. If I
went on and had to fight another battle with my three brigades now reduced to 900 men, 700 men and 1,000 respectively
[not easy to reconcile with casualty figures] we would probably meet with disaster. There are prisoners who were fighting
the Russians up in the Caucasus in the two new [Turkish]
divisions from the north. I have come to this conclusion with
great regret and sadness, but it is asking the men to do the
impossible. The effort of driving four divisions out of a fortified position has exhausted my division. The officers and men
have done splendidly.[10]

Nixon had no recourse but to approve this decision and the
British began their retirement. Oddly enough, so had the Turks.
A high-ranking Arab, whose band of cut-throats had been
scouting the area to the south for booty, clattered into Nur-ud-
Din's headquarters. He told the Turkish commander-in-chief
that the British force was arriving at Lajh in a defeated condition. Nur-ud-Din could hardly credit his senses. With a
defeated army he was contemplating a withdrawal and the
inevitable court-martial and now this rogue would have him
believe that he had won the battle. He was convinced that this
was a British plot. They wanted him to hold his present positions
so that they could administer the *coup-de-grâce*. Nur-ud-Din
accused the Arab of lying, worse—of being a spy. The man was
placed under arrest to await torture and hanging when a more
favourable opportunity presented itself. But other reports began
to come in which confirmed the Arab's story. Nur-ud-Din's
hopes began to rise. The deeply offended Arab was released with
apologies and promises of money but inside a few minutes he was
beaten into custody again. A messenger from the senior officer
of the party left behind by the Iraq Cavalry Brigade reported
that the British, having left four battalions and two gun batteries in front of the captured Turkish first line, were advancing
with the remainder of their strength in an attempt to outflank
him to the northwards. Undoubtedly what the officer had seen

was Melliss's cavalry brigade which had moved out to cover the
British retirement but this news firmly convinced Nur-ud-Din
that his original estimation of the situation was correct. The
British, having allowed time for the Arab traitor to spin his
story of the bogus retirement, were now attempting to cut off
his retreat. He gave orders for an immediate retirement to the
Diyala. The Iraq Cavalry Brigade was sent out to attempt to
hold back the British advance and the now considerably shaken
Turkish Army began its retirement, an orderly movement to
begin with, but as panic spread it became a shambles.

Fate was once more to take a hand. An overlooked party of
Turkish cavalry, not having received the order to retire, submitted a routine report that the British had retreated from
'V.P.' and that nobody was now in the old Turkish trenches
except a large number of Arabs who were seeing what profit
could be got out of the stores abandoned by the retreating
British. Nur-ud-Din cautiously sent a scouting party to confirm
this report and then issued orders for his army to retrace its
steps and reoccupy the abandoned second line. He also sentenced
the officer, who had wrongfully informed him of the British
advance, to death.

Nur-ud-Din's army, returning to its former positions, was
spotted by a British reconnaissance plane and it was reported to
Townshend that two large Turkish columns estimated at about
three divisions were again advancing from Diyala. One of the
columns was making its way down the left bank and the others
were moving away from the river and marching inland. It
should be mentioned that Nur-ud-Din had not given orders for
the latter movement. The column seen by the aircraft moving
inland was the 51st Division, which had once again lost its way.

By this time Nixon, after his trip downstream with his
staff, aboard the *Milimar*, had now arrived at Aziziya and was
having second thoughts. He cabled Townshend not to move
from Ctesiphon until he had received a coded cable which was
being despatched shortly. This read:

I do not like your retirement on Lajh for the following military reasons. At the present moment the enemy does not

apparently realise your state and they themselves are apprehensive of being attacked by you; and your resolute attitude
imposes on them. It is certain they will perceive their mistake
as soon as you abandon this attitude and they will recover
confidence and reoccupy Ctesiphon and probably move forward and attack you and turn all Arabs on to us everywhere.
You should have course to prepare a fortified position at
Lajh, on which to retire in case of necessity and to cover your
advanced base, but for [the] military reasons given above I
do not consider retirement desirable at present. No one can
deplore more than I do the sacrifices suffered by your gallant
troops but it is absolutely necessary to keep their spirits up.
[A] wing of West Kents and of 14th Hussars are on their
way to you and a strong brigade arrives in a week at Basra;
and our game is to play for time. There are men at Lajh
belonging to your battalions and you can get them up [to
Ctesiphon]. Picks and shovels can be replaced. Remember
the moral is to the physical as five to one.[11]

By the time Nixon's cables had arrived Townshend and his
force were back at Lajh. Townshend, on reading both messages
on his arrival, was resolute that his withdrawal from Ctesiphon
had been vital. Neither the promises of reinforcements, picks
and shovels nor his commander-in-chief's short homily on the
psychological aspects of warfare made any difference to this
conviction. Townshend cabled in reply:

I received your [telegram] this morning on arrival [at Lajh]
with the force. I adhere strongly to my [telegram] of 25
November. I consider that with 4,300 casualties—which is
the total—and when the brigades are [each] reduced to little
more than a full-strength British battalion, it would have
been madness to remain at Ctesiphon a moment longer than I
did. At 4 p.m. yesterday, two large columns of Turks estimated at 5,000 by air service were advancing from their
entrenched line covering the Diyala, north of Qusaiba, and at
5 p.m. were in sight, one moving along the river bank and one
at a turning distance inland while [a] hostile cavalry brigade
menaced Bustan. There is no question of my engaging such a

force in my present state with the men worn out, so I waited for darkness and moved off in the dark for Lajh, where I am now entrenching and going to make myself comfortable. From a military point of view it would be madness and nothing else to remain at Ctesiphon. Remember you agreed before to my Lajh reasons. I endeavoured to improve upon them at Ctesiphon and flatter myself that I extricated my force under good conditions of manœuvre, the hardest that can be imagined. Had I been attacked in the middle of such an operation, I should have been pinned down by one column and turned and cut off by the other. You must know what the result would have been. I know well. Here I remain and demonstrate up the right bank immediately. Air service reports that the enemy have reoccupied the second line of entrenchments at Ctesiphon and are now advancing. I do not think they will venture to cross the open [country] and attack without their beloved entrenchments. I hope you will approve of what I have done to the best of my judgement. Nothing will alter my opinion. I have acted for the best.[12]

Thus ended the battle of Ctesiphon. It had been a totally unnecessary battle, and, when it had ended, neither side knew who had really won. A few more false reports, or even some reliable ones, could have changed the outcome, especially at the later stage. One indisputable fact did emerge, however. Although the military evolutions were of the early twentieth century, the medical arrangements were not. The evacuation of the British wounded from Lajh was proving a problem. Nixon's estimate of 400 wounded having been far exceeded it was found that the steamers *Bloss Lynch* and *Musul*, neither of which had been prepared as hospital ships, could not possibly accommodate all the wounded. Nixon told the Mesopotamia Commission —a commission which was the result of the public outcry at the sufferings of the troops in that theatre—that 'the alternative before us was to bring the wounded down at any cost of suffering to them, or leave them exposed [to death and mutilation by the Arabs] before the regular Turkish troops had the chance to protect them'.[13] Crammed together on open decks, or covered merely by a thin canvas awning, the wounded left Lajh on the morning of 28 November by barge and steamer. Their sufferings were increased by heavy downpours of rain which saturated their clothing and blankets. Of course there was no means of drying these items. The wounded reached Basra on 17 December, twenty-three days after the battle, and as the ships lay in midstream waiting to be unloaded those downwind of the steamers became aware of a foul stench which came from the men huddled on the decks in pools of filth. When taken aboard the hospital ship *Varela* or admitted to the hospitals in Basra several men who had been put originally aboard the *Musul* and *Bloss Lynch* with comparatively light wounds were found to be dying of bedsores. Many were dead already. Yet Nixon sent a report to India which said: 'General condition of wounded satisfactory. Medical arrangements under circumstances of considerable difficulty worked splendidly.'[14]

Enemy losses too had been heavy. Official Turkish sources said their casualties at Ctesiphon were 9,500 killed and wounded. Nur-ud-Din's staff officer, however, has stated that this figure includes troops captured by the British and deserters, of which there had been many. Amin's estimate is 6,188 killed and wounded. The 51st Division had lost twelve per cent, the 35th twenty-five per cent and the 45th sixty-five per cent. The Turks captured only six or seven prisoners.

III

THE AFFAIR AT UMM AT TUBAL

At 9.10 a.m. on the morning of 27 November Townshend cabled
Nixon from Lajh, that although he possessed ample supplies of
ammunition his food was limited to ten days' rations for his
British troops and seven days' rations for the Indians. When
these became exhausted he proposed to fall back on Aziziya
where supplies could be replenished. He added that his present
position was too close to the enemy for manœuvre and some
friendly Arabs had told him that the area around Lajh was
normally completely flooded by rainstorms in the month of
December. He asked for an approximate date when reinforcements would reach him but concluded pessimistically that this
would probably take another two and a half months.

Shortly after Townshend had sent this message, however, it
was reported to him that a reconnaissance aircraft had sighted
two Turkish columns, numbering about 12,000 infantry plus
another 400 cavalry, advancing towards him. Townshend
decided to commence his retreat immediately. He wrote later:

> I began to see that there was no halting on the Baghdad side
> of Kut al Amara if the enemy really intended an offensive
> with big forces. If he once hooked into my little force I should
> be pinned down and surrounded. Basra was a long way from
> Lajh and I knew no reinforcements could reach me before
> late December.[1]

At 3.30 p.m. the British Cavalry Brigade moved out to cover
the retirement and one hour later the column, with the Turkish
prisoners and transport carts carrying supplies in the lead, began
its march southwards. For a short distance a number of Arab
raiding parties padded in the rear of the retreating column but
the lure of plunder, waiting back at Lajh, was too much for them

and at length they vanished into the mirage of the afternoon. For the remainder of that day the column marched onwards and with the fading light a cold north wind sprang up, biting through the thin drill uniforms—and then came the rain. The pace of the retreating troops was slow with frequent halts to allow stragglers and walking wounded to catch up. The night was intensely black and the tired troops groped their way on hands and knees across gulleys. Occasionally a shot rang out in the darkness and a man fell. This sniping was attributed to ancient firearms of the Arabs because of the long intervals between shots. At 2 a.m. there was a halt for two or three hours and then the march was resumed. The head of the column reached Aziziya just before 4 a.m. but it was not until 8 a.m. that the last troops tottered in. Townshend and his staff stood at the entrance to the camp until all his regiments had arrived.

According to the Turks, their infantry was not able to start in pursuit of the British force at once as the rain had turned the ground into a soggy mess, and when it did its progress had been slow. The Turkish steamers were unable to give chase until the mined obstruction across the river had been removed. Although some Turkish cavalry and camelry did make a half-hearted attack on the British mounted troops in the rear of the column, they were unable to make much impression.

Townshend halted at Aziziya for two days to rest his men and to give time for the wounded at the camp to be loaded on to a steamer, the *Mejidieh*, and some barges. Townshend was becoming completely disenchanted with his river transport. During the retreat from Lajh to Aziziya the steamers, encumbered by the barges which were lashed to either side of the vessels, had been unable to keep pace with the land force. This method was normal practice as the route of the Tigris was too tortuous to allow towing. Owing to the low state of the river, the barges frequently ran aground and were torn from the sides of the steamers. Because of the river's twists and turns the river transport had to travel almost twice the distance covered by the land force. The naval flotilla, which had remained behind at Lajh to burn abandoned stores and to act as rearguard to the other shipping, had fallen even further behind through constantly having to tow the wayward barges off mud banks. It became so delayed that on the night of the 28th the flotilla was still only four miles below Lajh. The *Comet* and *Shaitan* went aground eight miles above Aziziya and remained there all night with sniper's bullets making things rather uncomfortable for all those aboard the two gunboats.

On 28 November the reinforcements that Nixon had spoken of arrived at the British camp. The 14th Hussars joined the Cavalry Brigade and the 2nd Queen's Own Royal West Kent Regiment was added to the strength of Hamilton's 18th Brigade. On the same day the two Turkish Army Corps marched into Lajh on hearing from its scouting cavalry that it was clear of the British.

Shortly after mid-day, Townshend informed Nixon as follows:

Air service reports this morning are [that] large [Turkish] camps are being formed at Ctesiphon. One division of infantry, one cavalry and one artillery brigade [are] moving on Lajh from Bustan. Another column was reported east of Lajh.[2]

He followed this message two hours later with another:

It seems abundantly clear that the enemy has received large reinforcements and that [was] before the battle of Ctesiphon. The troops reported [at Lajh] in my telegram appear to be advanced guard of army corps being concentrated at Ctesiphon. I expect he will advance to Zor, but if he moves from that place to attack me here I shall again refuse battle and fall back to Kut in all probability; for Kut is the proper strategic point which we are bound to hold and is a concentrating point for reinforcements arriving from overseas. My principal object then is to gain time for my concentration with the reinforcements and I must avoid battle for the present, using Fabian tactics. Should he follow me to Kut then so much the better; we ought to destroy him in that case, but personally I do not think he will fight below Zor so far away from his beloved trenches at Ctesiphon. The further we get him from Baghdad the more chance of our next battle knocking him out altogether.[3]

There was more bad news from the river. The *Comet* had managed to get off the mud bank but the *Shaitan* had gone aground once too often and had sprung a leak. She was now resting on the bottom of the river with her gunwales awash. The ammunition was being removed from the sunken vessel while the *Firefly*, *Comet* and *Shushan* held off repeated attacks by Arabs who at the prospect of such riches were growing bolder each moment. Finally, at the request of the senior naval officer, Captain W. Nunn, R.N., Townshend despatched the Cavalry Brigade, the 7th Rajputs and a section of artillery who took the Arabs by surprise and drove them off without much difficulty.

It was while Captain Nunn, who had now steamed downstream in the *Comet*, was having a chat with Townshend, that the naval officer received a message from the *Firefly* that she was being shelled by some artillery on the left bank. Townshend correctly took this to indicate that the Turkish advance guard was not far away. Not long before Nunn's visit at 6 p.m. he had been informed that the main body of the Turkish force had reached Zor. Townshend therefore decided to march his force ten miles further south to Umm at Tubal at first light the following morning. Why Townshend had decided to march only ten miles the following day, knowing that the advance guard of the Turkish force was at his heels, requires some explanation. He said in his autobiography that if he had not had to guard the naval flotilla he would have made a forced march of some twenty to twenty-four miles the following day. Nunn, he said, had told him that the extreme limit of the naval flotilla's progress on the morrow would be Umm at Tubal where a guard would be required to protect the shipping from attack. Nunn emphatically denied saying anything of the sort, although he admitted that during his discussion with Townshend he mentioned the difficulties of navigation owing to the low state of the river. In fact, he said, on his arrival at Umm at Tubal the next afternoon he had pointed out to Townshend that it was regrettable having to order his shipping to anchor while there were still several hours of daylight left, which could be better utilised in getting further downstream.

Before marching off the following morning, however, Townshend received an urgent request for assistance from Nixon as his convoy of ships had run into some enemy opposition below Kut. The major-general despatched Melliss posthaste with the 30th Brigade, a cavalry regiment and some guns to rescue the British commander-in-chief.

The British force reached Umm at Tubal at about midday and spent the afternoon and evening digging trenches around the perimeter of the encampment. The camp was on a flat plain and was rectangular in shape with its southern face on the bank of the river. Each infantry brigade was made responsible for the defence of one face of the camp. The 16th held the west face, the 18th the north, and the 17th the east. During the afternoon the Cavalry Brigade probed out to the north for signs of pursuit but returned just before dusk having only sighted some hostile mounted Arabs advancing from the direction of Aziziya.

Nur-ud-Din, however, was not far behind. He had reached Aziziya during the afternoon and finding it vacated by the British had ordered an immediate advance on Umm at Tubal. But at 3.30 p.m. he had received an extraordinary message which was to be the curtain-raiser to a series of tragi-comic events, certainly without parallel in modern warfare. His cavalry commander had wirelessed the following:

Enemy is retiring from Aziziya. Patrols are following the enemy. The brigade is continuing its march towards Aziziya.[4]

If Nur-ud-Din noticed anything odd about this message he does not appear to have said so. It is certain that what the cavalry commander had identified as the British force was in actual fact the Turkish Army. Somehow the Turkish cavalry had managed to get behind the force for which it was supposed to be scouting. A further complication was added when the patrols, instead of following in pursuit as ordered, decided that enough had been done for one day. This conclusion was no doubt arrived at after the discovery of a considerable quantity of abandoned stores, including some alcoholic refreshment. The party, in which it appears the entire Turkish cavalry took part, was soon in full swing. According to the Turkish account, as soon as these troops reached Aziziya they went off duty and 'there passed the night in drunkenness among this priceless display of plunder'.[5]

Meanwhile the British troops had made themselves comfortable at Umm at Tubal. They discovered a considerable quantity of hay and straw with which to make 'nests' to protect them from the icy winds of night. The strenuous digging of trenches and the unaccustomed full stomachs had made them drowsy. All seemed at peace but this did not last long. An advance party composed of troops from the Turkish 45th and 51st Divisions, the latter maintaining its unblemished record for fallibility, blundered into a British outpost in the darkness. There was some sporadic firing and the Turks withdrew. The British came to the conclusion that the bullets had come from a party of would-be Arab marauders but nevertheless put out their fires and manned the trenches around the camp as a precautionary measure. Nur-ud-Din on the other hand was completely unaware that he had caught up with Townshend and thought that the shots had been exchanged with a small British rearguard party. He ordered the leading regiment of the 51st Division to advance once more with some guns and occupy Umm at Tubal as an outpost. It is almost superfluous to remark that this force got lost and straggled around in the darkness until it reached the river bank some distance to the south-westward of the British camp where it camped. Nur-ud-Din, on hearing nothing further from his wayward regiment, ordered his army to bivouac for the night and at 1.30 a.m. on 1 December he issued an order to the effect that the British force, having been driven from Umm at Tubal, was continuing its flight southwards and that he would take up the pursuit the following morning. He instructed his cavalry scouts by wireless to 'continue to maintain touch with the enemy and observe their movements'. If the roistering Turkish cavalry, oblivious by this time to any movements other than those of a few Arab girls, noticed anything significant about this order, it appears to have been drowned in a confused sea of alcohol and smashing bottles.

For some time now Townshend had realised that his force was in some danger but to what degree he was not quite sure. His wireless began to intercept messages which showed clearly that a large enemy force was out there in the darkness. The British troops in their shallow trenches had detected the rumble of gun and limber wheels on the frozen ground. The *Firefly* moored upstream had heard sounds of movement on the river bank, turned on a searchlight and opened fire. A Turkish shell in reply had scored a direct hit on the gunboat and the searchlight had been hurriedly extinguished. The firing had continued for a short time but had then ceased. Some of the light calibre shells had fallen into the British camp and although they had done no damage it was realised that Arab marauders could not have fired them. Townshend issued orders that if an enemy advance force was close at hand he would attack it at daybreak. He told his land transport to load up and be ready to move at first light. Nunn was instructed to move his flotilla southwards as soon as possible, leaving a gunboat to co-operate with the land force. He despatched a party of 7th Lancers after Melliss, who by now was ten miles towards Kut, ordering him to return with all possible speed with the 30th Brigade. Melliss was instructed to keep well to the north and fall on the enemy's flank. Realising that his party of Lancers might be annihilated before they had delivered this message, Townshend duplicated his orders and sent another party downstream by motor launch. The cavalry got through but the water-borne messengers were attacked. Of the three men in the boat, one was killed and the others were wounded.

At 5 a.m. Townshend assembled his brigade commanders and explained his plan for the dawn attack. By 6 a.m. his troops were in position, the 16th Brigade remained in their trenches on the north side of the camp, the other two brigades occupied a dry gulley which ran approximately north-west from the north-west corner of the camp. Before this, however, the transport column escorted by the 48th Pioneers had commenced to file out of camp and the British Cavalry Brigade had begun to move out to co-operate on the extreme right of the intended British attack.

According to the Turkish account, as the first rays of winter sunshine began to filter over the horizon an outpost battalion of the 51st Division saw the British transport column and its escort proceeding south-west and another British force marching north-west across its front. The commander of the 51st Division ordered his troops to prepare to attack. Its 9th Regiment was to direct its left on some low mounds about 2,000 yards to the north-west of the British camp, while the 7th was to follow in its rear. Nur-ud-Din, duly informed of the presence of a body of British troops, directed the 45th Division to co-operate by advancing on the right of the 51st Division.

Full daylight arrived at 6.45 a.m. with all the suddenness of the East and the situation became all too clear to both the British and the Turks. The two rival armies were encamped within two miles of each other. Townshend, although prepared for the worst, was as shocked as Nur-ud-Din with the numbers of those that opposed him. He ordered his artillery to open fire at once and sent messengers to his cavalry, instructing them to envelop the wing of the enemy that was closing towards his right and then charge it.

All the British guns, including those of the *Comet* and *Firefly*, opened fire simultaneously with terrible effect. The advance of the Turkish 45th Division and the two regiments of the 51st was brought to a standstill and thrown into complete disorder. The enemy began to retreat. The effect of the concentrated bombardment on the Turkish encampment itself was even more decisive. The whole XIIIth Army Corps fled in a panic. Muhammed Amin said of that morning:

This [artillery] fire opened with a *rafale* of shells which totally disorganised the XIIIth Army Corps [its commander was killed instantly and the commanders of the 35th and 38th divisions were wounded] and the 45th Division and kept them for hours out of the battle. From my own observations and experience I can say without exaggeration that had not the enemy's cavalry come up against the [Turkish] 7th Regiment and been forced to withdraw, they could have ridden over and taken prisoner the whole three Turkish divisions before they reached Aziziya.[6]

Townshend was quick to take advantage of the confusion and gave orders for an immediate retreat. He admitted later that he was tempted to order an advance. The 17th and 18th Brigades were instructed to cover the retirement of the transport and then to follow themselves. Townshend's attention was now drawn to the river where he could see that all was not going well. The *Firefly* was on fire and had gone aground and the *Comet* was desperately trying to tow her off.

The British gunboats had been under heavy fire from the river bank since the action had commenced. At 7 a.m. when the river transport had managed to get under way, Nunn, who was aboard the *Comet* signalled his gunboats to follow them downstream. At that moment a Turkish shell had destroyed the *Firefly*'s boiler room and she had drifted on to a mud bank. The *Comet* had immediately returned upstream, but she too had run aground and got wedged there by one of the *Firefly*'s barges which had broken adrift. The other gunboat, the *Sumana*, by this time well downstream and struggling with two large lighters herself, was signalled by Nunn to drop her two charges and return to his assistance. The *Sumana* steamed upstream once more and after passing a line made several attempts to tow the *Comet* off while the Turks poured shell, machine-gun and rifle fire into the ships. The *Comet*, as well as the *Firefly*, was soon on fire and Nunn was forced to abandon both. *Sumana* manœuvred alongside each burning ship in turn and took off the crews, coming under a tumult of fire at close range. She managed the rescue eventually and with her gunwales awash, due to the extra load, struggled off downstream pursued by shot and shell.

It had been the guns of the lost 45th Regiment of the 51st Division which had opened fire on the ships and caused this calamity. Calamity it certainly was, because aboard one of the two barges which the *Sumana* had been forced to abandon to the Turks were a large number of British sick and wounded. The other contained irreplaceable Royal Flying Corps spares and stores.

Meanwhile, the retreat of the British force was continuing at speed. The Turkish 51st Division followed for a short distance and then gave up the chase although some cavalry and horse artillery pursued the British column for another four hours.

The Turkish account said that Nur-ud-Din was not able to rally his badly shaken XIIIth Army Corps until noon. By this time the British force had slipped out of his grasp. Turkish casualties at Umm at Tubal were high. Seven hundred and forty-eight were killed and wounded of which 633 belonged to the XVIIIth Army Corps. Of these 488 came from the 51st Division. The British casualties were thirty-seven killed, 281 wounded and 218 missing. The Turks claimed to have captured 520 prisoners, 380 of whom were sick and wounded, found in an abandoned barge.

After the shrapnel of the Turkish horse artillery had ceased to whip at the heels of his rearguard, Townshend decided to shake off any further enemy pursuit by a forced march of twenty-six miles. His troops marched on, tired after their sleepless night, constantly harried by mounted Arabs who launched a series of stinging attacks against the flank and rear of the column. The trail to Kut now lay across a bare and dry desert, featureless except for some low scrub. All the regimental horses had been sent ahead with the divisional transport so even the officers had to march. Some troops, not up to the march, straggled behind and were picked off by the Arabs. As the day progressed it was difficult to keep the men pressing forward, but the main spur to progress was the padding camels of the Arabs.

The 17th Brigade, which was marching in the rear of the column, bore the worst of the Arab attacks. By this time the column had become so extended that the rearguard was a considerable distance behind the leading troops. The 17th's troops heard that in seven miles they would be halted and given food and water. Spirits revived, but luck was against them. By the time they had caught up with the main body of troops, Arab attacks with rifles and even machine-guns made further waiting out of the question and the forced march continued immediately.

All that day and into the night the march of the exhausted men continued. The night was moonless and it was impossible to see for any distance ahead. The route of the column was criss-crossed with dry gulleys which made the march exceedingly trying. At 2 a.m. the men of the rearguard saw the bivouac fires of the main body of troops ahead. As they shambled in they were told they could lie down as they were in column of route. Some tried to make a fire to warm cocoa in the mess tins, others dozed. The order came to move off in five minutes.

Meanwhile, the *Sumana* had come across some abandoned river craft containing wounded. She managed to take some of the desperately frightened men aboard but many had to be left behind. Because of these frequent halts the *Sumana* did not manage to catch up with Townshend that day and anchored for the night just below Bughaila. Next day she proceeded to Kut. During the evening of 1 December the Turkish Army marched for a short distance below Umm at Tubal before camping for the night.

When Townshend resumed his march on 2 December his hungry and exhausted men were barely able to carry on and many fell out during the day. Some were helped on by their comrades, others had to be left behind as the tired men hardly had the strength to march. A number of mule-drawn transport carts were ordered to follow in the rear to pick up as many stragglers as possible.

For another eighteen miles the march continued until over the almost flat horizon lifted the thin pencil shape of a minaret. Three miles from the town of Kut al Amara the British force bivouacked and was given hot food. The cavalry rode straight ahead into the town.

For twelve days Townshend's force, composed largely of young soldiers had been fighting continuously, marching or digging trenches with little food or water and almost without sleep. The last forty-four mile march had been completed in thirty-six hours.

The following day, on 3 December, Townshend's 6th Division marched into Kut. Oddly, the first sight that greeted the troops was a gibbet.

IV
KUT AL AMARA

Kut, Kôôt to the Arabs but pronounced by the British soldier
with his usual indifference to such subtleties to rhyme with 'nut',
huddled in the south and south-western corner of a peninsula
formed by a wide loop of the Tigris. This generally featureless
and flat promontory was about two miles long, a mile wide, and
in most places below the flood level of the river. The town
ranged along the left bank for almost half a mile and was perhaps a quarter of a mile in depth. A series of narrow streets ran
north and south, roughly parallel to each other, and at right-
angles to the river. At irregular intervals cross-roads ran from
east to west. Looking towards the town from the river bank, to
the left stood a legacy of Kut's former Turkish occupants, a
serai (military post) with offices, flag staff and barrack square.
Behind the serai was the mosque with its tall minaret topped by
a well-proportioned, turquoise-coloured dome.

Extending along the river bank to the right were the town's
two main bazaars, one parallel to the river, and the other, a
larger and more important one, at right-angles to it. Both had
the usual rush matting roof supported by wooden poles. In the
hot weather these bazaars afforded welcome shelter from the
fierce sun; in the winter they were dark, foul and squalid. The
internal arrangements were according to tradition—a series of
arches on a raised plinth in which the noisy vendors squatted
behind heaps of straw baskets, earthenware pots and jars. The
smaller stalls, run by less prosperous tradesmen, squeezed in
wherever possible, in gaps, nooks and crannies. When a British
soldier entered, the cacophony rose to a crescendo. The thin,
tugging fingers of the East tried to drag him from one stall to
the other or snatch away his wallet. The babble buffeted his ears
and the smell of camel dung and urine filled his nostrils. Food,

3   Kut al Amara, a view from the Tigris

4   A view of the foreshore, Kut

5   British river craft carrying stores on the Tigris to near-by
villages

cooked and uncooked, was presssed on him. Ancient curiosities, modern, mock and even authentic, were waved frantically under his nose. As he left the noise level would drop again. The tradesmen returned to keeping themselves adept by attempting to sell goods to each other. At night these markets were silent, the arches secure behind padlocked doors, attended only by a nightwatchman who patrolled or dozed as the fancy took him.

Further to the right along the river bank, private dwellings and gardens stretched away to the town's main gardens. Beyond these lay a bare, uneven stretch of bank which passed muster as a wharf. This was always cluttered with *mahailas*, the smaller *bellums* and an assortment of other river craft.

Scattered throughout the town, but mostly towards the western end were a few well-constructed two-storey houses, square in plan with verandahed rooms which opened on to an inner courtyard. This courtyard also contained the stairway to the roof and in the middle was a large drain leading to a larger cesspit beneath. After heavy rain these pits invariably over-flowed and amplified a condition which was never sweet at the best of times.

For the most part the inhabitants of Kut lived in smelly mud hovels with matting roofs. Some of these buildings were built around a central courtyard, the whole being enclosed by a sur-rounding wall which also embraced the one or two communal date palms and a mud oven. Here the Arab women sat winnow-ing or grinding corn for the '*kebaabs*' or played with their noisy, grubby, half-naked children. Most of these hovels had no drain-age at all and the refuse, human and otherwise, was shot out on to the narrow, filthy thoroughfares. The streets themselves had no drainage system; the inhabitants relied on the winter rains or the summer baking to provide relief. It never did. Townshend's senior medical officer, Colonel Hehir, told the Mesopotamia Commission that Kut was the most insanitary place that the British force had occupied in Mesopotamia—a no mean distinc-tion. Scattered along the thoroughfares were the much beloved coffee houses; where the Arabs squatted on the low, hard wooden benches, sipping the sickly-sweet brew and according to whim, either chatted, slumbered or invented rumours for the

c

edification of the British. Pre-war Kut had been the centre of a
busy trade in grain grown in the region of the Shatt al Hai but
now its granaries were fast becoming empty; some thought at a
suspicious speed. It was suspected that the Arabs feared that
the corn would be confiscated by the British. The 6,000 population, for the most part Arab but with a few Jews, Sabians and
Nestorian Christians, was ruled over by Sheikh Hajji Abbas al
Hali. He was a big, cheerful dignified man and respected by
Arab, Indian and Briton alike. His large strapping son, Sa'ad,
on the other hand, was fond of idling and sleeping and was held
in esteem by no one. Another local dignitary was the sheikh's
nephew, Mahommed Najeeb, an intelligent, enterprising man
who proved a valuable contact between the military authorities
and the riparian dwellers of Kut.

As the short, wintry days of November passed, those who had
to stay behind in Kut became oppressed by the feeling of being
left out of it all. At first troops and supplies had passed steadily
through the town on their way upstream to join Townshend's
division. The activity on the rickety wooden wharves, at the
river bank, had been feverish. Crowds of bewildered British and
Indian troops were disembarked and embarked again by shouting and Supply and Transport sergeants and worried-faced
officers. The work continued day and night, lit by the harsh,
white glare of naphtha flares. Seen through the continuous pall of
dust, the noisy, gesticulating soldiery and the cursed, sweating
native labourers projected an air of unreality. The 66th Punjabis, tireless off-duty footballers, bubbling with excitement,
fearful that they might be too late, swept on, leaving one officer
sweating in his tent with a temperature of 105 degrees, cursing
the attack of malaria which threatened to keep him out of the
coming battle. A day later he had been helped aboard a steamer
almost incoherent with gratitude.

Now all was quiet. Kut had become a backwater in a monu-
mental plan to be in Baghdad by Christmas. The troops of the
garrison wandered around the silent town wondering when the
great and final battle would be fought. Then the grapevine had
begun to work. The battle had commenced; the Turks had been
driven out of their positions at Ctesiphon; the enemy were being

pursued. Townshend had already announced in a communiqué the cogent fact that the Turkish soldier was endowed by nature with exceptionally strong knees, which made his withdrawals so effective because he could out-strip his pursuer. Baghdad was now a certainty but would the troops in Kut be allowed some Christmas leave in that city? Tattered guidebooks were consulted hopefully.

Inexplicably, after the news of the British success at Ctesiphon, there had been complete silence. The garrison thought enviously of belly-dancers and stumped around in gloom. The main off-duty occupation of the officers was a stroll out of the town with a shot-gun to bag a few sandgrouse. These dove-like birds with their strange, piercing cries buzzed and whirred about in large numbers and, as one sportsman observed, were 'best got in the morning when flying between eight and eleven o'clock'.[1]

Those with an eye for the squalid roved around Kut and its environs.

But the grapevine was at work again. The rumour had it that the Turks had counter-attacked at night and retaken the Ctesiphon positions. There had been heavy casualties and Townshend was retreating on Aziziya. Of course, it must be nonsense. The town Arabs encouraged and even started such stories. They were good for business as they tended to trigger off a wave of buying in the bazaars otherwise troops contemplating leave in Baghdad tended to husband their pay to the neglect of the local traders.

At garrison headquarters the news was positive. The telegraph chattered unceasingly in the wireless room, informing the garrison commander, Colonel Taylor, that the unbelievable had happened. This threw him into a quandary.

When Townshend's triumphant division had moved northwards it had been confidently presumed that henceforth Kut, at worst, would only have to be defended against those traditional roving thieves the Shammar Arabs—an almost laughable adversary. A suitable defence scheme was put in hand. Four blockhouses were to be constructed across the neck of the Kut peninsula which would be connected by a single barbed wire fence to a fort on the extreme right on the river bank. The fort, approximately 150 yards square, was to have ten-foot high mud walls pierced with loop-holes and provided with bastions at two corners to provide flanking rifle fire. The Arabs, unsupported by artillery, would have found this mud edifice a sufficient deterrent against any projected attack on the town in their eternal quest for loot.

In mid-October, while the 6th Division was still at Azizya, the sites for the fort and blockhouses had been selected and the contract for construction given to Lynch Brothers, the maid-of-all work contractors at Basra. By the beginning of November work on the blockhouses was well in hand and showed every sign of being completed by the end of the month; the barbed wire was in position and the work on the fort far advanced.

When the dreadful news of Ctesiphon began to arrive it was realised that these defences would be useless against an enemy with artillery, and there had to be an immediate reappraisal of the situation. Taylor was handicapped by a lack of time in which to effect any alterations and he knew that at best there could only be a compromise. It was recognised that in any attack on the town by a modern army the fort would occupy an extremely exposed and vulnerable position. The system of blockhouses and single barbed wire fences would be useless.

On 27 November a flotilla of steamers arrived at the river front, aboard one of which was the Army Commander, Sir John Nixon, and his staff. The steamers were hastily refuelled and on the following day the convoy continued its journey downstream, but were fired on in the region of Sheikh Saad and were forced to return two days later for an escort. It was understood that Townshend was sending one down to Kut but it never arrived. The steamer left for Basra once more on 1 December and after a short delay just below the fort managed to get downstream safely.

Nixon's adventure downstream had caused considerable anxiety in Kut. More rumours suggested that some 4,000 Turks with two guns had already arrived on the left bank of the Tigris just below Kut. The rumours had gained credence when Townshend wired from upstream that such an enemy force was moving down towards Kut. These fears, however, proved to be ground-less. Nixon had obviously mistaken an Arab raiding party, which had arrived in that area, for the rumoured Turkish force.

For some weeks past the military medical staff in Kut had been building two new hospitals complete with wards, store-rooms, operating rooms, dispensaries, kitchens, bathing places, isolation wards and offices. The construction of these wood and rush-matting buildings had been hampered by frequent inspec-tions by staff officers who, temporarily short of something to inspect, had turned their full attention on the hospitals. The medical officers had been only too pleased when the generals had departed upstream with Townshend at the beginning of November. The new building could accommodate some 500 to 600 patients. Nobody dreamed that the hospitals would ever be needed. It was the medical staff that received the first inkling of the extent of the tragedy of Ctesiphon. The message came from Townshend's headquarters. It said simply: 'Have evacuated 3,500.'[2]

This three-word message turned the prospects of a Christmas in Baghdad into a nightmare that none of them would ever forget. It was the finality of the message that so shocked the medical officers. Where could this number be accommodated? The consensus of opinion was that most of the boats carrying the wounded should be passed straight on to Amara or Basra but it was decided otherwise. Only one boat in six would go through. All the wounded aboard the rest must be disembarked and taken to the Kut hospitals. The doctors were dismayed. How could the hospitals, with accommodation for about 600, be expanded to house thousands? The medical staff started hastily to pitch tents.

A young medical officer stood gazing upstream in anticipation of the arrival of the wounded. He saw the black smoke of a steamer belching high in the air as it wound round the chicane-like sails of dozens of *mahailas*—the dhow of the Tigris. Slowly the pulsing smoke drew nearer. A steamer towing a large barge on either side gave a great gout of smoke, backed its paddle wheels with much churning of muddy water and bumped against the bank. The officer could scarcely believe what he saw.

Crammed and packed on the decks of the barges were the survivors of Ctesiphon in blood-soaked, filthy bandages. Many were already dead; some stiff with arms and legs in grotesque positions; others newly dead whose limbs rolled with the motion of the barges. The doctors were at first unable to reach those who were still alive because of the way that they had been jammed together. Some of the wounded whimpered, some cried with the low sobbing of desperation and loneliness, others were silent and just stared up at the stretcher bearers. From all came the stench of urine and corruption. Maggots crawled over the wound dressings and open wounds. Some men were covered by so many flies that they appeared to be wearing chain mail.

Night and day the medical staff laboured over the bodies of the wounded. As one of them wrote in his diary:

> We are strained to the utmost, boat after boat is unloaded; fetch and carry; accommodate and feed; examine and tend and treat is the order of the day—we do our best. Offers of aid by fatigues or by carts or in any way they can serve us, are sent in by our friends in the regiment and the battery, whilst a portion of a stranded field ambulance [unit] gives of its best.[3]

The wounded had to be taken by the springless transport carts to the hospitals which were about a mile from the river bank. A huge derelict two-decker barge was commandeered, strewn with hay and a hundred of the slighter cases bedded down on board. A stall was established on the river bank with hot milk and soup for the men. Then came urgent orders that all the wounded were to be repacked aboard the available river craft and sent downstream immediately.

News came that Townshend had detached a brigade which was hurrying down to Kut with all possible speed to prevent an early Turkish attack—then came news that the brigade had been recalled. An air of impending disaster hung over Kut. Conjecture was rife as to what the recall could mean. Some pessimists had already started to think that the end was near.

On 1 December the exhausted medical staff were sitting down

to a late breakfast when an unaccustomed but quite familiar sound stiffened them in their chairs. Faint at first, borne on the north wind, was the sound of guns. The officers ran outside the tent and listened. From out of billets, tents and shacks streamed dozens of soldiers. They stood silently, self-consciously, ears attuned. It came again, louder this time. There was a murmur from the listening men. The guns were silent now. An hour of suspense passed but nothing more was heard for the remainder of that day. During the afternoon of 2 December bugles began to sound. A defence officer rushed into the hospital and told the medical staff that every patient who could stand must fall in. Once more the quarters were emptied. Sightseers strained their eyes and binoculars to the north. Some noticed a cloud of dust on the horizon. From the dust emerged the leading troops of the retreating column. Ahead rode a mounted officer. Immediately behind him some more mounted troops, then a long winding irregular line of khaki uniforms. For some reason everybody in Kut heaved a deep sigh of relief. The column drew closer and the watchers could make out bobbing topees and brown turbans. The mounted officer at the head of the column rode into Kut, his face and uniform covered with dust. He was bedraggled and overwrought. He heaved himself from the saddle and asked for some food and water. It was obvious to everyone that the rider had undergone considerable strain. As he ate he babbled an incoherent story. Soon the rest of the column began to arrive. Guns pulled by oxen, then mules, camels, transport carts, cavalry with salt-stained horses, and finally the exhausted trudging, dusty infantry. Group by group they marched in, each followed by a chain of stragglers. One small party of British soldiers arrived with no kit at all. They smelled badly and explained that they had not removed their clothes for days, weeks in fact. Some asked for food but others were too cold and tired to eat. The main body of troops marched into Kut the following morning. At their head was General Townshend. Of the Turks, there was no sign at all.

As soon as Townshend arrived in Kut he had to choose whether to rest his troops and then continue his retreat downstream, or to stay where he was and take up a defensive position.

His decision to hold Kut has been expanded to include the theory that Townshend had a pathological inclination towards sieges. As a young officer he had been connected with Gordon's Khartoum. He himself had conducted a successful siege. He had got a C.B. out of Chitral; the possibilities of Kut were immense. A similar success but on a much grander scale would place him at the pinnacle of his profession and indelibly in the military treatises of which he was so fond. Townshend, it has been suggested, also had a morbid interest in the sieges of history and could quote their most obscure details from memory.

To the delight of his detractors, and unfortunately for Townshend, in his autobiography *My Campaign in Mesopotamia* he gave the exhausted and sorry state of his troops and their consequent inability to retreat further, until it was too late, as one of the main reasons for his decision to stay in Kut. This was strongly denied by General Delamain, who stated that the troops under his command could have continued the march on the day after their arrival at the town. This uncompromising statement has tended to support those theorists who believe that Townshend was not completely open-minded on the subject of retreat. Townshend's other reasons for making a stand at Kut appear to be valid. By holding Kut, which commanded the junction of the Shatt al Hai with the Tigris, he would block the advance of the Turkish Army as it was as dependent on the river for the transport of supplies as was Townshend. As long as the British guns controlled the river at Kut the Turkish ships could neither pass up or down the Tigris nor enter the Shatt al Hai. This would prevent the Turks from assuming the offensive and driving the British out of Mesopotamia altogether. If the Turkish advance was delayed, Nixon would be given time to assemble the small bodies of reinforcements which were beginning to arrive by sea at Basra into a cohesive fighting force and to move them upstream to Amara. In doing so he would give Nixon elbow room in which to manœuvre.

Townshend considered that by 'holding the neck of the bottle' at Kut the Turks would be unable to use the Shatt al Hai to advance on Nasiriya, which was being held by a small force consisting of three infantry battalions. This prevented

Nasiriya from becoming a stepping-stone to Basra, he said, or if
the Turkish Army was to suffer a reverse in the south, barred
the Euphrates, on which the town stood, for a retreat to Baghdad.

The only alternative to his decision to stand at Kut, Townshend reasoned, was to continue to retreat to the old Turkish
positions astride the Tigris at Es Sinn. But to hold this position,
which consisted of six miles of trenches on the left bank and
three miles of trenches on the right, would require three army
corps—about six times the strength of his force. Without
sufficient troops Townshend considered he would be overwhelmed before three days had elapsed. Townshend knew also
that he had neither sufficient shipping to move his munitions
and stores down to Es Sinn nor the time to resupply from downstream, if he proceeded to Es Sinn without them. The vagaries
of *mahaila* transport were well known. To move fresh supplies
upstream against the strong current from the nearest depot at
Amara would take a week. If sufficient supplies were not available at Amara the *mahailas* would take anything up to a month
to bring them from Basra.

Townshend admitted that as he weighed the arguments for
and against further retreat the spectres of Bazaine of Metz,
Mack of Ulm and Osman of Plevna were never far from his
mind. He recalled that Massena's defence of Genoa failed because the relieving army under no less a general than Napoleon
had not arrived in time and that Genoa succumbed because of
starvation. He knew that Bazaine's army, 'the flower of France',
had committed suicide by shutting itself up in Metz. The failure
of the Russian Army to arrive in time had caused Mack to
surrender at Ulm. And there, of course, was always Cornwallis
who was forced to surrender Yorktown when the Royal Navy
failed to reach him. Indeed, Townshend could not think of a
single instance of a force which, voluntarily or otherwise, had
been shut up in a besieged town and had later managed to effect
its self-deliverance. To Townshend it seemed that sieges were
extraordinarily bound up with capitulations.

On the other hand Townshend considered that he had ample
supplies of food and ammunition. As far as he knew reinforcements were arriving daily at Basra and were being built into a

potent force. Relief surely would not be long in coming. Town-shend decided to stay at Kut. He notified Sir John Nixon at once; Nixon wired his approval by return. The telegram read:

The Army Commander is glad to hear of your decision, and is convinced that your troops will continue to show the same spirit in the defence as they have shown throughout your operations. Reinforcements will be pushed up to you with all possible speed.[4]

Townshend issued the following communiqué to his troops:

I intend to defend Kut al Amara and not to retire any further. Reinforcements are being sent at once from Basra to relieve us. The honour of our mother country and the Empire demands that all work heart and soul in the defence of this place, we must dig in deep and dig in quickly, and then the enemy's shells will do little damage. We have ample food and ammunition, but commanding officers must husband the ammunition and not throw it away uselessly. The way you have managed to retire some eighty or ninety miles under the very noses of the Turks is nothing short of splendid and speaks eloquently for the courage and discipline of this force.[5]

The spectres of Gordon, Bazaine, Mack, Osman, Massena and Cornwallis smiled wanly.

Once Townshend had made up his mind to defend Kut the task of improving the defences of the peninsula and the town began in earnest. This work was to continue until Christmas.

Townshend agreed that the fort, because it could easily be isolated or cut off, was the main weak point but on the other hand it commanded two reaches of the Tigris and provided an excellent observation post for any guns sited near the town. It was, therefore, decided not to abandon it but to strengthen its defences by outside trenches, but the recently completed blockhouses must go. Townshend considered that these promin-ent structures were far too useful as ranging points for Turkish artillery and they were demolished with explosives. The block-houses were replaced by four strong redoubts known as 'A', 'B', 'C' and 'D'. Connecting these was the first or main line of

trenches which stretched from the river bank and across the
neck of the peninsula to the fort. Behind this line and parallel
to it was the second line. Later a third line, known appro-
priately as the 'middle line' was dug in between the first and
second lines. This was also completed by Christmas. Five communications trenches connected Kut to the three fire trenches.
These were named Gurkha C.T. (Communication Trench),
Reserve C.T., Hants C.T., Palm Grove C.T., and Brick Kilns
C.T. deriving their names from their locations or from the
troops that mainly used them. Emplacements for the artillery
were prepared. The largest cluster of guns was near the Brick
Kilns to the north-east of Kut town. The kilns themselves
were converted into observation posts. Townshend also considered that it was necessary to hold and fortify the small
village of Yakusub, or 'Woolpress' as it came to be called, across
the Tigris from Kut on the right bank. The village was cleared
of Arabs, entrenched and garrisoned by the 110th and 120th
Infantry of the 18th Brigade. This proved to be another weak
point in the defences, isolated as it was from Kut by a 500-yard-
wide river.

The whole defences were divided into four sections as follows:

a North-East Section. This comprised the fort, parts of the
first and middle lines and the appropriate communication
trenches. It was defended throughout the siege by Hoghton's
17th Brigade.

b North-West Section. This consisted of the remainder of the
first and middle lines and was defended alternately by the
16th Brigade (Delamain) or the 30th Brigade (Melliss).

c Second Line. This was manned by the General Reserve which
was normally stationed in Kut. The General Reserves were
alternately the 16th or the 18th Brigades depending on which
body of troops was in the North-West Section at the time.

d Woolpress village and Kut town itself. These were occupied
throughout by Hamilton's 18th Brigade. Half this brigade,
as mentioned earlier, was quartered in Woolpress while
the Norfolks and the 7th Rajputs lived in Kut itself and
provided men for picket duty.

It will be seen that the 17th Brigade, stationed in and near the fort, never left its positions or went into General Reserve in the same way as the other brigades. One reason given for keeping these troops permanently in these dangerous and arduous positions was because of the extreme distance from the town to the fort and the difficulty of getting troops there safely while under fire. This was probably true but there was also a far more sinister reason. Townshend firmly believed, and said so, that hostile bullets made better supervisors than sergeants. If troops were kept continually in dangerous positions they dug harder and faster and constantly strove to improve their lot purely out of man's primordial desire to keep a whole skin. So the 17th Brigade stayed put and suffered accordingly.

On the morning of 4 December, the day after the division's arrival in Kut, before the first blisters had begun to appear as the spades of the furiously digging troops struck the hard ground, Townshend wired Nixon as follows:

I am making Kut into an entrenched camp as far as possible in the time given, the enemy's advanced guard being some ten miles distant and the main body five miles beyond that. As it is reported that von der Goltz is in Baghdad now, in command of the Turkish Army of six divisions, I shall expect him to [pass] this place, leaving a force of observation at Kut to contain me. The relieving force will probably have to fight a second battle of Es Sinn. I have shut myself up at Kut reckoning with certainty on being relieved by large forces now arriving at Basra. The state of extreme weariness of my men demands instant rest. Our being at Kut will also delay von der Goltz's relieving force on the Amara–Ali Gharbi line. It is only violation of Economy of Force if you send up reinforcements in packets [small numbers]. Von der Goltz would take instant advantage of this. Eight hundred sick go down today.[6]

With the last of the seriously sick and wounded, Townshend sent his surplus river craft, tugs and barges. He knew that this transport would be vital to the Relief Force and it would be pointless to retain it at Kut. He did keep, however, the gun-

boat *Sumana*, four launches and six barges. These craft would be
vital to the maintenance of the garrison across the river at
Woolpress. Some fifty privately owned *mahailas* which were
on charter to the British military forces also remained at Kut.
The Arab owners of the craft did not appear too anxious to
leave the town and Townshend was only too pleased to have
these in addition. Townshend also decided that he would evict
the Arab population. He neither liked nor trusted the Arabs
and they were extra mouths to feed and would almost definitely
get under his feet. Sir Percy Cox, however, protested that this
would be nothing short of inhuman, as it was now bitterly cold
and the women and children would undoubtedly die of starvation and exposure if the Shammar, the traditional enemies of
the marsh Arabs, did not kill them first. The deleterious political
effects of such an act would be hard to underestimate, said
Cox. After making a few preliminary enquiries about the quantities of food in Kut, Townshend relented. He contented himself with ejecting about 700 Arabs who were not normally
resident in the town. Cox was perhaps lucky that he went
downstream with the last of the river craft. Townshend did
not cease to regret that he allowed the Arabs to remain in the
town, and railed against those who had persuaded him to do so.

As the last ships to leave Kut got up steam those aboard
shouted that they would be back inside three weeks. Those left
standing on the river bank fervently hoped that they were right.

All the 6th Division's ammunition, equipment and stores
that had been carried by the ships were disembarked and piled
on the bank. The troops who could be spared from trench
digging were put to work transferring the equipment to closely-
guarded dumps. The ammunition not immediately required
was taken to a number of underground storehouses in Kut
itself. Arab working parties were impressed to help shift the
food and ammunition to safety, and so zealously threw themselves into this work that a large quantity of stores was never
found again. Townshend was furious. Seven Arabs caught
looting were hanged. The major-general rounded up twenty
hostages against the future good behaviour of the town's
population.

That evening and during the night the sniping started. The bullets whizzed through the canvas walls of tents; they dropped from above; they ricocheted along alleys and avenues. There was very little doubt that the bullets came from inside the town itself and were part of an Arab campaign to discourage the British occupation. Early next morning a number of search parties combed the Arab dwellings for firearms. Townshend decreed that any Arab found in possession of a rifle in future would be shot.

Townshend reviewed his position. His field state showed that he had a total of 10,398 combatants under his command of which 1,555 were cavalry and consequently not much use in a siege. There were 7,411 infantry, including the West Kents that had joined him at Aziziya. (The *Official History of the War* puts Townshend's strength on 6 December after the cavalry had been sent downstream, at 11,607 plus 3,530 non-combatants and camp followers. Excluding the sick and wounded, artillery, cavalry and technical troops, this made about 7,000 'effectives'.)

Townshend had 2,700 yards of front to defend and for this he considered he was considerably undermanned. According to the book, three to five men per running yard was demanded. A calculation was enough to show Townshend that he did not even have enough troops to defend Kut on the landward side, let alone along the river where an attack could never be considered unlikely. In addition he had to defend Woolpress village. Nevertheless, he had 800 rounds of ammunition per rifle and 600 rounds per gun in his magazines which if husbanded carefully would be adequate for his needs.

In his storerooms he had sixty days' full rations of food for both his British and Indian troops and twenty-one days' rations of fuel in Kut and another thirty-three days' fuel across the river in a mud building known as the Liquorice Factory. He considered that the town Arabs had enough food for three months but he authorised the town's military governor, Colonel Taylor, to buy up all the grain to ensure a fair distribution.

Townshend received a disquieting telegram from Nixon which said that alternatives to Townshend's decision to hold Kut had been considered at headquarters but had been found wanting, and that the Army Commander could only approve of the commander of the 6th Division's plan. The telegram continued that every effort for the relief of Kut was being made and it was hoped to be able to do so within two months. In view of this it was suggested that all mounted troops and all shipping and gunboats that Townshend could spare, should be sent downstream to Ali Gharbi in order to facilitate the advance of the Relief Force and 'save mouths to feed'. The main concentration of troops would now be at Amara, with an advance or covering force at Ali Gharbi.

Although Townshend was in agreement with the recommendation concerning the cavalry and shipping (indeed he had already sent the steamers downriver) he was concerned by the casual reference to 'two months' in the telegram. He thought long and profoundly about this and began to have the first twinge of regret about his decision to hold Kut. Townshend, however, was not downcast for long. He could deal with Nixon later. He must tackle the immediate problem of getting the cavalry away downstream before he was surrounded and cut off. He sent for his divisional engineer commander, Colonel Rimington, R.E. The Turks could not be far off now and as it was known that they were making their advance down the Kut, or left side, of the Tigris, it was considered that the Cavalry Brigade stood the best chance of a safe journey down to Ali Gharbi by the opposite, or right bank. The job of constructing a bridge across the river near the fort was given to the 6th Division's bridging expert, Captain E. W. C. Sandes, R.E. and his 'Bridging Train'.

For a few days past a party of Indian sappers (Sirmurs) had been engaged in improving an old Turkish bridge of *gissaras* (small native craft) lying about a mile downstream. This was to have been used had the 6th Division decided to continue its retreat to Ali Gharbi. When it became known that Townshend had decided to stand at Kut orders were given for this bridge to be dismantled and brought upstream. There was also a considerable quantity of planks and bulks of timber at a dump near the fort which had arrived from Amara by *mahaila* at the

end of November. As most of the division's bridging material
had been lost or abandoned during the retreat it was proposed
to improvise a bridge from the planks and *gissaras*. Labouring
up to their chests in the cold waters the engineers commenced
their task and the bridge began to take shape and stretch from
the left bank towards the right bank. The *gissaras* were lashed
gunwale to gunwale and over these, massive nine-inch square
by forty-foot long wooden beams were placed and covered with
planking. The structure was kept pointing in the right direction
despite the river current by cables attached to anchors which
were dropped to the bed of the river. In eight hours, their
bodies numbed from the cold water, the engineers took the
bridge to within ten yards of the other bank. The tired and
hungry men heaved two trestles and a wooden ramp in position,
and the bridge was complete.

The commander of the Cavalry Brigade, Brigadier-General
Roberts, came down to the river bank during the afternoon and
watched the progress of the work but as dusk began to fall he
decided not to order his brigade to cross that night. He had
doubts about a stretch of shallow water some twenty yards
wide which separated the far end of the bridge from the river
bank. Captain Sandes was dismayed by this decision. It had
already been reported to him that although the water at the
end of the bridge was three feet deep, the bottom of the river
was safe and hard. Roberts was adamant and refused to cross
until the following morning. The cavalry commander's caution
created a trying situation for Sandes who, owing to the
aged and sinking condition of the *gissaras*, was forced to keep
his exhausted men working all night patching holes in the rotten
craft and baling them out to prevent the bridge from sinking.

At 9 a.m. the following morning, the Cavalry Brigade began
to arrive at the fort. After much struggling, kicking and biting
the first horses were coaxed on to the bridge and the crossing
began. At first the horses crossed without incident but as the
sand at the other end of the bridge, which Roberts distrusted,
got churned up by the horses' hooves it became a quicksand.
Horses floundered and fell pinning their riders under them.
The men were rescued with much difficulty. A Royal Horse

Artillery gun battery decided to take the final treacherous twenty yards at the gallop but crashed into the oozing swamp with horses struggling and screaming. This made further crossing impossible. The left bank approaches to the bridge became a mass of guns, waggons, cavalry, camels, mule transport carts and donkeys. The frightened animals kicked and screamed as the riders and handlers tried to keep them in check. One shell from the Turkish artillery would have been enough to turn the animals into an uncontrollable stampede.

Baulks of timber, trestles and planks were laid across the quicksand by the enginners and after another hour and a half, the crossing began again. The last vehicle to cross was a heavy, lumbering Royal Flying Corps motor car which threatened to plunge into the river but after much shunting backwards and forwards it bumped off the end of the bridge, miraculoulsy ploughed through the stretch of quicksand and planks, and lumbered on to the bank with a loud toot of its horn. After the military were clear some 800 camels with their Arab drivers crossed the bridge and took off after the cavalry in the hope of protection. A soldier tapped Sandes' arm. The eyes of the officer followed the line of the man's finger. Near the mouth of the Shatt al Hai was a force of about a thousand mounted Shammar watching the debouchment with interest. They now began to lope in pursuit. Later it was learned that these Arabs had made a weak attack on the cavalry and then turned their full attention to the camels in the rear. Most of the camels were stolen and nearly a hundred of their drivers killed.

The weary Sandes was sitting on the river bank smoking a cigarette watching the disappearing Arabs when he received orders to dismantle the bridge immediately. He was about to order his flagging workers off their haunches but noticed to his surprise that the Indian sentries who were supposed to be guarding the outlying approaches of the bridge about 300 yards away had disappeared. Several armed Arabs were walking in his direction and others were appearing over the brow of a sandhill, the closest Arabs suddenly broke into a run. Sandes and his men were pursued by bullets into the fort where they found the missing Indian sentries seated on ammunition boxes.

An engineer corporal asked them why they had not warned the 'Bridging Train' of the approach of the hostile party. The Indians grinned broadly. Sandes' men mused on the difference in the sense of humour of the Asian and that of the European.

Sandes thought it wiser to postpone the dismantling of the bridge until nightfall thus hoping to avoid the attention of the Arabs who appeared to be arriving in large numbers. Even more important, a squadron of 14th Hussars on scout duty (Townshend had retained a small body of cavalry for reconnaissance purposes) had come under hostile shell and rifle fire. There was still no sign of the Turkish advance guard.

That evening Townshend decided he would take Nixon up over his telegram of the previous day. He wired that relief in the two months quoted would almost certainly mean the loss of the 6th Division as before long he expected some six Turkish divisions to be around him. If such a considerable delay was unavoidable, said Townshend, it would be better for him to attempt to retire to Ali Gharbi and join up with Major General F. Aylmer's force. (Townshend had been informed that Aylmer had taken command of what became known as the Relief Force.) If he acted immediately he could take with him his heavy guns and most of the ammunition. Townshend pointed out that the loss of the 6th Division would not only be a dangerous blow to British prestige in Mesopotamia but would also have a disastrous effect in India from where most of the troops, of which the 6th Division was composed, came. He asked if there was any news of a Russian move towards Baghdad as if this was so maybe it would compel von der Goltz to forget Kut and concentrate all his energies on the defence of Baghdad.

In his diary for that day Townshend wrote:

Amongst other disadvantages, an entrenched camp can never guarantee even shelter from fire for a force occupying it. A hostile battery manages to get into *son pli de terrain* and firing, even at chance, is sufficient to cause confusion and alarm.[7]

On 5 December Turkish shells began to drop into Kut. They appeared to be coming from the north-east and from the left bank. There were still no signs of regular Turkish infantry on either bank or shellfire from the right bank. Shrapnel screamed over the western palm grove and some landed in the hospital just beyond. Colonel Hehir realised that his hospital occupied an exposed position and began to look for another site. A number of medical staff and orderlies who had never been under shellfire before tended to take it all very calmly. They even laughed at the frantic efforts of their comrades who threw themselves into holes and ditches and under transport carts, but a few near misses remedied this and the novices began to join the rush for safety with the best of them. Much to the chagrin of their traditional occupants Hehir decided the bazaars on the river front would provide safe accommodation for his sick and wounded and at 8 p.m. on 6 December every available sweeper was impressed and the work of cleaning the bazaars commenced. It took 200 men the best part of two days to make any noticeable improvement in the insanitary conditions of the bazaars. The work was hampered by the Arab shopkeepers and hired loafers who sat behind the stalls and refused to move. They had to be carried from their arches and out of the building.

Because of the intensive trench digging that was in progress Townshend was unable to supply working parties to carry the sick and wounded from the hospitals to the bazaars. The task was considerable as these amounted to over 2,000. (Only the seriously wounded had been sent downstream by steamer. Those who looked as if they would shortly be fit for duty had been retained.) In fact the problem solved itself. The chronically ill were transferred by stretcher. Those who were capable of making the mile-long journey unaided were instructed to do so. The remainder were told that transport carts would be provided after the medical staff had had some dinner. The doctors returned from their meal and found that the hospital wards were empty. The offer of a ride on a transport cart had been enough and the patients had limped, carried each other and even crawled down to the bazaars rather than face such a journey again.

It is an interesting comment on human nature that while the Turks were virtually at the gates of Kut and there was more than a chance that the town would be overwhelmed immediately a small food shop at the river end of one bazaar was doing a roaring trade. Soldiers were buying large stocks of food, tobacco and other goods, doubtless for sale at a higher price later. In some, it seems, the instinct for self-advancement is far stronger than that of self-preservation.

On the evening of 6 December Townshend received a lengthy reply to his telegram. Nixon said:

First Point: 'Relieved by the period of two months' was an outside limit, calculated to arrival of last reinforcements and the time that would elapse before a general forward movement could be made. It is hoped to quicken this up.

Second Point: So far as we know, you are not yet invested, nor is the river line cut. Younghusband with the 28th Brigade and Cavalry Brigade should be established at Ali Gharbi and Sheikh Saad within the next week and enable supplies to be pushed up to you.

Third Point: Retirement from Kut would open Shatt al Hai to the Turks, and have a bad effect, and does not at present seem to be demanded as a military necessity. Of the actual dispositions for occupation of Kut you are the best judge. Do you think it possible they [the Turks] have shot their bolt for the time being? They have only five steamers against our three times that number and more [are] coming. You have some 10,000 as against 12,000 and you have superiority of artillery.

Fourth Point: You speak of six [Turkish] divisions. Does this include the 52nd last reported to be in Baghdad, and 26th rumoured to be at or near Faluja but not in any way confirmed? On 5 December you spoke of only three divisions in front of you. You should send aeroplane reconnaissance to see what is going on at Badrah.

Fifth Point: Retirement from Kut should only be resorted to as last extremity. In any case Es Sinn seems indicated as point of retirement, not Ali Gharbi where you will be on top of Younghusband. Russians on 4 December were reported three marches from Hamadan and twenty-three marches

from Baghdad and Army Commander is wiring Chief of the
General Staff to expedite their advance. It may be possible
enemy merely wishes to contain you while concentrating on
Nasariya. Have you considered this? We are reinforcing
Nasiriya at once to provide against this contingency.

Sixth Point: Remember that our large reinforcements,
arriving daily, will have a good moral effect throughout
Basra vilayet. Army commander has asked for another
division and more heavy guns. As long as you remain at Kut
enemy is in ignorance of your plan, and you are fulfilling
duties of a detachment by holding up superior numbers.

Seventh Point: Your 169G received. The concentration [of
British troops] at Sheikh Saad and Ali Gharbi will be carried
out. Army Commander does not approve of your proposal to
fall back on Ali Gharbi.[8]

Thus it was finally settled that a stand was to be made at Kut.
Townshend, under promise of early relief, considered that it was
sound strategy to do so. The number of approaching enemy
troops was overwhelming and if he had chosen to meet them in
the open he would have been annihilated. There was one point,
however, that completely bewildered Townshend. For Nixon
to imply in his telegram that 'being on top of Younghusband
at Ali Gharbi' was an undesirable situation to be in seemed to
Townshend to be thoughtless nonsense. He could not think of
anywhere he would rather be at that particular moment.

On 7 December Townshend replied to Nixon:

That Younghusband with the 28th Brigade and the Cavalry
Brigade will be at Sheikh Saad and Ali Gharbi within the
next week is what I asked for in my 169G, and I am glad
you can do it, as it altogether alters my situation here. All
the reasons you give that I should remain at Kut were fully
considered by me before I decided to shut myself up at Kut,
knowing well by history the fate that generally awaits any
force which shuts itself up in a fortress or entrenched camp.
It was your statement that you hoped to relieve me within
two months which made my situation critical. Your placing

Younghusband's command and cavalry at Sheikh Saad altogether alters matters.[9]

That afternoon the diggers at the front line to the north of Kut had seen the enemy infantry advancing towards them on an extended front and had thrown themselves into their uncompleted trenches. The British artillery at the fort and among the palm groves opened up on the Turks as they pressed forward. It was immediately concluded that the enemy had decided to take Kut by assault without any of the usual preliminaries. The British and Indian troops in the front line of trenches fired and reloaded their rifles frantically. Over their heads whistled the British shells which burst with deadly effect amongst the advancing Turks. The lines of yellow-clad soldiers surged onwards seemingly indifferent to their heavy casualties. Then suddenly, within 400 yards of the British line, the Turks flung themselves down and began to dig in. It was a sight to remember. The Turkish shovel-work was impeccable. Farm labourers from Kent and Oxford, 'navvies' from Beckenham, Camberwell and Ilford, and ploughboys from the Punjab, were completely astonished at the speed at which the earth flew as the Turks hefted their picks and shovels. It was already known that the Turks had unusually strong knees; now the digging troops gave ample evidence that their arms and shoulders were more than equal to the task. Doubters might suggest that any troops under similar conditions would be enthusiastic and effective diggers, but even when this was taken into account the Anatolian peasant was unashamedly admired for his prowess.

The mud of Mesopotamia, as was amply demonstrated in the months to come, is unusual and deserves special mention. A young English subaltern of the 66th Punjabis wrote:

It is as disagreeable as, but rather more glutinous, than most other brands and when baked hard by the sun is singularly inpenetrable to rifle bullets. All the rules in military pocket-books were upset by it, some eight inches of the best variety is enough to stop any bullet. For the same reason trench digging in many places was slow and tedious work as the ground at that time [December] was dry and hard, it was more like cast iron. As a wag commented: Truly the spade of the Prophet is as mighty as his sword.[10]

The 'Bridging Train' having worked all night dismantling the bridge by the fort were given instructions to re-erect it further upstream with all possible speed.

The real reason for this bridge is obscure. It was generally believed by most in Kut that the bridge was intended solely as an escape route by which the 6th Division could fall back on Ali Gharbi before the siege commenced. In his autobiography Townshend said that had his troops been fit enough to work and had managed to complete this second bridge with a fortified bridgehead at the other end on the right bank it would have made all the difference in the world to his position at Kut. He wrote:

> I would be able to throw the principal mass of my force to either bank of the Tigris in an offensive against any isolated fraction of the enemy. I should manœuvre in battle just as if I were fighting an offensive/defensive battle and, if necessary, I could abandon Kut at need and fall back by the right bank on the approach of the relieving force who would stretch out a helping arm to me.[11]

Townshend was writing his memoirs for posterity and his reference to an offensive/defensive role was most probably a mental exercise for military strategists. Also Townshend's memory was at fault. The bridge was completed and a bridgehead was established on the other side of the river. Townshend's offensive/defensive role was unhappily demonstrated.

To protect the bridge builders the Oxfords were taken to the other bank in a barge towed by the *Sumana*. Sandes and his engineers, by now slit-eyed with fatigue, set to work and managed to complete about 120 yards of bridge by nightfall, when work ceased until the next morning.

The dawn of 8 December was fine. The sky was a deep blue and uncluttered by a single cloud. It was sunny but cold. Sandes assembled his party and noticing that the *Sumana* was moored at the right bank presumed that the gunboat had already taken the covering party across the river. The engineers set about their task with vigour. There was a loud hail from the *Sumana*. The engineers glanced up from their work and saw a large and apparently derelict *mahaila* coming down swiftly with the current. It was about 200 yards away and there was little the engineers could do but wait on the rolling bridge and attempt to cushion the blow. The sixty tons of *mahaila* would undoubtedly smash the bridge to pieces. A small boat, vigorously rowed by two seamen, was seen to pull away from the *Sumana*. The sailors managed to overhaul and keep abreast with the Arab craft. A sailor throwing down his oars, stood up and deftly passed a line aboard the *mahaila*, secured it then threw the attached anchor from the rowing boat. The *mahaila* drove on, checked violently, slewed around in her own length and halted with her stern a few feet from the bridge.

Sandes later congratulated the commander of the *Sumana*, Lieutenant L. C. P. Tudway, R.N., on the presence of mind of his crew which had undoubtedly saved the bridge from destruction. He suspected that the drifting *mahaila* had been a deliberate attempt by the Turks to destroy the bridge. Tudway thought it was more probably an Act of God. 'But whose God?' someone muttered drily.[12]

Work continued on the bridge for the remainder of that day. Sandes was informed that a large party of Turkish infantry had been seen on the right bank to the north-west of Kut but as he had seen no signs of activity by the covering party across the river he was not concerned. At last the bridge was completed. Sandes was surprised to see no movement from the trenches at the end of the bridge as he walked across to the other side. Staring into the mud hole he found it empty. He quickly walked up the right bank to the *Sumana*, casting anxious glances towards the sandhills that surrounded him and asked Tudway the whereabouts of the covering party. Tudway said that he had received no instructions to bring any troops across the river that morning, and that he thought Sandes had known this. 'In that case I think I should mention that a couple of Turkish officers have been watching you and your bridge for some time.' Tudway indicated a straggle of sandhills some 300

yards upstream from where they were standing. Leaving Sandes
to mull over this piece of information Tudway ordered his radio
operator to inform headquarters in Kut of the situation.
Within half an hour two hundred 67th Punjabis arrived on the
left bank, walked across the bridge and threw themselves into
the trenches. The immediate anxiety was over.

As the *Sumana*, her work finished, steamed upstream to Kut
that evening she was fired on from the right bank as she rounded
the bend by what was estimated to be eight Turkish guns. The
aim was bad as dusk was falling rapidly and she arrived without mishap.

Sandes received a visit from no less a personage than Townshend, who inspected the bridge, complimented the engineers
on a fine piece of work but omitted to explain the reason for the
bridge; Sandes was too tired to ask him.

Early the following morning of 9 December the engineers
were working on the bridge, repairing leaks in the *gissaras*,
adjusting planks, tightening lashings and listening to the
occasional rifle shot upstream, when Sandes was handed a note
by a messenger from Townshend's headquarters in Kut instructing him to destroy the bridge forthwith. Cursing, the
engineers started to pull their bridge to pieces. The rifle fire
from upstream became heavier and the covering party on the
right bank returned the fire. Bullets kicked up the sand on
the hills. The fusillade increased in volume. Looking upstream
the engineers on the bridge saw the yellow uniforms of about a
dozen soldiers running down the bank towards the bridge.
Another cloud of Turkish soldiers appeared over the brow of the
sandhills. The engineers ran back across the bridge to the left
bank, bullets throwing up slivers of wood around them. They
assembled at Sandes' work barge to draw rifles and ammunition.
Using a field telephone set, Sandes informed headquarters in
Kut that the bridge was being attacked. By now the tumult on
the right bank had increased in ferocity. Turkish infantry, led
by an officer waving a sword, advanced towards the bridge in
short rushes. They were screened to a degree by some hollows
in the ground—probably the remains of old irrigation ditches—
and by the sandhills. The Punjabis suffered accordingly. The

Turks advanced as far as the sandhills nearest to the bridge, regrouped and poured heavy fire down on the covering party. Captain Gribbon, in command of the 200 men, realised that his position was becoming serious and decided to retreat across the bridge before he was overwhelmed. The Punjabis crawled from their trenches and, carrying their wounded, ran to the bridge and commenced to cross. The Turks neglected to take the initiative, contenting themselves with firing at the fleeing troops. The Punjabis, tripping and falling on the partially dismantled bridge, managed to make the left bank and throwing themselves down on the exposed ground returned the fire. Sandes, in his barge, glanced at his watch. It was only 9 a.m.

Major-General Melliss, commanding the 30th Brigade (then in General Reserve) arrived on the scene, sent for Gribbon and asked him to explain why he had withdrawn his covering party from the other bank. Gribbon said that he had only 200 troops and this was too few to defend the approaches of the bridge against the Turkish attacking force. The major-general disagreed and ordered Gribbon and his party back across the bridge immediately to attack the sandhills and dislodge the enemy. Strong measures were the only way to prevent seizure of the bridgehead, Melliss informed him.

Gribbon and his Punjabis crossed the bridge and advanced towards the sandhills at the double. A burst of rifle fire could be heard but the scuffling troops had kicked up the sand to such a degree that a heavy pall of dust obscured what was happening to the watchers on the other bank. Melliss himself crossed the bridge. Gribbon's covering party was being cut to pieces. Gribbon was hit three times and fell mortally wounded while leading his men in yet another attempt to dislodge the Turkish troops; his second in command, with a chest wound, was trying to encourage the survivors. Melliss ordered the retreat and the remnants of the force struggled back across the bridge being shot down as they fled.

The Turks left the sandhills and advanced to the trenches at the end of the bridge. The survivors of the covering party, together with the engineers, crouched in a shallow, foul-smelling ditch, barely eighteen inches deep, which gave scant cover. Melliss retired to a small mud hut about a hundred yards away in isolation.

To everybody's relief reinforcements of the 7th Gurkhas were sighted advancing across the open plain from Kut. The Turks were now trying to rush across the bridge but so far they were being prevented from doing so by machine-gun fire. The Gurkhas arrived and a general rifle duel across the river ensued. There were several Arabs amongst the Turkish infantry distinguishable by their coloured headcloths. One Arab was particularly noticeable by the way he pushed his rifle over the parapet of the trench and let fly without any pretensions of taking aim.

For seven hours until the sun went down the Gurkhas, Engineers, and the survivors of the covering party crouched in the nullah. It became obvious that the bridge—the back-door into Kut—must be destroyed. It would be a comparatively simple operation to cut it from its moorings on the left bank but it was considered that this would be handing the Turks a complete bridge. If the bridge was to be kept in British hands it would have to be cut at the Turkish end.

Lieutenant A. B. Mathews volunteered to lead this enter-prise. A 50 lb gun-cotton charge was lashed to each end of a plank. The distance between the charges was the same width as the bridge, ensuring that if the plank was placed at right angles to the length of the bridge each of the charges would be located over its strengthening beams where they would do the maximum damage. Slow-burning fuses were attached to the charges.

At just after midnight, Mathews, accompanied by Lieuten-ant Sweet of the 7th Gurkhas, and a small party of his men, crept across the bridge. Several of the *gissaras* had succumbed to the rifle fire and had filled with water and sunk. Two sections of the bridge were under water, and had to be negotiated by wading up to the armpits in the cold, black water. Some of the 'bodies' lying on the bridge were still alive. One man started crying out as the Gurkhas attempted to move him and they held his head under the water until he drowned. Mathews crawled ahead and placed the charges as near to the Turkish end of the bridge as he could. As he lay on his back, searching for his matches, all was silent. The stars overhead were as large as lanterns and seemed to crackle emphasising the chill of the night. Faintly he could hear Turkish voices seemingly raised in argument. Mathews had never heard Turkish spoken before and it sounded strange and throaty. Striking a match which made a sound that reminded him of a door slamming he lit the two fuses and crawled back across the river. A loud explosion followed quickly by another shattered the silence. There was a furious outburst of firing from the other bank. The bridge began to swing. Unfortunately the force of the concussions had split the bridge into sections and these began to float downstream. Nothing could be done to recover them. Townshend recommended Mathews and Sweet for the Victoria Cross. They received the Military Cross.

The Turkish force which Captain Gribbon's party of Punjabis had tried to dislodge from the sandhills was part of a complete Turkish division. This division crossed the Shatt al Hai about five miles down the channel from its junction with the Tigris and approached the eastern flank of the Kut peninsula. In this way Kut was completely surrounded, and the siege begun.

V

THE HOLD TIGHTENS

Despite heavy British artillery fire in a few days the Turkish
forces to the north of Kut had dug a vast network of fire and
communication trenches entirely closing off the neck of the
peninsula. Guns were placed around Townshend's force, as he
described it, 'at all points of the compass, and on both banks'.
The major-general also observed:

> The chief disadvantage of an entrenched camp such as this,
> shaped like the great Indian peninsula with water on all
> sides except north, was that fire from our guns went from the
> centre to the circumference [and] so was divergent and
> disseminated, while that of the enemy was directed from the
> circumference to the centre and thus converged and con-
> centrated.[1]

Townshend was also worried about the low morale of his
Indian troops of which the major part of his force was composed. He attributed this to a shortage of British regular
officers owing to the heavy casualties at Ctesiphon and described it as a 'dangerous and serious factor in the defence of
Kut'. He went as far as to state that this offered a threat to the
successful defence of Kut as the few British Indian Army
reserve officers with his division, although full of zeal, were
untrained and had difficulty in keeping the Indian troops under
control. The discipline had degenerated, he remarked, until they
were little better than armed bands; not entirely unruly ones
though, he added. He deplored the decline of the Indian Army
from the days of the East India Company which had insisted
on a full complement of British officers. He wrote in his diary:

We have now some 8,900 combatants of whom infantry

number 7,000; the British battalions [Norfolks, Dorsets, Oxfords and a half battalion of West Kents] are practically [reduced] to the strength of double companies in peacetime. The want of British officers in some of the Indian battalions is most serious. For example the 110th [Mahrattas] had one British officer; the list of sickly and weakly men unable to march is a depressing one.[2]

Why Townshend was so despondent is not easy to understand. A day or so earlier he had received a jolly telegram from Nixon which read:

I am delighted to send you this just received from Chief, India [Sir Beauchamp Duff]. Begins 'Please convey to General Townshend and all under his command my appreciation of the skill and gallantry displayed in their admirably conducted retirement on Kut al Amara in face of greatly superior numbers'. Following private message from home says: 'All England and Paris are talking of your wonderful success and brilliant achievements.' And so they ought. Army Commander.[3]

Which success was not specified and gives rise to some mystification unless, of course, the two cities were agog over the advance to Ctesiphon which, in the circumstances, would have been extremely tactless of Nixon to mention. Of the retirement to Kut the public, as yet, knew nothing.

Townshend, at the request of his Royal Flying Corps commander, gave permission for his three serviceable aeroplanes to fly downstream to Ali Gharbi, agreeing that they would merely be destroyed by shell fire if they remained in Kut. Despite the overt attention of Turkish snipers, two of the aircraft took off safely and vanished eastwards. One aeroplane broke down, its engine refusing to start again, and it was trundled away to join two other crippled birds stored under tarpaulins to the north of the town. The Engineers were given permission to remove the engines which reappeared again later in a most unexpected role.

Townshend's field telephone at his headquarters rang and he

was informed that a Turkish officer under a white flag was asking to see him. The Turkish *yuzbashi* (equivalent to a captain, literally means the commander of 100 troops) was ushered into the office still blindfolded. The blindfolding of envoys or even prisoners being brought through one's lines was *de rigueur*. The Turkish officer, according to one witness, was smartly dressed and wore 'riding breeches of immaculate cut'.[4] Another officer was 'amazed to find the *yuzbashi* so tall'.[5] What height was expected was not mentioned but it seems that British astonishment at the stature of foreigners is so prevalent as to amount to a national characteristic.

The officer handed Townshend a letter from Nur-ud-Din which requested him to lay down his arms to avoid useless bloodshed. It continued that it was known that the British and Indian garrison was weak and a serious attack would overwhelm it. This was the traditional approach but the Turkish commander also had another. He complained that the occupation of Kut was against the laws of civilised war and by doing so Townshend was exposing the peaceful inhabitants of the town to the horrors of war.

Townshend was more than equal to this challenge. He sent the *yuzbashi* back to his master with a written reply stating that such an absurd demand to lay down his arms was unthinkable. Although he thanked the Turk for his courtesy in conforming to the usual custom in summoning the commander of a besieged town to surrender before starting to bombard it, Nur-ud-Din was 'curiously and extraordinarily in error' in imagining that the defence of a town was against the laws of civilised warfare. In fact, Townshend informed him, there had never been a siege or battle of consequence in Europe which had not included a town or a village. Townshend concluded tartly that Nur-ud-Din's German friends even made a point of involving civilians in their sieges.

Feeling slightly elated, Townshend decided to issue a communiqué to his troops. The major-general was, with a certain amount of justification, a firm believer in this means of bolstering morale. Referring to Nur-ud-Din's unsuccessful overtures, he told his troops that bombardment was imminent but the effect of heavy guns was more mental than material. He continued:

> Stray mules are knocked over, a cart or the corner of a house are destroyed; but let the men remain quietly in their dug-outs and they are not touched. They must keep quiet and reserve their ammunition, both rifle and gun, for the hostile infantry.[6]

He concluded by saying that reinforcements for the Relief Force were now concentrating at Sheikh Saad. This would be completed within the next week.

Townshend was quite accurate with his first prognostication. That afternoon the Turkish artillery began to destroy the town. The shelling up to that time had been for ranging purposes only. Throughout the siege an unusually high proportion of unexploded shells landed in Kut but this deficiency was more than made up for by the quantity. The Turkish guns, ranged around Kut, were estimated to consist of about thirty field-guns, five howitzers and, curiously enough, one of the ancient brass mortars which Townshend's force had found near 'High Wall' at Ctesiphon. The two 4-inch naval guns aboard the captured gunboat *Firefly* very seldom fired on Kut because, it was believed, the Turks wanted to keep the gunboat intact. To bring her in range would have brought her also within range of the heavier British guns.

The main grouping of British artillery strength was near the Brick Kilns, located roughly in the centre of the peninsula. Here there were two 5-inch field guns and four 5-inch howitzers. One field-gun battery was located behind the middle line trenches and another in a palm grove upstream of the town. Early in the siege two 4-inch field-guns were also in this grove but were later moved to another palm grove to the rear. Two 15-pounder field-guns were stationed at the fort and two more near the North-West Section trenches. At various sites in Kut town itself were four naval guns—two 5-inch, one 18-pounder and one 13-pounder. There were four 4·7-inch naval guns mounted precariously in horse boats moored at the river bank and one 3-pounder in the *Sumana*.

Neither the Turkish artillery outside or that of the British inside fired high-explosive shells during the siege. All the shells were 'lyddite' or its Turkish equivalent and, as Townshend remarked, had more bang than bite. Only a direct hit did damage, except of course for the murderous shrapnel shells with their distinctive powder-puffs of white smoke.

The garrison of the fort formed a subordinate command under Lieutenant-Colonel W. H. Brown (103rd Mahrattas) and comprised the 103rd Mahrattas, 119th Infantry, fifty 'bombers' of the Oxfords, the two 15-pounders of the Volunteer Artillery Battery plus the Maxim Machine Gun Battery. The trenches in front of the fort were manned alternately by the Oxfords and the 22nd Punjabis, the battalion not in the trenches forming the local reserve.

The medical authorities had begun to discover that their new hospitals in the bazaars did not occupy the most salubrious of positions. The artillery had also discovered that the immediate vicinity of the bazaars was an ideal situation and had soon established four field-guns within a few yards of one of them. Endeavouring to silence these guns the Turkish artillery on the right bank began to score direct hits on the hospitals, killing patients and staff alike. On 9 December seven Indian stretcher bearers and an orderly were killed outright by one shell.

Townshend was extremely apprehensive of a strong Turkish infantry assault but the enemy confined himself to digging trenches and general shelling. It was still possible to wander along the river bank after dusk as the Turks were as yet too busy to take up sniping as a full-time occupation. The little shop near the bazaar had now closed its doors. It was shortly a pile of rubble.

Across the river at Woolpress village the trench digging by both the British and the Turks was proceeding at speed but the Anatolians were forging ahead by sheer enthusiasm.

A British reconnaissance aeroplane from Ali Gharbi passed over Kut and vanished upstream. The pilot reported to Townshend, via his base, that at Shumran, five and a half miles upstream, there were three Turkish camps of considerable size. Moored next to one of the camps were three paddle steamers,

D

one tug and ten barges. The pilot said that four miles above
Kut on the left bank of the river a line of Turkish trenches ran
in a south-easterly direction. On the right bank of the river,
just behind the sandhills, about 500 Turkish infantry were
bivouacked. With them were four guns. No other troops were
observed on the right bank. About 2,000 enemy were encamped
to the north-east of Kut and there were tents at the Es Sinn
position which the pilot said looked as if they were occupied.

Townshend was still convinced that the Arabs had a concealed arsenal of weapons somewhere in the town. Fearing an
insurrection he issued orders that all officers and men were to
carry arms when moving around Kut and that working parties
must have an armed escort. He forbade any troops from entering the Arab coffee shops. The lull was having a bad effect on
the major-general's nerves. He complained bitterly that Indian
troops were not over-punctilious in saluting officers. He threatened that any further breaches of discipline in this respect
would be severly punished.

The commanding officer of the 48th Indian Pioneers, Colonel
A. J. Hayward, also had his cross to bear. His daily orders
read:

It has been noticed that the communication trench running
from the mess behind the Quarter Guard has been used at
night as a latrine. This trench is not intended for use as a
latrine and must not be used as such. Tins for this purpose are
supplied by the medical officer.[7]

Townshend received a wire from Kitchener asking him briskly
for details of his position at Kut and the relative dispositions
of the Tigris, Shatt al Hai, Kut town and Es Sinn. He asked
Townshend if he had a boat bridge connecting both banks of the
Tigris.

Townshend seemed to misunderstand the reason for Kitchener's enquiry and innocently gave him what almost
amounted to a travelogue. He informed the Secretary of State
for War that his 'entrenched camp was in the peninsula of land
formed by the loop of the Tigris on which the town of Kut
stands, at the most southerly point of the said peninsula'.

From this southerly point, the entrenched camp extends to the northward some 3,200 yards, its breadth is roughly 1,700 yards. We are invested on all sides except the west as yet. The boat bridge which I had brought from its old site outside the sphere of my entrenched camp and placed east of Kut town, had to be demolished last night by volunteers with explosives—a most gallant affair, as the enemy had made a determined attack on the bridge during the day driving in the bridgehead detachment and occupying the bank and the bridgehead. I have no means of gaining the right bank except by the gunboat *Sumana* and a barge. We are heavily shelled by enfilade fire all day. I had 199 casualties yesterday. I occupy the Liquorice Factory and the village on the right bank with two battalions. Es Sinn is seven miles north-east as the crow flies.[8]

A telegram in reply from Kitchener came back in about ninety minutes. As Townshend put it Kitchener was 'evidently anxious'. The following questions were to be answered forthwith:

1. Have the Turks heavy guns superior to ours?

2. What barges have been captured or destroyed, and what did they contain?

3. What is your present view of the situation? How long do you suppose you can hold out? Health and spirit of troops and anything you may want to bring to the attention of the War Committee.

4. How are you employing the 4·7-inch guns and where is the *Shushan*?[9]

Townshend replied:

1. The Turks have four 10·5 centimetre guns which are certainly superior to our 5-inch guns in rapidity and range.

2. No. 1 coal and oil barge, nearly empty; No. 28 barge, containing naval ammunition tents; No. 4 barge, supply and transport stores; No. 11 barge, supply and transport stores, sick men unable to march and a few wounded, 220 boxes of small arms ammunition and 445 rounds for 13-pounder gun;

No. 31 barge, aviation stores; two L. Class launches. All
bridge pontoons and several dannocks sunk by rifle from
bank.

3. My view of the situation is that our strategic offensive
received the usual check, common enough in history when
the offensive has not sufficient troops nor a constant flow of
reinforcements to keep its offensive up to its high water
mark; while the defender, retiring more and more into the
interior, gains time for above factors to weaken the offensive,
and draws nearer supplies and reinforcements not available
to him at the outset of the struggle.

This situation can be quickly remedied by rapid concentration of forces and relief of my beleaguered force, uniting all
forces at Kut for final advance to Baghdad; example Welling-
ton's resumption of the offensive after his retreat from Burgos
to the Portuguese frontier.

The fighting value of my troops has naturally much decreased since Ctesiphon, though discipline maintains. I am
very anxious as to result if enemy makes a determined
onslaught with very superior numbers. We are constantly
shelled all day and I am very anxious to be relieved in, say
ten to fifteen days. I am doing all I can by appealing to the
troops on the ground of their good name and patriotism.
I have 800 sick and am convinced there should not be more
than 300 at the outside. When we are relieved these troops
require rest on the line of communication.

4. My 4·7-inch guns are in horse-boats, but I am endeavouring to mount them on land.

Townshend's reference to the excessive number of sick was
attributed by him later to malingering among his Indian troops.
On 10 December Aylmer officially announced his arrival
from India, to command the Relief Force in a telegram to
Townshend, which read:

Have assumed command Tigris line. Have utmost confidence
in defender of Chitral and his gallant troops to keep flag
flying till we can relieve them. Heartiest congratulations on
brilliant deeds of yourself and your command.

Townshend replied in the same spirit:

Thanks from 6th Division and troops attached for your inspiriting message. Your confidence shall not be misplaced. Grateful thanks from myself for your message. Am proud to serve under you.[10]

Even as the major-general was preparing his reply to Aylmer the Turkish gunfire began to increase in severity. The enemy artillery had been firing shells into Kut all day but as nightfall drew near it became obvious to Townshend that something else was intended. Artillery fire was contagious. As the guns on one side commenced to fire so a corresponding number of guns on the other side began to reply, hoping to either knock its opponent out or cause it to cease fire through sheer funk. In this way guns became 'paired' and an almost 'if you don't, I won't; but if you do, God help you' arrangement existed between rival gun crews.

With the fading light shells began to drop into Kut town, the fort and middle line. The front line was ignored, presumably because the Turks wished to capture it intact. Suddenly the Turkish gunfire ceased. The soldiers feared this silence more than the shells.

A sound of shouting came from along the whole Turkish front line, then from the exits poured the infantry. Their first few paces were unsure and unsteady, with legs stiff and unaccustomed to running but gradually gaining speed, they raced on, accompanied by the jingle of equipment and thudding of feet on the frozen ground. Forward they came, their curiously long bayonets held out before them as though they were shields. Orders were shouted from the British line and the troops along the parapets took aim. Shrill voices. A crackle then a roar as the rifles opened fire. The Turks in the front of the advance staggered and fell, quite slowly and gracefully; lips moving silently and hands stretched skywards. Others sank to their knees and pressed their heads to the ground. They were passed by their fellows. Cold hands in the British trenches worked their rifle bolts. The cartridge cases flew out and clattered to the earth. Bolts crashed as they were rammed home. The fire rippled out

again. The Turks started to shout again, some screaming with
excitement, some with the long-drawn-out baying of fear.
Another volley; the riflemen in the trenches had got into their
stride. The Turks were falling in dozens, rolling on the ground,
lying still. Shrapnel flailing into the running men, earth shooting skywards as if pushed from underneath. Whistles. The
enemy halted as if frozen. More fell, then they began to retreat.
Cheering broke from the British trenches. Some of the yellow
figures on the ground waved their arms; one made a dull
repetitive honking. No one could help them until after dark
and by that time most of them had bled to death. The Turks
attacked four more times before the assault was abandoned.
The British fired 61,000 rounds of rifle ammunition.

During the day's bombardment seven 40-pounder shells
landed in the hospitals, killing six and wounding many more.
Several town Arabs were hit by shell splinters. A five-year-old
child was carried into the hospital with a huge shell wound
which had torn off most of her buttocks; tissue and bone. She
had made a full recovery by the end of March.

Sunrise on the 11th brought another heavy assault. Above
the pandemonium of shrieking shells and clattering rifles, the
long wail of the muezzin—the call to prayer of Islam—echoed
out across Kut from high on the minaret. A young rifleman wrote.
in his diary that he thought the muezzin was beautiful and the
squabble that was going on around him squalid and grubby.
A shell set the matting roof of one of the hospitals on fire. The
casualties began to roll in. The single Turkish infantry attack
lacked sting, however, and was repulsed. The British casualties
for the evening and morning attacks were 202 killed and
wounded. The enemy's losses were unknown.

But the Turks were learning. On the following day they
waited until they knew that the British troops were eating their
breakfast. The trundle of the transport carts which had brought
up the rations to the front line was just dying away when a
heavy rifle barrage opened up on the British first line, particularly in the vicinity of 'D' redoubt. The British troops threw
down their food and lined the parapets of the fire trench. It was
still dark as the enemy launched his attack on the trenches.

The British artillery opened up immediately and flung shrapnel into the tightly massed advancing infantry. Despite heavy losses, small parties of enemy troops managed to reach the barbed wire in front of the British line but were wiped out as they attemped to cut their way through. It grew light but the assault continued until 9 a.m. and was then abandoned. British losses were eighty-eight killed and wounded. The same heavy rifle fire had been opened up on the Liquorice Factory and Woolpress village, but either it was just a feint or the Turks reconsidered their plan to attack, for none was launched. The Turks tried again at dawn on the 13th and met with similar losses and lack of success. Turkish casualties were thought to be heavy.

A staff officer wrote in his diary for these three days how much he admired the companies of Indian soldiers of the 16th Brigade when under attack. These had no British officers and were commanded by their own countrymen. This opinion conflicted completely with Townshend's view of the fighting capacity of his Indian troops.

The hospitals suffered badly. A 'whizz-bang' (see Appendix H) burst inside one of the wards, fatally wounding two orderlies and seriously wounding two more. Another shell smashed into a dispensary, completely destroying all the medical supplies, and yet another exploded in one of the old bazaar arches now doing service as a ward and showered bricks and debris over the three inmates. An Indian *havildar* (sergeant) with a broken leg had the leg broken again, his scalp torn open and eight additional wounds. One of the medical officers, Major Charles Barber, became convinced that his office was the focal point of the Turkish artillery with some justification. A shell burst outside his door, a second inside his office and a third—Barber by this time had moved—demolished the office completely. This last shell was of the heavy type known as 'Windy Lizzies'. Fortunately for the garrison of Kut, and Barber, the shellfire ceased just after noon and decreased in severity for the next ten days.

Normally the medical units were equipped and staffed to deal with 650 wounded. Because of the persistent Turkish infantry attacks and shellfire the daily average reached over 1,000. By

Christmas 1,140 sick and wounded were accommodated in the hospitals. This congestion threatened to cause a breakdown in the medical arrangements and so the old Turkish *serai* was used as a convalescent depot to relieve the pressure. At the beginning of the siege those wounded in the first line were carried or found their own way from the trenches to dugouts with shrapnel-proof roofs in the palm groves to the north of the town. Here the temporary dressings were removed, the wounds examined and redressed. Ideally the patients were fed and rested before being transferred to the bazaar hospitals on the river front. But because of the increased Turkish sniping and shellfire, which prevented movement above ground in daylight, the wounded had to wait in the trenches, or at the fort, until after dark, when it was possible for the stretcher bearers, or if neces-sary the pain-inflicting transport carts, to collect them. Before the construction of the communication trenches, even at night the collection of the wounded from the trenches had to be carried out under persistent sniping and sometimes heavy rifle fire. There was always a shortage of medical staff in the trenches as the bazaar hospitals took precedence for personnel. This shortage, already a serious one because of the below standard medical establishment of the Indian Army, was aggravated by Ctesiphon where eight doctors were lost. A number of medical staff had also been sent downstream with the wounded. Sub-sequently three doctors were killed by shellfire in Kut and another two died of disease.

Although the artillery quietened down, the Turkish infantry, still engaged in digging, began to display another character-istic at which they excelled. Persistent sniping at the northern front, including the fort, and across the river from the right bank became the order of the day. Hardly anywhere, unless among the houses of the town, was there any respite from the attention of these riflemen. They fired at anything that moved and a continuous stream of wounded soldiers and town Arabs taxed the resources of the dispensaries and hospitals.

Although these Turkish sharpshooters took a heavy toll their enterprise and tirelessness earned for them a grudging admira-tion. Under cover of darkness they would crawl to shallow ditches or depressions, sometimes within thirty or forty yards of the British lines. As soon as it became light enough to see, these marksmen began their grim business, defying every attempt to dislodge them. Others of less stern stuff in the enemy trenches would merely point their rifles in the air in the general direction of Kut and pull the triggers. These spent bullets ripped through the tents of the reserve troops near the middle line inflicting a considerable number of head and chest wounds. Most of the British and Indian troops avowed that it was safer in the front line trenches where these bullets hardly ever fell. The Turkish snipers lay in their hollows existing on a handful of dates, a military biscuit or two and a mouthful of water despite the bitter cold weather and the biting wind.

The cold was particularly felt in the trenches. The days were cold and the nights were freezing. Apart from greatcoats which few possessed neither the British nor the Indian troops had clothing even approaching the thickness adequate for the low temperatures. The men in their cotton drill clustered together, cupping hands around cigarettes for warmth. Oil lamps were forbidden, to conserve fuel supplies. Wood fires in the trenches were out of the question as the smoke drew the attention of the Turkish gunners. The Indian soldiers suffered especially from the cold. They started to wear blankets over their heads and shoulders. Townshend heartlessly strictly forbade this practice as 'unsoldierly'. A soldier wrote in a letter: 'The washing water was frozen over this morning. Thank Christ I'm not a bleeding officer.' On 12 December Colonel Hayward of the 48th Pioneers triumphed in his persistent war against breaches of discipline. Bhistie (sweeper) Nehada of 'C' Company was apprehended for 'committing a nuisance in an unauthorised place' and fined one rupee (1s. 4d.).

Oberleutant von Kiesling in his book *Mit Feldmarschall von der Goltz Pasha im Mesopotamien und Persien* attributes the lull in the Turkish infantry attacks to the arrival of von der Goltz at Nur-ud-Din's headquarters at Kut. According to Kiesling, the new supreme commander forbade any further attempt to take Kut by storm; they had cost the Turks, so far, some 800 dead and numerous wounded. Nur-ud-Din had been under the impression that only a portion of Townshend's force was still inside Kut. Goltz, however, knew the truth and to him it appeared to be a better plan to starve the garrison into submission. If Nur-ud-Din was not pleased to see von der Goltz, a certain British lieutenant of artillery had no such reservations.

This officer, in charge of an emplacement near the Brick Kilns, was supervising the cleaning and oiling of his field gun. While staring through the sighting tube, ever vigilant for that speck of rust, he was distracted from his purpose. Striding along near some enemy trenches at about 700 yards' range was a gaggle of senior Turkish officers and, above all, the portly form of Field Marshal von der Goltz. A shell was slammed into the breach; a quick turn of a wheel realigned the field piece; a hand crashed down on the firing handle. The British officer was gratified to see a heavy shower of mud and flying field service caps, pickelhaubes and 'enverris' as the enemy officers scrambled into a nearby trench. The shot had missed and there was no opportunity for another but the officer would have a good story to tell in the mess later that evening. Almost before the sound of the shot had died away the matter was reported to Townshend. The major-general was furious. He considered that von der Goltz was one of the world's foremost military strategists and his idol's summary treatment at the hands of a mere subaltern was intolerable. The offending officer (Townshend does not give his name) was 'severely reprimanded'. From the tone of Townshend's account of the incident he seems fortunate not to have been court martialled.

Captain Sandes' 'Bridging Train' was still hard at work. Townshend's plan of defence included the improvement of the western, southern and south-eastern parts of Kut. The system provided for a slow withdrawal, with house to house fighting, if the Turks had been successful in piercing the northern front or effecting a landing on the river bank (southern front). The Tigris by now was at such a low state that it was feared that if the level continued to drop at its present rate the Turks might be able to wade across the river. To enable Townshend's slender military resources to be transferred quickly from one defensive quarter to another the construction of a series of 'emergency roads' was put in hand. A sufficient number of north–south roads were already in existence but only a few narrow mud alleys ran from east to west. Sandes was given the job of driving new roads through the town.

There is no doubt that this work caused the townsfolk considerable hardship and distress. Sandes thus described his endeavours:

> It was rather amusing work knocking these 'rabbit runs' through these houses. I was supposed to get official leave from the Military Governor before boring into a house but time did not permit so, after a few enquiries to avoid the risk of inconveniencing any influential Arab, I would set my men to attacking the selected wall with picks and crowbars and in time a small hole would appear right through the wall backed by the protesting face of an Arab shouting 'Makoo, Makoo' [no, no]. He was politely waved aside with 'Akoo, Akoo' [yes, yes] and soon we were climbing through into one of his downstairs rooms and out into his courtyard where we started the same again towards the next house while the recently made hole was enlarged into a good doorway. The 'emergency roads' were thus completed in three weeks. There was always a pleasing uncertainty as to where one was going to come out and this added to the fascination of knocking things down felt by most males. The Arab owners were liberally compensated and were given sheets of matting to act as screens. They quickly recovered from any injury when shining rupees began to trickle into their palms.[11]

At the beginning of the siege the water requirements of Townshend's force, with its large numbers of horses, mules, donkeys and battery-bullocks, had been met by working parties with buckets and cans from the Tigris. The increasing activity of the Turkish snipers from across the river had now put a stop to this method and now water was delivered by two pump-houses on the river bank to two 7,500 gallon canvas 'tanks' in the palm groves. Because of the fear of contamination or the introduction of poison the Arabs were forbidden to approach these military reservoirs. This order was the cause of more hardship and even death to the town's native population. As the sniping had increased tunnels had been dug under the north–south roads in order that they might be crossed during daylight hours. The roads themselves, however, had been rendered unusable until mud-filled kerosene-can walls had been built across their ends near the river. At dusk the Arab womenfolk, the traditional carriers of water, began to gather behind these walls carrying their long-necked earthenware jars. They chattered nervously, their voices rising in pitch as the occasional bullet, from across the river, struck a wall with a swish and a thwack.

As it grew darker the women began to venture from the protection of the walls and make for the river, some sixty yards away. At first one, then another and then a long, black stream. There would be a crack of a rifle and a thud, but the women would continue with the task of filling their water vessels. Occasionally a woman would fall to the ground. This resulted in a general stampede back to the walls. Weeping relatives would wait until well after dark before collecting the body of the latest victim to carry her home or, more often than not, fruitlessly to one of the hospitals. Every night the same little drama would be played out. After a shooting the river bank would be deserted for an hour or two except for scavenging dogs and then the water-carriers would continue their dangerous task.

The Turkish artillery still occasionally lobbed shells into Kut, it was thought for ranging purposes, after shifting the site of a gun. A 'Windy Lizzie' (see Appendix H) crashed through the roof of a dugout in which eight warrant officers were seated playing cards. One was killed outright and two others died shortly afterwards; the survivors were treated in hospital and recovered. Captain Sandes had a narrow escape. A shell burst so close to him that he contracted bronchitis from the fumes. He remembers thanking God that 'Adbul' had no poison gas shells.

Major Dashwood, a medical officer with the Punjabis, devised a different, if dangerous, way of passing the time. He collected 'danger spots'. These were found along the river bank and distinguishable by bullet-pitted walls and perhaps a few blood stains. These marked a Turkish sniper's aiming point. Dashwood used to test these 'danger spots' for potency by leaping into view. He would then collect a few of his cronies and demonstrate the accuracy of the sniper's fire. Unfortunately for Dashwood another officer had a fondness for the same hobby. Dashwood became the second one to find a 'danger spot' and the sniper was waiting for him. He narrowly escaped with his life.

By mid-December the Turks had dug so hard and well that on the extreme right of the British line they were only about fifty yards away from the fort. The digging could be heard quite plainly by working parties on both sides. As a precaution against surprise attack the garrison of the fort was reinforced by 150 Norfolks from the 'General Reserve'.

During the night of 14 December, the Woolpress troops launched a successful attack and drove their besiegers from their trenches. The imperturbable Turks dug some more further away.

Although the garrison's morale was high and popular opinion put the probable date of relief at about Christmas, Townshend continued to be seriously worried by his Indian troops. He informed Aylmer by radio that he had withdrawn an Indian battalion from the fort because he doubted its discipline under pressure of a concerted attack. He had good reasons for this despondency. On that day No. 1748 Sepoy Sheo Chand, of 'C' Company, 48th Pioneers, had received a gun-shot wound on his right hand. The enquiry and court martial established that the sepoy had wrapped his right hand in a piece of cloth, placed it over the muzzle of his rifle, pulled the trigger and blown off the middle two fingers. He was sentenced to five years' imprisonment. On the same day another sepoy, of the 120th Infantry, had deserted his post and committeed a similar act. The Indian was sentenced to be shot but Townshend refused to confirm the sentence and it was commuted to seven years' imprisonment. Townshend also said he was becoming concerned by the number of casualties, which he placed at between 100 and 200 a day.

Another aerial reconnaissance from Ali Gharbi informed him via base that his estimate that he was surrounded by about 12,000 enemy troops with thirty-three guns was roughly correct. Townshend placed the distribution of the enemy as some 8,500 on the left bank, including 3,000 in the Turkish front line trenches, 1,000 scattered around Kut in small detachments on the right bank, plus some 2,000 horsemen. This body of mounted troops were seen later moving down the right bank in the direction of Es Sinn. The effective strength of Townshend's force was 9,185.

More bad news was on the way. One of the Turkish snipers had over-stepped himself and having been ringed by rifle fire had been forced to surrender. The Turk told his captors that although the surrounding force still only consisted of the four divisions which had defeated them at Ctesiphon (35th, 38th, 45th and 51st), two more divisions, the 26th and 52nd, were expected to arrive shortly. Any suspicion that this was a bluff and that a 'willing' prisoner had fallen into British hands was swiftly dispelled by a report from Intelligence at Basra which said that one of the expected Turkish divisions (52nd) was just finishing its reorganisation at Baghad. Townshend cabled Nixon forthwith, saying that he trusted the Russians were being asked to put pressure on Baghdad by advancing in that direction and so taking the strain off him.

Townshend's chief of artillery, Brigadier-General G. B. Smith, an elderly man whose health was declining, had been relieved from duty. His successor, Colonel Grier, had hardly been installed in his place when he was wounded in the head by a spent bullet. Colonel Courtenay, R.G.A., was appointed in his place. Informing Nixon of these changes Townshend also took the opportunity to preach his gospel about the relatively few British officers in his Indian regiments. He said that a policy which made it necessary for inexperienced captains and even subalterns to be put in command of battalions was nothing short of 'criminally foolish'.[12] These young officers could barely keep control. Townshend's remarks were ignored by Nixon. In return he received a summary of telegrams which had arrived at Baghdad. One cable from the Secretary of State for India,

Austen Chamberlain, informed him that the Russians intended to advance on Kermanshah and Khanaqin in Persia to the neglect of Baghdad. Townshend then realised that any movement on Baghdad would be of a limited nature if indeed there was any at all.

To add to Townshend's worries it had been reported that it was becoming increasingly difficult to obtain dairy produce in Kut. On Saturday, 18 December 1915, the following announcement appeared in all regimental orders:

Supplies. All troops and followers and interpreters are strictly forbidden to buy local produce such as fowls, eggs, milk, etc., which are urgently required for the sick and wounded. All produce will be bought up by the L.P.O. [Local Produce Officer] who will, after meeting the requirements of the hospitals, issue the remainder, on cash payment. Any infringement of this order will be severely dealt with.[13]

Townshend also decided on further economies. From this time all British troops had their meat (beef) ration reduced to twelve ounces and fresh potatoes to six ounces. The Indians had their ration of dhall (lentils) reduced to two ounces. The other rations remained at the standard issue. These minor reductions caused little or no hardship.

Townshend was in the habit of taking an evening stroll around the town with Spot his fox terrier. Unlike his master, Spot was no Dog of War. Even the 'brrph' of a shell being sped on its way was enough to terrify the animal and he would take off for home, leaving his master dogless—almost a state of nakedness for an officer of the Indian Army. Townshend was not a little self-conscious of his dog's blatant cowardice in the face of the enemy. Any reference to it was taboo. This, of course, turned it into a standing joke. One evening the whine of a shell had set Spot off on his usual retreat and Townshend had turned off his accustomed beat into one of the 'emergency roads' in an endeavour to intercept the fleeing animal. Sprawled, half-slumbering, in a doorway with a blanket about his shoulders, was No. 2017 Sepoy Jodha. Indian soldiers were not at the height of their popularity with Townshend. Idling and blanket-wearing were anathema. The man was reported to his unit, charged with malingering and being improperly dressed, found guilty and sentenced to twelve lashes of the cat-o'-nine-tails. All regimental orders for the following day carried the following announcement:

> Discipline. The G.O.C. regrets to observe the slovenly appearance of the troops in the streets of the town and draws immediate attention to this matter of all officers commanding regiments and admin. units. The movements of hospital patients at the convalescent stage should be limited to certain prescribed areas near the hospital.[14]

Townshend had enough on his plate as it was. Aylmer had telegraphed him to ask how he thought the Relief Force could enter Kut when it had advanced upstream. He wondered if the major-general would be able to put his force across the river to the right bank to link up with the Relief Force. Townshend had been informed by his engineering commander that a bridge to the other bank was out of the question. There was an acute shortage of bridging materials as the remains of Sandes' bridge had been sunk by gunfire when it had threatened to drift to the Turkish side of the river. Townshend wired to Aylmer and said that it would be better if the Relief Force approached Kut along the left bank, thus obviating the necessity of crossing the river. The major-general considered that the task of ferrying his infantry across the river for the proposed link-up would be perilous. His only means of crossing the river was now by the *Sumana*, launches and barges. He did have the fifty *mahailas* but as these were engineless they would be unmanageable and would be swept downstream under the Turkish guns. With the engine-driven craft at his disposal Townshend calculated that it would take two hours to embark 700 men (the capacity of his fleet), ferry them across the Tigris, disembark and return the empty transport to the embarkation point. By a straightforward multiplication the major-general arrived at a total of twenty hours to put his 7,000 infantry across the river. Another twenty hours would be required to ferry his 3,000 animals, such as officers' chargers, field batteries and Maxim gun mules;

his field ambulances would take another six hours and thirty transport carts fifteen hours more. If time were added for the transference of his stores and supplies a total of about nine days would be required to complete the job. Townshend thought that this might be reduced to six days if the ferrying was continued through the day as well as at night but he shuddered to think what the Turkish artillery might do to his force while this was taking place. Townshend told Aylmer that the only alternative to an advance up the left bank was for the Relief Force commander to bring his own bridge.

An unreasoned rumour took hold of the Kut garrison which said that the military post office was open and that letters and parcels were being distributed. Why anyone could have credited this is hard to imagine. Townshend's force had been besieged now for almost a month and out of reach of ordinary communications for considerably longer but crowds gathered at the battered post office on the river front only to find it closed. The rumour was probably the manifestation of the men's loneliness. The 'what are we doing here anyway' feeling was beginning to take hold. A probable basis for the rumour was that Townshend was allowing his senior officers to make a small number of private radio messages to Basra. This practice was later extended to other officers. The rank and file were excluded. The crowd at the post office watched miserably as the shattered body of a sepoy was carried into the hospital near by. A 'whizz-bang' had torn off both the Indian soldier's legs. He died later that evening. The following day a Turkish shell obligingly destroyed the post office—and all future rumours of letters from home.

VI
THE ASSAULT

Townshend's 'emergency roads', now complete, opened up entirely new vistas of Kut for those with the time, interest and authority to wander along them. Each one had its appropriate letter ('A', 'B', 'C' or 'D'), painted on wooden boards at the junctions with the north–south roads or at difficult corners where an influential Arab's house had caused the road to swerve or sidestep. Because of this it was often difficult to keep to the correct lane.

A stroller, entering 'A' road from the west side of Kut, passed down the landward side of the riverside bazaar hospital, and entered a khan (inn) through a hole in the wall. This khan, in common with all the others in the town, was a filthy, smelly area of hard mud surrounded by a verandah which let off into five-foot square, low, mud-walled, dark chambers, or stables, as the occasion or the traveller demanded. Leaving through the wall at the other side of the khan, the wanderer passed through the corner of a matting-roofed, noisome hovel, collected a number of insects, mostly fleas and spiders, which parachuted from above into the hair, and stumbled into an old flea-bitten Arab pony; a great favourite with the troops until it disappeared mysteriously later to fill a more urgent need.

Emerging into the daylight again, one passed through one nondescript courtyard into another. The continuous sounds of hammering, sawing and filing identified the headquarters of the Royal Engineers where sinister experiments were constantly taking place. Inside the stable-like building the walls were festooned with various instruments of death, palpable or in embryo. Parts of guns and rifles, mirrors, metal pipes and coïls of wire covered the benches. Townshend's division was not equipped with trench mortars and the engineers were making some out of wood and baling wire. The 70 h.p. Gnome engines from the crippled aircraft stood to one side and Captain R. E. Stace had removed one of the pot-shaped cylinders and was tinkering with it on a bench to the left. It was in this building that 'jam pot' grenades, or bombs, were made. These were jam tins containing gun-cotton charges which were then topped up with pieces of metal, old rusty nails, broken glass, Turkish shrapnel picked up at the fort; in fact anything that would cut bruise, tear or maim, when the fuse was lit and the bomb tossed among advancing enemy infantry. This was the basis of the design for the grenades which were lobbed from the wooden mortars.

One private, working on another bench, was constantly referring to a page torn from an illustrated magazine which gave an account and a photograph of a 'hyposcope'. This was a rifle mounted on a frame with a periscope fitted near the back sight. This device, said to have been invented by an Australian private serving in France, allowed the weapon to be aimed and fired without the rifleman bringing his head above a trench parapet and receiving a bullet through it as a consequence. Three 'hyposcopes' had been constructed and set up at the fort and were found to be extremely useful against snipers. Ordinary periscopes for safe observation from trenches and even Roman-style catapults were also constructed here. Leaving this palace of home-made slaughter, one walked past a jumble of dugouts occupied by infantry and shielded from the snipers aross the river by a wall of sand-filled kerosene cans. Here the road dipped through a tunnel under an unprotected north-bound road, up to ground level again, through some troops' quarters and straight into the Turkish bath. This was a domed and vaulted building and looked like the crypt of a cathedral, and as dark; lit by an oil lamp or by the cooking fires of the Hindus who had adopted the building. Another dip beneath a road, through a hole in a wall and into the living-room of a house occupied by the Rajputs. Outside one could hear the thuds and shouts of the enthusiastic Rajput footballers and see their breath in the cold air. The traveller had now arrived at the other side of the town.

A climb up the usual winding staircase set in the usual wall of the usual courtyard brought one on to the flat roof of the Punjabis' mess. On three sides was a four-foot high mud brick wall loopholed at intervals of three yards. On the remaining side which faced east a sheet of corrugated iron had been erected to the height of the other walls. The loopholes were surrounded by sandbags. Two or three snipers or observers were usually on duty here. Each man sat on a brick or two with his eye to a telescope. Within reach were a few spare cartridge clips. Occasionally there would be a sharp crack as a rifleman spotted a Turkish head.

This roof was about forty feet from the ground and commanded a good view of Kut, the river, and the surrounding country. Immediately below, on the river side, rolled the *mahailas*, the tips of their tall masts describing circles. Straight across the river was the mouth of the Shatt al Hai, the connecting link between the Tigris and the Euphrates. At this time of the year the Hai was shallow and, in many places, dry. On either side of the channel and stretching along the river bank as far as the Woolpress village were the Turkish trenches. In these the Turkish infantrymen and Arabs could be seen as they passed small gaps in the parapets, a sight welcomed by the British snipers. Woolpress village occupied about a quarter of a mile of river bank opposite the west end of Kut and consisted of a hundred or so flat-roofed mud houses. High above them was the iron structure of the woolpress. Beyond and to the rear of the village were more Turkish trenches.

Away to the west, on the skyline, one could see the great white mass of tents of the Turkish camp at Shumran, as well as the masts and funnels of their river craft, including those of the captured gunboat *Firefly*. On the right-hand bank, stretching between Shumran and the Sinn ridge, ran a raised mud road. There was always something moving here, a camel train or straggling infantry. Towards the north-east the river curved round to Fort Magasis and perhaps thirty miles beyond were the peaks of the Pusht-i-Kuh, which stood out a milky pink in the fading sunlight of evening. To the north spread Kut town; a heterogeneous collection of flat housetops with, here and there, a watcher gazing through a telescope or an Arab woman strutting about a courtyard, and a line of guns limbers in the shelter of a wall. Beyond the houses and gardens was a conglomeration of debris, rubbish, with possibly a dead horse or mule with its legs stuck stiffly in the air, old broken transport carts and scavenging dogs.

Behind the rubbish dump, in the middle distance, standing above the plain like truncated Martello towers, were the Brick Kilns. Three of the kilns had been turned into artillery observation posts and the heads of watching soldiers could be seen above the sandbag eyries at the tops. Around the bases of these kilns were irregularities in the ground marking the gun emplacements. Then came the flat plain stretching away to the British first line with the fort on its extreme right.

Between 7 and 18 December the Turks, working night and day, had established six lines of deep trenches which ran parallel to, and the foremost within 150 yards of, the north-east face of the fort. Then they had begun to dig saps, sticking out like fingers towards the fort, getting closer day be day. Nothing could be seen of the Turkish diggers except shovelfuls of earth thrown up from below.

Intensive efforts were being made to destroy the British barbed-wire entanglements in front of the fort. Some sort of machine was being used to throw spherical bombs from the nearest Turkish trench. They pitched like cricket balls about fifty yards from the wire and bounced across the hard ground into the entanglements and then exploded. By 23 December most of the wire and its supporting posts opposite the fort's north-eastern bastion and eastern corner had been destroyed. While this destruction was in progress the Turks kept up an incessant rifle fire against the fort's mud walls. Occasionally a bullet snicked through a loophole claiming a victim. By far the more serious hazard, however, was the 'lobbed' bullets, those fired high in the air which descended without warning inside the fort. The wounds received in this way were seldom mortal but this activity accounted for about twenty casualties a day, causing a continual drain on the working parties inside the fort. The rifle fire was supplemented by intermittent artillery bombardments which more or less kept to a schedule. These 'hates' as the bombardments were termed, could be expected from 7.30 a.m. to 9.30 a.m. and from 4 p.m. to 6 p.m. with the guns also opening up for a brief period at noon.

At first the gunfire was directed at the south-east bastion, but then it turned its attention to the north-east bastion. A dangerous situation almost developed when a series of shells killed eight Sirmur sappers located in this bastion and destroyed their equipment. The surviving sappers managed to prevent a fire spreading to their explosives stored in a dugout near-by. The north-east bastion was then neglected by the enemy artillery in favour of the east wall, the observation tower, and the river wall, each in turn. This observation tower was an extremely vulnerable forty-foot-high stack of mud-filled sacks. At the top sat two observation officers who were forward spotters for the artillery near the Brick Kilns to which they were connected by field telephone. The Turkish gunners were not tardy and usually shifted their guns overnight and opened fire from a fresh position each morning. It was the observation officer's duty each dawn to spot the new emplacements and report them to the artillery commander for subsequent treatment.

As far as the limited daily allowance of ammunition would allow, the British artillery tried to delay the progress of the enemy's saps. The fort's two 15-pounder field-guns manned by the Volunteer Artillery Battery also took part in this work. This battery was a territorial unit raised in India and was composed almost entirely of Anglo-Indians (the sons of mixed British and Indian parentage). Most of its members were little more than schoolboys. One private was a fifteen-year-old who persistently claimed he was at least seventeen.

In the early days of the siege the lives of those unfortunate enough to be stationed at the fort had been short without the usual compensating feature of being merry. Due to the restricted nature of its original conception the interior of the fort was completely devoid of cover. For the first fortnight all troops who could be spared from the work on the main defences of the peninsula worked in three-hour shifts (three hours' digging and three hours' resting), often until 4 a.m. the following day, preparing dugouts inside the fort until at last on 23 December the fort's garrison could eat and rest in comparative safety underground. But the work of maintaining the defences was without end. When they could be spared, parties of sappers and 48th Pioneers from Kut assisted the garrison in repairing the walls that were constantly being breached by gunfire. This continuous work took its toll of the garrison in partial and even complete collapse through exhaustion.

As the days passed the Turks pushed their saps closer. The British replied by pushing out some of their own from the trenches in front of the fort. It then became a matter of waiting until the Turks dug themselves into the range of the 'jam pot' bombers. The Turks, strangely, countered with pamphlets tied to sticks, but as they always fell short of the British saps the defending troops had to contain their curiosity until later in the siege.

The wooden mortars arrived from the R.E. workshops and received a cool reception. The wooden barrels dried out after about twenty rounds had been fired, then contracted and choked the grenades with sensational results. The firers of these Elizabethan weapons became extremely fast sprinters. These guns did, however, stop the Turks sapping closer for a considerable period. As one operator observed: 'Whether this was because of the fear of the grenade or of the exploding wooden gun itself will remain a mystery.'

The answer to the problem of the wooden mortars was supplied by Captain Stace's modifications to the Gnome aircraft engines. He had converted the cylinders of the radial engines into mortars and two of these arrived at the fort. At first they threw 3-lb. T.N.T. aeroplane bombs which were fairly accurate up to a range of 300 yards but occasionally snags occurred. Loose collars were attached to the bomb so they would fit snugly in the cylinder. These sometimes failed to drop off when fired and spoiled the projectile's trajectory. This failure often caused the bomb to land inside the fort. The mortar gunners developed skills similar to those of ornithologists and could spot a 'collared' or 'collarless' bomb

immediately and remove themselves quickly from the vicinity
of the explosion. Captain Stace, however, solved the problem by
adapting the gun so that it could fire the 'jam pot' bombs
which fitted snugly in the barrels of the Gnome mortars without
collars.

The Turkish practice of concentrating artillery on various
parts of the fort's defences in turn made it obvious that it was
only a matter of time before an infantry assault was launched
on this sector. With this conviction another fear took hold—of
underground burrowing. Mining, as it was called, was often
resorted to by an attacking force in order to destroy the enemy's
defences. Tunnels, sometimes hundreds of yards long and as
much as fifty feet down, would be dug until they reached the
defenders' positions. A large explosive charge was then placed
at the end of the tunnel and detonated with disastrous effect.
It was decided that the only way to find out if the Turks were
digging a mine was to make a sortie and take a look.

On 17 December, just after dark had fallen, a party of sappers
crept out to the barbed wire and prepared two channels through
it and then lay there in the dark ready to stave off any surprise
Turkish attack. The moon came up, bathing the pock-marked
landscape with white light. The sappers lay motionless. The
moon was due to set just before dawn and this confined the
sortie to the short interval between moonset and the coming
of daylight. No. 1 Sortie Party, waiting in the north-east
bastion, was composed of fifty men of the 103rd Mahrattas,
four 'jam pot' bombers, and six sappers, led by a British officer,
and carrying explosive to destroy the Turkish mines if any were
found. No. 2 Sortie Party, stationed in the trenches outside the
fort, had fifty men of the 119th Infantry, four 'jam pot' bombers
and six sappers, led by an Indian jemadar (lieutenant). The
two parties watched the moon fade in the black sky and dashed
through the channels in the barbed wire towards the enemy
trenches. The digging Turks were taken by surprise and were
bayoneted before they could drop their shovels and grab
rifles. The British parties then worked their way along the
Turkish trenches and saps. A fierce fight developed with a party
of Turks trapped in the third sap opposite the north face of the

fort but eventually they were wiped out by the 'jam pot' bombers. The five saps were explored but no traces of mining were found. The two parties returned to the fort, just as the first wafer of dawn was appearing in the eastern sky, with twelve prisoners and a quantity of rifles and trenching tools. They reported that forty Turks had been killed. One of the British troops was slightly wounded. The British officer was awarded the Military Cross for this exploit. The news that no mining was in progress considerably lightened the hearts of those in the fort but in the ensuing days the Turks redoubled their efforts to destroy the barbed wire with mortars and the spherical bombs.

Christmas Eve commenced with a heavy Turkish bombardment of the fort, Woolpress village and the northern end of the British first line. The fire on the fort was concentrated on the north-east bastion by an estimated twenty guns placed in a semi-circle from the north-west to the river on the south-east. Almost immediately the Volunteer Artillery Battery's two 15-pounders were destroyed and, more seriously, the telephonic communication between the observation tower and artillery headquarters was cut. Shortly after 8.30 a.m. the Turkish artillery ceased its bombardment of Woolpress village and joined the remainder in pounding the fort. The noise was deafening. Shells slammed into the fort and the walls crumbled to heaps of rubble. The bombardment turned the trenches along the inside of the walls into graves. The men lining the loopholes of the eastern wall were buried under the cascading debris. The north-east bastion had degenerated into a ruin and its former occupants, thirty men of the Oxfords, withdrew behind the stockade. This was a wall of *bhoosa* (compressed animal fodder) bales some yards to the rear. They were joined by the gunless survivors of the Volunteer Artillery Battery.

The bombardment of the fort continued until 11.30 a.m. when it suddenly ceased. The men were ordered out of their dugouts. The air was thick with smoke and dust. The men at the stockade peered ahead trying to see what was happening, shielding their eyes from the dust. The 103rd Mahrattas moved up to their flank on both sides.

A loud cry from overhead was heard. One of the artillery

spotters in his roost of mud sacks was shouting and pointing. They could hear it now; the pounding of feet, the jingle of equipment and a growing murmur of voices.

Some yellow-uniformed figures crouched low over their long bayonets appeared in the gap where the north-east bastion had stood. Rifles crashed out, 'jam pot' bombs were thrown, and the Gnome mortars hissed and banged. The air was clearing quickly now and the riflemen along the loopholes kept up a continuous crackle of fire. Some Turkish infantrymen threw themselves into the ditch in front of the fort walls and holding haversacks on bayonets attempted to cover the loopholes. They were shot down instantly.

Another attack had been launched against the eastern point of the fort. Fighting their way across the British trenches about a hundred Turkish infantry clambered over the debris of the wall and although a stout defence was put up by the 119th Infantry they were being pressed back further into the fort area. Major A. J. Anderson, the commander of the Volunteer Artillery Battery, who had forsaken his useless telephone on top of the observation tower and was trying to join his men at the stockade, found his way blocked by the desperately fighting men. The 119th Infantry had lost all but two of its officers and lacked cohesion. Anderson threw in his lot with the retreating men, rallied them and they began to hold their ground. Exchanging bayonet jab for bayonet jab they drove the Turks back across the debris. The Rajput company of the 119th Infantry led by Captain W. F. C. Gilchrist, which had been temporarily swamped when the Turks had overrun the trenches outside, began to put in some effective riflework from the enemy's rear, raking the desperately fighting Turks from end to end.

At the stockade the Oxfords and the Mahrattas were still pelting the enemy with bombs and keeping up heavy machine-gun fire. The artillery gunners at the Brick Kilns, by now having realised that the fort was being attacked, opened fire on the Turkish trenches in front of the fort, killing the enemy troops as they emerged to reinforce their comrades in the attack. Although a few Turks braved the British artillery fire and advanced, their numbers were not enough and the enemy attack began to waver and fall back. The defenders, shouting and cheering, pursued them through the breaches in the walls. The Turks turned and ran back to their trenches. Immediately, the defenders set about piling the debris into something that resembled defensive walls and to collect the wounded lying among the crumpled brickwork. These were taken to the fort's dugout hospital where they would have to remain until nightfall before being transferred to the bazaar hospitals.

The workers at the walls and bastions drank mouthful after mouthful of water; their thirst assuaged they continued to drink as a nervous reaction. They smoked cigarettes and stared at the Turkish trenches.

The Turks were bringing up large numbers of reinforcements and it was obvious that they were not prepared to let matters rest as they were. The enemy artillery, however, which had ceased firing just before the attack, remained silent. A solitary shrapnel shell burst overhead and wounded a British lieutenant in the face. He was carried to the dugout hospital.

At 1 p.m. reinforcements began to arrive at the fort. The remainder of the Oxfords, some 200 who had been in the brigade reserve, were detailed to defend the section from the north-east bastion to the fort's north-eastern corner to replace the 119th Infantry who had suffered heavily. The company of Oxfords at the stockade was reinforced by ten men. The Rajputs remained in their trenches outside the fort. The commander of the fort, Colonel Brown, also ordered the Mahrattas to maintain their position on the flanks of the stockade but instructed them to fall back if the Turkish infantry once more attacked through the north-east bastion breach. They were to retire to side galleries (small trenches) thus allowing crossfire from the right and left, as well as from the stockade, to bear on the attackers.

At dusk a Turkish shell swept the top of Townshend's headquarters in the town where a collection of officers were peering towards the fort. Captain Begg, R.G.A., was killed instantly and the acting artillery commander, Lieutenant-Colonel Courtenay, and his staff officer, Captain C. L. Garrett, R.F.A., were badly wounded. The colonel's leg and arm were broken but he dragged himself on to his good leg and, leaning on a helping shoulder, hopped below. These officers' wounds were to prove mortal.

Two hours after darkness had fallen the battlefield in front of the fort was lit by a moon partially obscured by clouds. At 8 p.m. the Turks attacked. The enemy infantry, fronted by a line of 'bombers', dashed once more at the breached north-east bastion and gained entry. The Mahrattas fled to the right and left thus allowing the converging fire to cut swathes through the attackers. Flares were fired but the smoke and dust almost

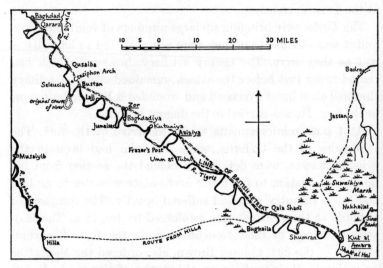

The Tigris from Kut al Amara to Baghad

completely obscured the advancing infantry. Using the confusion to best advantage the Turks lobbed bombs amongst the Mahrattas in the side galleries with terrible results. The casualties among the British troops at the stockade began to mount; it seemed as though the bhoosa bale wall was about to be outflanked. The bursting bombs, the continuous machine-gun and rifle fire, the shouts and screams of the fighting men created a terrific din. The British artillery at the Brick Kilns fired salvo after salvo of lyddite, shrapnel and starshells at the Turkish trenches.

For almost an hour the desperate grappling in front of the stockade continued, the enemy just being kept at bay, the defenders suffering severe losses. A machine-gun at the top of the stockade was put out of action when the sepoys manning the gun were killed. Captain L. H. G. Dorling, R.F.A., another of the personnel from the observation tower, took over the gun but after firing a few bursts was severely wounded and collapsed. The Turkish 'bombers' advanced to the stockade and lobbed bombs amongst its defenders, killing or wounding all those on the right-hand half of the wall. Major Anderson appeared through the smoke and rallying enough men managed to keep the Turks to the other side of the wall. The fight at the stockade then settled down to a bayonet and bomb fight at close quarters.

The other main part of the Turkish attack, against the northeast wall, was reduced to driblets by the rifle and machine-gun fire of the Oxfords at the wall and the Rajputs in the trenches in front of it. Assisted by the starshells overhead they kept the assault exits of the Turkish trenches under a continual barrage.

At 11 p.m., three hours after the attack had commenced, 200 48th Pioneers who had been acting as a second line of defence just outside the fort were ordered to move inside and reinforce the stockade. The first thirty men, including their commander, Captain C. W. Neumann, who was wounded in the face, were shot down. Another rush by the Pioneers, under Lieutenant C. A. Raynor, succeeded in joining the survivors. Together they managed to defeat all further Turkish attempts to get over or around the stockade. The assault began to weaken and then at about midnight the Turkish infantry melted into the smoke. Once more the defenders attempted to repair the walls, stack their dead and remove the wounded to the dugout, which fortunately had been cleared since the last attack.

The moon grew larger and brighter, illuminating the battlefield between the Turkish trenches and the fort. The landscape was littered with Turkish dead and wounded; some lay still, others groaned or cried and called out for help, waving their arms. It was pitiful to hear. At 2.30 a.m. the rifles under the walls of the fort crackled out again. In the moonlight the

defenders could see the Turkish infantry emerging from the
exits of their trenches and running towards the fort. This final
attack was half-hearted. The Turks reached the north-east wall
but repeated salvoes of rifle and machine-gun fire set them
back on their heels and they began to retire almost immediately.

British losses at the fort were 315 killed and wounded
including seventeen British officers. The fighting at the north-
east bastion and in the vicinity of the stockade was responsible
for a large proportion of the casualties. Of the original party of
thirty Oxfords at the stockade, no less than twenty-three were
killed and wounded. Of the Volunteer Artillery Battery,
numbering thirty-three, fourteen remained unwounded. The
103rd Mahrattas suffered 103 casualties; the 119th Infantry,
sixty-three and the Oxfords, other than those at the stockade,
twenty-five. The Turkish shellfire on Christmas Eve (it was
estimated that about 500 shells fell on Kut town alone) accounted for another sixty-three killed and wounded elsewhere.

The assault on the fort was delivered by the Turkish 52nd
Division which Townshend had heard earlier was reforming at
Baghdad after journeying from the Caucasus. British estimates
placed the Turkish losses at about 2,000 killed and wounded.
Commandant Moukbil Bey wrote that the dead were 907 of
all ranks.[1]

According to von Kiesling, Nur-ud-Din carried out the attack
in von der Goltz's absence and against his express orders.
Evidently the German field marshal was at or on his way to
Kermanshah at the time. Although Kiesling's theory has
considerable charm it is hard to believe that the over-cautious
Nur-ud-Din would have done anything of the kind. Certainly
von der Goltz never mentioned in his despatches that this was
a 'sneak' attack. Townshend, in his autobiography, comes
down hard on Nur-ud-Din for his failure. He wrote:

> The Turkish officer who commanded the assault should not
> have been pardoned for his failure. In attacks of this nature
> the reserve should be crammed on the heels of the assaulting
> detachments. It is only by piling on your masses that you

can succeed. If your advance parties succeed in effecting a
lodgement in the work and are driven out again—as ours
were at the Redan in 1855—it is the fault of the commander
of the attack. The Turkish division engaged in this assault
had just arrived from the Caucasus and had not lost morale.
Its commander was to blame. It was no time to think of
loss of life, for if you cannot afford to lose heavily you should
not try to assault.[2]

The other mistakes made by the Turkish commander listed
by Townshend were warning the British of the pending assault
with the preliminary bombardment and neglecting to make a
feint attack elsewhere to prevent reinforcements being sent to
the fort.

Christmas Day dawned in perfect peace; not a shell or rifle
bullet broke the calm. The ground was solid with frost and in
the distance the Pusht-i-Kuh reared their snow-covered summits high into the perfect blue of the sky. Smoke from the
cooking fires ascended in tall thin wands in the still air. But out
on the barbed wire the bodies of the Turkish soldiers hung like
dummies. Occasionally one flapped his arm, showing he was still
alive. One with his jaw shot away made a brittle rattling noise.
It would be quiet for an hour or so and then the rattling would
start again. The British troops attempted to bring in a few of
the seriously wounded Turks who lay immediately in front of
the fort but this activity was stopped by Turkish snipers who
had obviously been ordered to stop their comrades being taken
prisoner. A few managed to crawl to the fort unaided. Out on
the wire the rattler continued in isolation.

Underground it was quiet, uncannily so. Some found it
ominous and thought it presaged something worse. In dugouts
and billets all over Kut the British troops, wrapped in their
blankets and greatcoats, thought of those at home and wondered what they were thinking.

Christmas Eve in England was unusually warm and mild.
The *Morning Post* deplored the high temperature and said that
this Christmas would never be remembered like the 'good old

days of yore with snow covering the ground and skaters indulging in their favourite pastime'. The newspaper also carried an appeal on behalf of King Albert's troops in Flanders. 'Remember Belgium's Martyrdom—and do not forget her wounded soldiers.' The Marchioness of Townshend and Mrs. Algernon Paget invited all wounded officers to join them for a musical tea between four and seven at the Knightsbridge Hotel.

King George's message to the wounded in the 3rd London General Hospital was read by Princess Louise, Duchess of Argyll. His Majesty's one wish was that all in hospital might make a speedy recovery. 'The men', said the *Morning Post*, 'rose spontaneously and sung the National Anthem.' There was also an article entitled 'The Tommies' Christmas' (from a Correspondent). It concluded:

It is still raining on a grey Christmas Eve. Are they downhearted? Most decidedly, NO. They make their jokes until the whistle blows and the women at the carriage doors sprinkle them with tears in laughing at them. We take our hats off to them as the troop train special glides past us. We are proud of our Tommies. We hope they are proud of us.

Another article points out that 'trench feet was more commonly known as frostbite'.

Readers of the *Daily Graphic* were invited to write for a coloured print which depicted an angel and a British soldier who looked as if he had dozed off. There was, however, a poignant significance about the flags around his head. It was entitled *The Great Sacrifice* and cost a shilling.

There was very little news from the war front. One report told of an artillery bombardment south of the Lille-Armentières Line. Everywhere else, it was reported, activity was 'normal'. Downpage there were two small items. 'Major Winston Churchill returned to France yesterday on expiration of his leave of absence' and 'The Indian Army has left France for another field of action'.

Three days later the news of the fighting at Kut was released which gave the impression that it was a front-line town 'somewhere near the Persian Gulf'. Nobody knew that 12,000

6   A street in Kut

7 Artillery officers observing and range-finding from a
mobile observation ladder

British and Indian troops were besieged in the town. Another two months were to elapse before the 'tiny coaling station on the River Tigris' was to get any prominence at all.

The remainder of the daylight hours at Kut passed in peace. The rank and file were given a Christmas dinner of beef, baked potatoes, tinned fruit, bread, jam and tea. There was a Christmas Day message from King George on regimental orders.

Special. The King-Emperor commands the following to be published in all orders on Christmas Day. Begins.
Buckingham Palace.
Another Christmas finds all the resources of the Empire still engaged in war as I desire to convey on my own behalf, and on behalf of the Queen, a heartfelt Christmas greeting and our good wishes for the New Year to all who on land and sea are upholding the honour of the British name. In the officers and men of my Navy on which the security of the Empire depends I repose, in common with all my subjects, a trust that is absolute. On the officers and men of all my Armies, whether now in France, in the East or in other fields I rely with faith, confident that their valour and self-sacrifice will be under God's guidance and lead to Victory and honourable peace. There are many of their comrades alas in hospital and to these brave men also I desire, with the Queen, to express our deep gratitude and our earnest prayers for their recovery. Officers and Men of the Navy or Army, another year is drawing to a close as it began, in toil, bloodshed and suffering, but I rejoice to know that the goal to which you are striving draws nearer into sight. May God bless you and all your undertakings.[3]

The men read this message with thanks. It showed they were not forgotten even though they had to be content with a side reference. In one set of orders the last word of the King's message had been transcribed as 'undertakers'. One pauses to wonder if the great men at home who sat down and composed these messages ever bore in mind the fact that thousands of miles away they would be transcribed by a non-English orderly on a rusty typewriter and suffer as a consequence.

There was also a message from Townshend to Colonel Brown. It read:

1. Please convey to your garrison my appreciation of their splendid defence under your command.
2. Kindly wish all ranks from me Christmas greetings and say I am grateful to all for their splendid conduct and trust that soon we will keep proper Christmas.[4]

There was one from Nixon to Townshend. It read:

Army Commander to G.O.C. Sixth Division.
Good again Sixth Division. Please congratulate garrison of fort who pluckily kept their end up and went in on 25th–26th. I am proud to command such troops.[5]

The officers at Kut enjoyed themselves in a more splendid manner. In the Royal Engineers Officers' Mess those not on duty sat down to a five-course meal including a plum pudding 'of sorts' and asparagus with Scotch whisky with filtered Tigris water. In the Medical Officers' Mess they even had duck. Colonel Hehir complimented the corporal cook on this unexpected treat and said that it really seemed a shame to kill the duck after it had survived a month of shellfire. The cook told him not to be concerned as lately the duck had 'not been very well' and that it would have probably died on the morrow anyway. The medical officers stared thoughtfully at the back of the retreating soldier. After Christmas dinner in the Officers' Mess of the 66th Punjabis, a young subaltern, clutching his glass, rose unsteadily to his feet and said: 'I don't know if you chaps have noticed anything but it is Christmas Day and wants only four hours to midnight. Where's the Relief Force?'[6] He was told to sit down and shut up. He did.

But a strong cheerful rumour was sweeping swiftly through the messes, trenches, redoubts and hospitals. The Relief Force under Aylmer was preparing to advance to Ali Gharbi en route to attack the Turkish positions at Sheikh Saad. Popular opinion now put the date of probable relief at 15 January 1916. The mail order catalogue of the Army and Navy Stores in Bombay was in great demand. Officers began to make out lists of what to order when their first letters got through to Basra.

Later that evening the familiar clatter of rifle and artillery fire began again. By 10 p.m. the tumult was in full swing. It was concluded that the lull had only lasted until the Turks could bring up fresh supplies of ammunition from Shumran.

During the hours of darkness further and more successful attempts were made by the British troops to bring in the wounded Turks from the stretch of ground immediately in front of the fort. Rescue parties were actually able to remove some men from the barbed wire. One with barbed wire wrapped round his neck and a leg partially severed and some others who could neither be extricated from the entanglements nor moved without a stretcher had to be left to die of loss of blood or exposure. Movements on the wire and cries confirmed that some were still alive up to four days after the assault.

Captain Sandes' 'Bridging Train' soon had their festive spirit dissolved by the discovery that sometime during Christmas Eve the barge containing most of their stores had broken away from its moorings and drifted downstream to the sandbank on the other side of the river from the fort. As the barge had been strongly secured the Engineers were convinced that Arabs had swum across the Tigris in the dark and cut the mooring lines. This could never be confirmed. Sandes and his men stared sourly at the stranded barge which contained books, instruments, tents and some personal effects. To deprive the enemy of the use of the equipment thus gained, the guns in the fort opened up on the craft, setting it afire. The flames took hold with such ferocity that the watching Engineers were puzzled until it was recalled, with added sorrow, that there had been some cases of whisky and vermouth aboard. The burnt-out derelict was later used as a sniping post by the Turks and then one day if drifted off downstream; evidence to all that the shot holes in the hull were all above the waterline. The barge was subsequently used by the Turks as a ferry at Fort Maqasis.

At the hospitals the doctors began to experience a large

number of cases of influenza and, even more serious, tetanus
was detected. An outbreak of this disease was feared but it was
kept under control. Colonel Hehir asked Townshend if an
aeroplane from Ali Gharbi could drop some anti-tetanus serum.
The message was passed on.

Two large Turkish columns, estimated at two divisions, were
seen crossing from the left to the right bank by a pontoon
bridge at Shumran bend. The troops halted about seven to
eight miles to the west of Kut town and pitched tents. This and
other activity to the westward was watched with great interest
by Townshend. He came to the conclusion that the Turks were
retreating but further observation revealed that the enemy
commander was merely deploying his force more equally on
both sides of the river. Having his hopes thus dashed Townshend
was not in the mood to be informed that two sepoys of the
22nd and 66th Punjabis had climbed out of the British first line
trenches and had fled to the Turkish positions before they could
be stopped. Townshend recalled: 'Both were fired on, but
unfortunately not hit.' The major-general attributed this fresh
outbreak of unrest to some pamphlets which had been laid
against the British barbed wire near the fort. Although the
bundles had been carefully collected some of them had undoubtedly fallen into the hands of the Indians.

The pamphlets, printed in Urdu, Pushtu and Punjabi, were
published, they informed the reader, by the Indian National
Society, Chicago (see Appendix F). These effusions were
treated by the majority of the British troops as rather humorous
but the Indians, at whom they were directed, tended to take
them more seriously, containing as they did just enough truth
to give credence to the rest. Townshend was firmly convinced
that the pamphlets were highly inflammatory and he received
proof in the increasing number of desertions.

As the year drew to a close the main occupation was getting
the fort back into some kind of defensive order. The walls were
breached in many places and full of rents and holes. Piles of
debris lay everywhere. Timber, sheets of corrugated iron and
equipment and stores lay buried under heaps of rubble and
rubbish. The trenches at the fort had been almost completely

obliterated by the bombardment and required re-digging. At
night parties would crawl out to the wire with mallets wrapped
in cloth to replace the entangments. Everyone was thankful
that the Turks had not yet received any artillery which fired
high-explosive shells. If this had been so no one at the fort, or
even at Kut, would have remained alive. For the most part the
Turkish guns were 40-pounders and 15-pounders of German
origin and mostly of Krupp manufacture. The 40-pounder
shells, filled with 'black powder', burst on impact with a terrific
detonation but unless a direct hit was scored or the explosion
occurred within a confined space, such as a dugout, they
seldom did more than puncture eardrums and severely shock
those within close range. The 18-pounders fired shrapnel and
were much feared. Later the Turks employed howitzers which
fired small calibre high-explosive shells.

Apart from the morning, noon and evening 'hates', which
were now inflicted on all parts of the town and trenches as well
as the fort, the days following Christmas were fairly quiet. The
sniping, however, increased to an unprecedented peak and
wounds, mainly from 'overs', kept the hospitals busy. The
water-collecting Arab women continued to suffer. According to
Townshend the Turks used 'hollow bullets' against the womenfolk which inflicted large, gaping wounds. Counter-sniping
parties were organised which used captured Turkish rifles with
a flat trajectory up to 400 yards in preference to the Short
Magazine Lee Enfield (S.M.L.E.), the standard British weapon.

On 28 December, a division of enemy troops were seen
marching eastwards down the left bank towards Es Sinn
followed by a column of transport vehicles and camels. The
following day Aylmer cabled Townshend to inform him that
the Relief Force was now composed of two divisions plus one
cavalry brigade. He asked for details of the Kut defences, which
Townshend supplied. Townshend also heard from Nixon that
the Russians were definitely putting pressure on Kermanshah
to the neglect of Baghdad.

The usual blue sky became overcast. Rain clouds scudded
from the south but apart from a few flecks of rain the days
remained dry and cold.

At the fort the Turks were becoming offensive in a different way. Even those among the garrison with strong constitutions were losing their appetite for food because of the stench from the 180 decomposing bodies on the wire. The Turks seemed to be suffering similarly for on 29 December a white flag appeared above an enemy parapet. Across no-man's land came a bim-bashi (major) with a letter for Townshend from the command-ing officer of the 52nd Division requesting an armistice to bury the dead. Townshend told the envoy that as the proposal had come from a local commander it could not be considered. An armistice would only be granted if Nur-ud-Din himself re-quested one and even then only if he gave an undertaking that the truce would not be used to bring troops up to the forward positions as had recently been the case at Gallipoli. Townshend said that he would reserve the right to open fire on the burial parties if he even suspected that this subterfuge was being employed. Four smelly days elapsed before Nur-ud-Din replied. Some witnesses said that this time the bimbashi was drunk but if this was so Townshend does not have appeared to have noticed it. The Turkish officer informed Townshend that Captain Gribbon, who had been badly wounded and captured during the mêlée at the bridgehead, had died of his wounds and had been buried with full military honours. Townshend gratefully acknowledged this courtesy but then changed the subject and asked the Turkish officer if he knew anything about a projected Turkish expedition into Persia. Was this why von der Goltz had vanished from the scene? The bimbashi was non-committal. Townshend persisted. If this was so, Townshend said, why should the Turks stop at Persia? Why not Afghan-istan—or even India itself? The Turk replied enigmatically that von der Goltz was an old man and then asked Townshend about the burial armistice, saying that Nur-ud-Din would agree to Townshend's conditions. Townshend, however, thought he would play the Turks at what he described as their own traditional game. He said he would let Nur-ud-Din know to-morrow. He did, however, send the Turkish officer back with a present of a box of fifty cigarettes for the Turkish general. Soon after the bimbashi had returned to his lines a furious artillery bombardment opened up. Townshend said the Turks pumped shell after shell into Kut. One passed through his headquarters and injured his radio operator and inflicted twenty-four other casualties. Townshend thought that it was most ungrateful of Nur-ud-Din after the present of what Townshend described as 'my last box of Masperos'.[7] It is a minor point but the Turks told exactly the same story but they said that it was Nur-ud-Din who presented the cigarettes and Townshend who supplied the bombardment. It is certain, however, that nothing came of the proposals for a truce and the corpses were left for the rats, which were appearing in increasing numbers, and flocks of sparrows and starlings. That these birds participated in this gruesome feast provided an interesting sequel which will be dealt with later.

There were twelve more cases of self-mutilation among the Indian troops. In each case the offenders had bound a piece of cloth around their right hand before discharging the rifle. There were more desertions. No. 1050 Halvadar Jodha of the 48th Pioneers was charged with 'In the presence of the enemy misbehaving in such a way as to show cowardice'.[8] He was given 'seven years rigorous imprisonment'. A sepoy of the 103rd Mahrattas on sentry duty at the fort suddenly fired two shots at an Indian officer and jumping from the trench tried to desert. He tripped, fell and was captured. He was tried by a summary general court martial, found guilty, condemned and was shot that evening.

And so 1916 came and the old year died. The days grew longer and colder. There was a hint of rain in the air. The troops were getting enough to eat and were reasonably content. Relief was expected within a fortnight and then they would be sent home on leave to Britain or India. The great urge to get to Baghdad had evaporated; now the troops wanted to go home. Health was generally good. It is true that influenza and bronchitis were on the increase but apart from a small number of cases of pneumonia and beri-beri this was not considered much to worry about.

Between 14 and 31 December there had been 1,774 casualties, either killed or seriously wounded. Slight wounds and wounds of a less than serious nature were not included in this figure.

Townshend wished 'good luck and happiness in the New Year to all my commanders of all ranks Sixth Division and troops attached and a speedy end to our Mesopotamian labours.'

VII

MUD AND MUDDLE

On 17 December 1915, Sir George Buchanan, chairman and for fifteen years chief engineer of the port of Rangoon, then at home on leave in England, received the following letter from the Government of India:

> It has been decided that you should proceed to Basra at the earliest opportunity in order that you may be in a position to give immediate assistance to General Sir John Nixon, K.C.B. in all matters connected with the port of Basra, its administration, engineering works, and river conservancy. Your designation will be 'Director General of Port Administration and River Conservancy' but the exact delimitation of your duties will be fixed by Sir John Nixon in consultation with you, the Government of India being advised of the decision arrived at.[1]

Buchanan took shipment almost at once and arrived in Mesopotamia on a bitterly cold Friday two weeks later. Buchanan wrote later:

> I had never before in my life seen such a hopeless mess and muddle and I wondered whether this was the usual accompaniment of war. It seemed incredible that we should have been in occupation of Basra for over a year, so little had been done in the time.[2]

The engineer was directed to Nixon's headquarters where he was greeted by a staff officer. Buchanan showed him his letter of instructions and the officer hurried away only to return some minutes later to ask if he could come back the following Monday. Buchanan protested that a meeting with Nixon was a matter of urgency. The officer informed him blandly that the

Army Commander was constantly having to deal with urgent matters and that was why he was being asked to return at 10 a.m. Monday morning. Another officer did helpfully suggest that if the new port administrator was not otherwise engaged over the weekend he might arrange for the removal of the carcass of a mule which was on the river bank and was making its presence felt in no uncertain manner.

After arranging temporary quarters Buchanan took a look around down by the Shatt al Arab. It took little time for him to realise that the main port of Mesopotamia, through which all troops and supplies had to pass on their way up to the Relief Force, was nothing more than an anchorage and a swamp. The original force had been small and required little base accommodation but although the size of the Expedition was increasing daily, there was no corresponding expansion of the port facilities. On arrival the various military departments—Supply and Transport, Ordnance, Engineers, Marine Transport, etc., just spread themselves along the dry parts of the bank. Now a huge conglomeration of stores, supplies and equipment stretched for three miles up the right bank of the Shatt al Arab. A few jetties had been built which, although sufficient for an emergency landing, had not been added to or improved and were even falling into decay. No proper floating pontoons or landing stages had yet been constructed. A number of sheds of reed matting had been built but wind and weather was reducing them to ruins. These should have been replaced by corrugated iron sheds months ago. Even explosives and ammunition were stored in highly inflammable temporary sheds. The entire camp was a huge quagmire scattered about with heaps of rotting stores. At the main landing point matters were chaotic. There had been heavy rain and horses, mules and troops floundered in liquid mud fifteen inches deep trying to rescue guns, limbers and stores.

Buchanan enquired about fourteen ships waiting at the anchorage and discovered that, although troop transports received priority for disembarkation, ships carrying stores could wait as long as six weeks before being discharged. The reason for this was no mystery to Buchanan at least. The ships,

using their derricks, could swiftly unload but the *mahailas*
which ferried the stores to the jetties had to be unloaded by
hand and this could take three or four days. There was not one
shore-based crane in the entire port.

An elementary knowledge of cargo handling seemed to
be lacking. Buchanan noticed a large pile of wooden packing cases of all shapes and sizes. He was informed that the
wooden boxes had been shipped from India intact to be
used as fuel rations for the troops. Buchanan could scarcely
believe that anyone in his senses would send firewood all
the way from India without first chopping it up to save cargo
space.

And where was the river transport to take the supplies upstream? Buchanan was informed that nobody was quite sure
when this would arrive in Mesopotamia. All the river craft were
at the time upstream with the Relief Force. There were of course
the *mahailas*.

Buchanan was deeply concerned, especially so as his son was
a subaltern in the Black Watch which formed part of the
recently arrived 7th Division. The engineer tried to locate his
son but was told that he had been sent up to the front. He was
also informed that the division had arrived ahead of its medical
units. These were now on their way from France. Buchanan was
horrified. He had never before heard of an army going into the
field without its ambulances or medical supplies. Buchanan
needed to be convinced that this was so. Why hadn't anyone
heard about this shocking state of affairs in England? He was
informed that the military censors at Basra ruthlessly deleted
anything from the troops' home-going letters critical of the
organisation. He was told of an instance where a dying officer's
last letter had been suppressed because it contained the words
'. . . and the medical treatment such as it is . . .'[3] This was only
one of many such instances.

Buchanan was a calm man. All this could boil down to
ignorance of how to run a port; and this was why he was here.
To him it was just a problem of simple arithmetic: *a.* the
requirements of the army at the front in tons per day, delivered
where required, including extra steamers for special services;

b. the tonnage capacity of the river fleet and number of vessels available for all purposes. If *a.* exceeded *b.* something unpleasant was bound to happen.

Armed with this ammunition Buchanan was at Nixon's headquarters on Monday before his appointed time. As he entered Nixon's office he could see that the general was a worried and probably sick man. Buchanan sat quietly while his letter was read. At length the general said that he could not understand what the letter was about. The title of 'Director of Port Administration' was nonsense because there was no port to administer. All the jetties and landing stages were military and surely these would not be within Buchanan's province even though he had now assumed military uniform.

Buchanan patiently explained the meaning of 'port administration' and pointed out that a military port required traffic management in precisely the same way as any civilian port. Nixon did not agree but he thought that maybe Buchanan might be found work directing the dredging of the Tigris or the Hammer Lake. He made it clear that he regarded Buchanan as a nuisance and then ended the interview. It had lasted just fifteen minutes. Buchanan at first thought that he might as well leave the country but he realised that this would not help matters and stayed on in Mesopotamia. He was never able to do much while Nixon remained in control.

Why Nixon had dealt with Buchanan so summarily is impossible to discover. He was exhausted and his health was fast declining but this was no excuse for his rejection of men who were extremely knowledgeable in their own fields and could have at least eased the rapidly deteriorating situation. Nixon constantly railed against 'experts from Oxford' who were continually arriving at Basra with the express purpose of interfering with his war. He once quite innocently informed a colleague that one such adviser, with no knowledge of warfare or for that matter Mesopotamia apart from an archaeological 'dig' at Qurna, had sought an interview and told him that the Arabs might be induced to turn against the Turks if approached in the correct way. Nixon remembered that the young man had a nervous tic and that he chain-smoked cigarettes. The general said that he had sent the fellow packing. Nixon's visitor was T. E. Lawrence.

On 1 January Townshend received a telegram from Aylmer outlining his proposals for the relief of Kut which cautiously stated that it should be realised that in drawing up the appreciation it had been necessary to give 'safe' dates. The Relief Force would not be able to form into a composite force until it reached Ali Gharbi and any dates given were based on the arrival of the necessary river transport from Basra. Aylmer stated his objections to pushing forward from Ali Gharbi prematurely. For example, he said, he could send a column forward immediately if required and provided it did not meet with any opposition it could possibly reach Nakhailat on 3 January. If troops were despatched from Basra directly to Nakhailat without the usual interruption of journey at Ali Gharbi, Aylmer calculated he could assemble a complete division there by that date. Aylmer continued: 'If the enemy do not [make a] stand between Nakhailat and Kut such a column could join you at Kut on the 4th. The remainder of the [Tigris] Corps could not possibly reach Nakhailat till the 8th and Kut till the 9th.

I would greatly prefer to make a start from Ali Gharbi with one division on 3 January. In such a case, if your condition demanded it, one division could be at Nakhailat on the 5th and the rest of the Corps on the 8th.

By far the best plan, however, from the point of view of the Relief Force, would be to advance altogether from Sheikh Saad, or its vicinity, as a combined Corps. Nakhailat could be possibly reached on the 8th though the 9th would be the safer date. Such a plan, though slower, would be far more certain to gain its objective. It is essential to postpone adoption of actual method of advance as long as possible, as having [here two words were omitted but almost certainly these were 'few ships'] means want of organisation and consequently decrease of efficiency. You may, however, rest assured that everything possible will be done to hurry relief to the utmost if your circumstances demand it. I know you will give full weight to such consideration before you give any definite date by which you must be relieved.[4]

The actual wording of Townshend's reply is not known, but in his autobiography he said that he told Aylmer that he should unite his force before moving upstream from Ali Gharbi, although he thought an advance guard should be sent forward to Sheikh Saad. Townshend said that he would only ask for help from the advance guard if it became essential but he doubted if this would be the case as the Turks seemed more concerned about preventing the advance of the Relief Force than with attacking Kut at that time. According to his version Townshend made no reference to any date by which he must be relieved but it is now normally accepted that Townshend pleaded for relief by 15 January. Edmund Candler wrote about Townshend's 'visionary hour-glass'[5] as a direct reference to such a request. Townshend subsequently denied that he insisted on one but it will be recalled that it was strongly believed in Kut that relief would be effected by 15 January. In a later telegram (23 January) Townshend certainly referred to 15 January as the date by which he had been promised relief.

The Turks did not seem keen on making any further infantry assaults on Kut but the three daily bombardments never abated. Once more a 'whizz bang' burst on the doorway of one of the arches of a bazaar hospital in which two men were lying. One of the men lay with his head within a foot of the door. His clothes, bed and blanket were riddled with iron shell fragments and the explosion burst his ear drums but otherwise he was unharmed. The other patient was similarly unscathed but the shell fragment collapsed his hot water bottle and slashed the belts and other equipment, which was hanging by his head, to ribbons.

Now shelling at night came into vogue. An officer wrote in his diary:

You try to doze off, but are intermittently awakened by the sizzing scream of an approaching 'obus'. You cock up an interested ear to judge whether you are exactly in the line of its flight or not, and if you are, and you have no dugout, you await its fall with still greater interest, only equalled by your relief when it bursts clear or landed with a wump on a neighbouring mud hut. A 'whizz bang' on the other hand gives no warning. It comes hissing through the mud wall and there is a tremendous explosion and segments are scattered all over the place, filling the air with its poisonous fumes. They are annoying little beasts and are on you before you have a chance to move.[6]

On 3 January a Turkish 'deserter'—a corporal—informed Townshend's force that a new division had just arrived and in confirmation of this a large body of enemy troops, estimated at two divisions at least, were seen moving eastwards from the Turkish camp at Shumran. It was at first believed that the intention was to attack the fort but the troops marched past the anxiously watching garrison and vanished downstream on the left bank. The mind boggles at the idea of a Turk deserting into Kut at this stage of the siege but Townshend did not doubt that the man was genuine.

The funeral of Colonel Courtenay, who had succumbed to the wounds received on the roof of Townshend's headquarters on Christmas Eve was held with full ceremony and attended by every officer not on duty. A solemn procession wound through Kut, out to the little cemetery to the north of the town. The burial ground was enclosed by a low mud wall. Beneath the palm trees was a rapidly growing plantation of wooden crosses. It was a lonely place and always made a strong impression on those who visited the graves of their fallen comrades. Because of an outbreak of wooden-cross stealing there was always an armed guard on duty at the gate. As the troops returned from the cemetery it began to rain, lightly at first, and then a full Mesopotamian rain storm. The men in the trenches crouched in the lee of the mud walls, thrust their hands deeper in their pockets, shivered and brooded.

On 5 January a telegram from Aylmer asked Townshend if he agreed with an estimate by Nixon of the numbers and distribution of the Turkish forces. The Army Commander was of the opinion that on the right bank, nine miles west of Kut at the Shumran bend, were the 45th and 36th Divisions totalling 11,500 infantry with forty-one guns; on the left bank facing Kut, the 5th Composite Division, 51st and 38th Divisions totalling 12,900 infantry with twenty-four guns; on the left bank at Es Sinn, the 35th Division of 2,500 infantry with eighteen guns. At Sheikh Saad, it was believed, were two full battalions, 800 cavalry and 1,200 camel corps. A grand total of nearly 30,000 combatants with eighty-three guns. Townshend replied that although he agreed with the distribution he considered that the numbers were probably exaggerated. He thought that the strength was more like 20,000 with eighty-three guns. He pointed out that the Turks must have lost between 4,000 and 5,000 men in and around Kut since the siege had begun. Nixon's estimate, however, proved to be accurate. The Relief Force, Townshend was informed later in the day, was composed of two Indian divisions which had come from the fighting in France; the 3rd (Lahore) and 7th (Meerut) Divisions.

Now, for the first and only time, the Turks moved the captured *Firefly* downstream with the intention of shelling Kut with her 4·7-inch forward mounted guns. The British 5-inch guns opened up on the gunboat and she withdrew out of range.

Towards evening two reconnaissance planes flew low over Kut. There was wild cheering from the British groups. Here at last was tangible proof that relief was at hand. Morale rose accordingly. The spotters on the Rajput roof watched the aeroplanes fade into the distance. About an hour later they heard another aeroplane approaching, this time from the west. It was also heading straight for Kut. Lieutenant Saunders, on the roof, envied the pilot his job as the aircraft drew near. It was flying very low. Saunders waved vigorously; he was answered by the ping of bullets from across the river but the British officer did not care. It was good to see the aeroplane; he kept waving and shouting. The aeroplane passed almost directly overhead. Saunders could easily see the head of the pilot. On the tail of the aircraft was painted an Iron Cross.

The aircraft landed in a flurry of dust near Shumran camp. If the news of the arrival of the German aeroplane was not bad enough there was some more food for gloom on the way. Kut had recently been receiving Reuter's telegrams which contained 'potted' news of the outside world. These were eagerly looked for. The telegram for this day informed the Kut garrison that the Peninsula and Orient steamer S.S. *Persia* had been sunk with all hands by a submarine in the Indian Ocean. There were few details but 650 had perished and the disaster was considered to be on a par with the loss of the *Lusitania*. The troops were exceedingly angry about this atrocious act, especially as the *Persia* would have undoubtedly been carrying mail for Mesopotamia.

The supply of fresh meat was now exhausted and eight ounces of 'bully' (approximating to corned beef) per man was issued in its place. The officers, however, got an unexpected ration of beef when an enemy sniper so severely wounded one of the heavy battery bullocks that it had to be destroyed.

More large bodies of Turkish troops were seen moving in the direction of Es Sinn during the afternoon of 5 January under low banks of cloud that rolled continuously from the south and south-east. Next day the clouds still blackened the sky and there was a faint rumble in the distance. At first it was thought that it was thunder but the more experienced troops said assuredly that it was gunfire. Jubilation swept through Kut. It was the first time that they had actually heard the guns of the Relief Force.

Although Aylmer had received a number of reports which indicated that at least 20,000 Turkish troops with sixty-three guns were moving down the left bank of the Tigris, he very much doubted if much more than an advance guard had proceeded to Sheikh Saad. Aylmer considered that Nur-ud-Din would be content to occupy the more easily defensible positions at Es Sinn and wait to do battle with the British force there. The Relief Force commander also calculated that the Sheikh Saad positions on the right bank would be lightly defended because the Turks had limited means of transferring troops to that side of the river. The enemy was known to have only a few barges and the remains of a boat bridge below Kut. Aylmer wanted to teach the Turks a lesson. If the small enemy force on the right bank at Sheikh Saad could be trapped and heavily punished this would have an excellent morale effect on his 7th Division. Not that he had reason for much concern in this respect. The newly arrived division had seen action in France and were quite optimistic about the outcome of any battles with the Turks, whom they considered to be vastly inferior to German troops. The hardened campaigners of Loos and Givenchy were confident that the Turks could easily be flushed out of their positions. After all Townshend's force had been beaten only by overwhelming numbers at Ctesiphon. With the arrival of the Black Watch the organisation of the 7th Division was complete. It was true, of course, that the division was nowhere as fully equipped as it had been on the Western Front as it had been rushed out of Marseilles by the urgent need to relieve Kut. It would have been wiser to regroup the division in Egypt but there had been no time. It had arrived without its transport waggons, its mules and its five field ambulances. Items of equipment such as bombs, rifle grenades, rangefinders, signal pistols and cartridges, and 'hyposcopes' or periscopic rifles, as they had now come to be called, were still on the high seas. There was a shortage of wire-cutters and telephone equipment.

On 4 January Major-General G. J. Younghusband was ordered to move his 7th Division forward to the region of Sheikh Saad. The advance proceeded up both banks; the land transport, nearest the river, shielded on either side by the marching infantry. Between the two columns was the river transport led by the gunboats *Butterfly*, *Cranefly* and *Dragonfly*.

From an aerial reconnaissance it appeared that the Turkish force, estimated at about 10,000, was entrenched about two and a half miles below Sheikh Saad. The enemy troops were divided in two equal parts in trenches which extended roughly 2,000 yards on either side of the river.

On 5 January after two days of marching, Younghusband's columns reached the eastern end of Musandaq reach where it encamped. Enemy interference with the advance had been slight; the only opposition was on the right bank where two squadrons of Turkish cavalry and about 300 Arabs had been driven off without difficulty. Younghusband explained his plan for the morrow's advance and attack to his subordinate commanders. He intended to threaten the Turkish positions on the left bank while pushing forward on the right bank, so as to drive the Turks back into the Sheikh Saad loop. There he would destroy it. He thought that the loss of Sheikh Saad would expose the Turkish trenches on the left bank to enfilade fire which would cause them to be abandoned. The column which was to threaten the Turkish left bank positions would be commanded by Brigadier-General G. B. H. Rice and would consist of the 35th, 19th and 21st Brigades. The main force on the right bank was composed of an advance column of one troop 16th Cavalry, a section of the 9th Brigade, R.F.A., 56th Rifles and one company of 128th Pioneers. The main body of troops under the command of Major-General G. V. Kemball would move forward in two parallel columns. The right-hand column, advancing along the track nearest the river would consist of the column headquarters, the 9th Field Artillery Brigade, 92nd Punjabis, one company of 128th Pioneers and three field ambulance sections. The left column consisted of half-company of 13th Sappers, Brigade Machine-Gun Company, 2nd Leicesters 51st and 53rd Sikhs. The Cavalry Brigade would advance two miles out to the left of the marching columns.

The advance commenced the following morning in a dense mist which, when it lifted at 10 a.m., revealed to all that the surrounding landscape was an infantryman's nightmare. The country was completely flat and devoid of cover. It was grass-less and a monotonous mud-brown colour. At 11 a.m. the head of the right-bank column reached the western end of the Musan-daq reach which was about two miles from the enemy trenches.

The attack began at noon and came immediately under heavy rifle fire. As the main body of troops pressed home the attack on the right bank it became obvious that the Turkish line of trenches extended considerably further to the left than had been reported by the aerial reconnaissance. Instead of outflanking the Turkish positions as intended the British troops on the left of the attack found they were outflanked themselves. The Cavalry Brigade, under heavy fire from the Turkish trenches and attacked on their left flank and rear by a strong body of Arab horsemen, was brought to a standstill.

Meanwhile on the left bank, Rice's leading troops had arrived within 800 yards of a strong line of trenches. The attacking troops (37th Dogras) came under heavy rifle and artillery fire. By 3.30 p.m. all the Dogras had been absorbed into the firing line and were digging themselves in about 800 yards from the Turkish trenches; the 97th Infantry had moved up their support and the 102nd Grenadiers had come up on the Dogras' right. The remaining battalion of the 35th Brigade (1/5th Buffs) was still in reserve and about a quarter of a mile to the rear were the three battalions of the 19th Brigade.

By this time the 28th Brigade on the right bank had gradually closed on the Turkish trenches. The 56th, 128th Pioneers and 53rd Sikhs were within 300 yards of them; on their left the Leicesters, under heavy enfilade fire and partly mixed with the Indian troops, were about 500 yards from the enemy trenches. Because of the featureless country and the low-lying Turkish trenches which were almost imperceptible until the troops were right on top of them, the attackers on both banks were suffering heavily. To make matters worse a mirage so distorted the view that nobody was quite sure where they were.

At 3.45 p.m. Kemball ordered up the 92nd Punjabis to add weight to his attack but the movement had hardly started when Younghusband intervened and called off the battle for the day. He had come to the conclusion that as sunset was at 5.10 p.m. the determined resistance of the Turkish troops precluded any possibility that Kemball's column would be able to gain an advantage before darkness fell. He also called off the attack on the left bank. The 35th Brigade was meeting with such stiff opposition that Younghusband knew that he would have to commit his whole force before any progress was possible. Younghusband told the leading brigades on both banks (28th and 35th) to take up battle outposts and maintain pressure on the enemy throughout the night.

7 January dawned misty and close; not a breath of wind ruffled the rushes at the river banks. The British troops continued the attack. Aylmer rode forward to meet Younghusband and was informed that the Relief Force had suffered over 600

casualties during the preceding day's fighting. Aylmer came to the conclusion that the 7th Division was so completely committed that it gave him very little freedom of manœuvre in the forthcoming battle. In fact it looked as if the Turks might even be able to surround and annihilate his 35th Brigade. Aylmer, however, had been presented with some information with which, if put to use, he might achieve a swift victory. During the night an Arab horseman had blundered into a British patrol. A search had revealed that the man was in fact a despatch rider from the Turkish commander on the right bank. From a document thus obtained it appeared that the main Turkish force was not on the left bank as had been supposed but had somehow managed to cross to the right bank despite the lack of river transport or a bridge. Although this despatch was suspiciously informative Aylmer decided to throw all his available strength against the enemy's weaker force in the left bank. Younghusband commanded the attack while Kemball was transferred to the right bank. The battle now came under Aylmer's personal direction.

The attack on the left bank was launched with the sun blinding the advancing British infantry. A mirage so disrupted observation that covering fire from Aylmer's artillery was minimal. The enemy rifle and machine-gun fire from the low-sited trenches was heavy, accurate and well-directed. The veterans from France had experienced nothing like it before. By dusk the British line had advanced to within 300 to 400 yards of the Turkish trenches. Any further attempts to advance by individuals or parties were swiftly checked, the participants becoming casualties. A company of Seaforths which managed to reach a point forty yards from the Turkish trenches was contained there by such heavy fire that they were unable either to progress or retreat. The Black Watch and the Jats each incurred 400 casualties including their commanding officers. The Seaforths and 125th Rifles both lost 300 men, including the Seaforths' commanding officer.

On the right bank the British met with more success than would have been thought possible against the quantity of defending troops indicated by the captured Turkish document.

At about 4 p.m. the Leicesters and the 51st and 53rd Punjabis made the final assault over 300 yards' distance and swept into the Turkish front line. The captured trenches were found to contain 300 enemy dead and wounded. Six hundred Turks were taken prisoner. Any further advance was, however, out of the question because of heavy hostile rifle fire to the front and flank. The whole right bank of the river was slashed with old irrigation ditches which provided excellent defensive cover. Unable to proceed any further Kemball's troops consolidated the captured positions for the night. The losses had been heavy. During the two days' fighting the Leicesters had incurred over 300 casualties and the Indian frontier force battalions (51st, 53rd and 56th) each lost over 200 officers and men.

With darkness the usual cold wind sprang up but this time it was accompanied by heavy rain. Under heavy Turkish rifle fire parties of British and Indian soldiers wallowed through the deep mud searching for wounded. Many were found to have drowned in the water-filled shellholes. Other troops formed digging parties which accompanied the transport carts, loaded with wounded, to the river bank and the steamers. The carts constantly plunged into ditches throwing the already soaking wounded into the churned-up mud. At 9.30 p.m. Aylmer gave orders that the attack was to be continued the following morning. He reported to Nixon that he appeared to have the whole Turkish force against him, except some 4,000 to 5,000 who were besieging Kut. After a wet, cold and sleepless night the troops once again sloshed their way towards the Turkish lines. On the night of 8 January Aylmer reported to Nixon that he was unable to make any further progress until his exhausted troops had been given a chance to rest. He estimated that he was opposed by 15,000 Turks. His troops once again spent the night searching the battlefield for their comrades and carrying the wounded to the now congested river bank. The morning of 9 January broke with a dense mist despite the heavy rain. There was complete silence from the enemy positions. The British troops began to advance, slipping and slithering in the glutinous mud. There was still no response from the enemy. At 11.45 a.m. Aylmer issued orders for a general advance along both banks to Sheikh Saad. As the weather was too bad for aerial reconnaissance he sent his cavalry to probe forward for signs of the enemy. The leading troops of the 28th Brigade occupied Sheikh Saad just before 2 p.m. One hour later the cavalry reported that the Turkish trenches to the west of Sheikh Saad were empty. The enemy, after inflicting grievous losses to the attackers, had withdrawn during the night. The following day Aylmer reported to Nixon that the fighting for Sheikh Saad had resulted in 3,799 British and Indian casualties and that owing to 'inadequate' medical units he was having great difficulty in evacuating the wounded. He said that his men were too exhausted to pursue the enemy. The Turks had lost heavily also. Over 4,000 dead and wounded were found lying in the waterlogged trenches.

At the British camp near the river there were scenes which witnesses described as being reminiscent of the Crimea. After fifteen months there still was not one hospital ship in the whole of Mesopotamia. The British and Indian wounded just could not believe that such little provision had been made for their treatment and comfort. They were used to conditions in France; even at their hardest the elements of medical treatment had been present. But the 7th Division's doctors, field ambulances and medical equipment were still on their way from Marseilles. As the battle had progressed over a thousand wounded had clustered around one medical tent in which were three doctors and an assistant. It was obvious to the wounded men that something had gone terribly wrong. They had strewn themselves on the ground and waited, lying all night in the mud and the rain. Later a few Red Cross tents appeared. A small cemetery grew on the right bank of the river. Wrapped in blankets, the dead were placed in shallow, water-filled graves near the river bank amongst the kicking mules and gurgling camels.

Three days earlier Townshend had received a cable from Aylmer which told him that the Relief Force commander was of the opinion that Younghusband was up against the whole Turkish force apart from those surrounding Kut. He added:

'Will you consider the advisability of making a sortie and let
me know?'[7]

Townshend read between the lines and concluded that
Younghusband was being roughly handled. He replied immediately:

> I was unaware of the fighting below Sheikh Saad—on the
> left bank, I suppose. I do not know what numbers contain
> me here. The Turks are hidden in trenches which surround
> me. No reconnaissance came over on the 7th as promised.
> I have contemplated a sortie to harass the Turks on their
> retreat past me on the left bank. I have also been thinking
> out what to do if you are repulsed, and it is in my mind, in
> such a case, to attempt to cut my way out; it would be
> well worth trying if I could even carry off even two-thirds of
> the garrison in doing so. Such a step means the abandonment
> of all guns and all wounded and such. We have no means of
> reaching the right bank in sufficient rapidity and secrecy to
> make the effort successful. I think I could fight my way out
> on the land side, left bank, crossing the maze by portable
> ramps which I am having made now. Such a step would only
> be a desperate necessity. It cannot be in any way advisable
> at this juncture. I trust and hope you can give me better
> news soon. If the Turkish forces have gone to meet you they
> cannot be strongly entrenched and their convoys of ammu-
> nition have to go all the way from here.[8]

Townshend repeated his message to Nixon and the Army
Commander's comments on his proposals came with surprising
speed. Nixon's telegram read:

> Army Commander directs you not to resort to expedient of
> cutting your way out except in desperate extremity. We
> have plenty of reinforcements which are being sent up [from
> Basra] as soon as empty shipping is returned from upriver.
> Will Corps please keep Townshend fully informed of situa-
> tion.[9]

Aylmer, realising that his knuckles had been rapped, cabled
Townshend:

On 5 January aeroplane reported enemy strongly entrenched astride the river about two miles west of Sheikh Saad. Numbers as follows: 4,500 on north side of river, 6,500 on south side. The latter included some 2,000 cavalry. Enemy have no bridge with them.[10]

Another followed hard on its heels. It read:

In asking you to consider advisability of making sortie, of course I only meant by way of creating a diversion and thus relieving pressure here. There is absolutely no idea yet of you having to cut your way out. I do, however, contemplate some delay in reaching you as I am opposed by very considerable numbers.[11]

And then came the first piece of bad news. The brief cable ran:

Owing to the fatigue of the troops on account of yesterday's efforts I have been unable to make any progress today.[12]

Townshend asked his supply and Transport officers to report on the food stocks in Kut.

Meanwhile the rain was becoming heavier and continuous. Torrential deluges produced puddles in the trenches which deepened then united. The men were soon up to their ankles and sometimes knees in the chilly water. The trench sides began to cave in and the troops stood in a stiff porridge of mud and water. The situation was aggravated by lack of fuel supplies for the fires. Strange things began to happen in Kut. Notice-boards vanished overnight. An observation post built on the roof poles of a two-storey house collapsed burying the three duty observers and the Arabs residing below. They were all dug out unscathed. A subsequent investigation revealed that the roof poles were missing. The following notice was contained in all regimental orders:

Theft. Picquets and maules placed at the sides of communication trenches for fixing therein barbed wire trestles are being stolen. This is an offence triable by summary general court martial endangering as it may the fences. Offenders will be severely punished. There have also been numerous complaints from the inhabitants of Kut of the removal from their houses of such articles as mats and wood. All ranks are warned that this amounts to theft and as such will meet with instant and severe punishment.[13]

In the trenches life was somewhat enlivened by a plague of green frogs. In spare moments frog races were held but one night the champion of the Norfolks disappeared from its tin and it was suggested that the Indians had eaten it. The Indians protested vigorously. Such persiflage was cut short, however, by a far more unpopular plague. With the rains came the lice season. They infested underclothes, shirts and blankets. Killing lice became a constant preoccupation; picking them out singly or destroying them *in situ* in their dozens. The patients in the hospitals would sit for hours searching for the live and became expert. One patient claimed to have found—and killed—247 lice, and then another 420 a few hours later. The claim was not disputed.

Mesopotamia had a complete cycle of insect pests. The lice lasted until the spring, and then, with the coming of the warmer weather they vanished as suddenly as they had appeared. Hard on their heels came armies of fleas which, though not as numerous as their predecessors, far exceeded them in agility and biting power. After the fleas came the sand-flies with a sting reminiscent of a hot needle thrust into the flesh. But ubiquitous was the common fly which abounded in incredible numbers the entire year round. The recommended method of eating a sandwich of bread and jam was to place it in between the hands in rather the same way as a harmonica player might hold his instrument. All the effort was in vain, however, and a ring of mutilated flies lay on the sandwich where the bite had been inflicted. In addition there was the malarial mosquito, a large stinging centipede and the scorpion.

The British troops, exhausted by the work of rebuilding the subsiding trench walls, paused in their labours and watched the large numbers of enemy troops marching downstream by the left and right banks. They knew that they were on their way to fight

Aylmer's Relief Force, to dig in and wait for him, but their confidence in the eventual outcome never waned. There was some hopeful news from home. A Reuter's telegram talked of conscription at home—'compulsion' was the expression used—and everybody in Kut seemed to think that this was a good thing. 'Too many bachelors are not with the colours', was a typical comment. Townshend's supply officer, Colonel Annersley, reported that there were thirty full day's rations for the British troops and twenty-nine days' for the Indians. In addition there was eighty days' grain, seven days' fresh meat and tea for fifteen days. Townshend decided to cut the troops' rations to half. On the same day Nixon telegraphed Townshend that because of ill-health he was relinquishing his command and would be leaving Mesopotamia in seven days or so. He hoped that Aylmer would have relieved Kut by then. He said that he had informed the commander-in-chief of the Indian Army, Sir Beauchamp Duff, that he was handing over to Aylmer as next senior in Mesopotamia and that he had recommended Townshend for the command of the Tigris Corps. Evidently Beauchamp Duff thought otherwise for this was not to be. It was announced that the commander-in-chief's own Chief of Staff, Sir Percy Lake, was coming from India to take charge.

That morning (9 January) the observers on the Kut roofs noticed that the steamers at Shumran bend were decked with bunting. Cheering, bugling and volleys of rifle fire came from the Turkish trenches. The British troops were somewhat mystified by this cheerful demonstration until the answer was supplied by the Arab coffee shops. It was bad news indeed. The British troops were being evacuated from Gallipoli after suffering heavy losses. The soldiers in the first line trenches at Kut tried to dampen the exuberance of the celebrating Turkish soldiery with a few well-directed mud pies. It is extremely unlikely that anyone was capable of throwing a handful of mud for 400 yards but the British troops had made their gesture and felt better for it. On the afternoon of 10 January four or five parties of wounded Turkish soldiers straggled past Kut on the left bank coming from downstream. Aylmer telegraphed Townshend to tell him that his losses at Sheikh Saad had been

heavy but that the fight was continuing. Three days later
Townshend's wireless operators reported that from the hubbub
of messages overheard on the radio, it would appear that
Aylmer was attacking the Turkish positions at the Wadi on
the right bank of the Tigris. Townshend waited patiently.

On 11 January Aylmer was informed that the Turks were
entrenching on the right bank of the Wadi—a stream which
connected the Pusht-i-Kuh with the Tigris. Behind the Turks
were the Suwaikiya marshes, the most southerly edge of which
reached within about a mile and a half of the Tigris, almost
blocking the enemy's line of retreat. Aylmer thought that this
would afford him an almost unique opportunity. If he could
outflank the Turks swiftly and place his troops in the line of
Turkish retreat the entire enemy army of 15,000 could be
rounded up. His plan was a simple one. Younghusband's 7th
Division was to move forward swiftly and undetected from
Sheikh Saad to an assembly point about three miles from the
Wadi. At 6.30 a.m. on 13 January the division was to advance,
cross the Wadi and envelope the enemy's flank with a wide
turning movement. The 28th Brigade was to advance straight
up the river bank, cross the Wadi and hold the Turks in the
southern portion of their trenches and prevent any escape. The
British artillery was to cut the trapped enemy to pieces.

The night of 12–13 January was ideal for Aylmer's purpose.
It was cold but clear with just the faintest suggestion of moonlight. The ground was smooth and the 7th Division reached their
assembly point without mishap. Dawn broke on the 13th with a
thick mist which lifted at about 7 a.m. when the sun rose. The
7th Division which was delayed slightly by the mist advanced
in echelon from the left. In the lead was the 21st Brigade with
the 20th Field Artillery Battery, followed by the remainder of
the artillery, then the 19th Brigade and then the 35th. The
Cavalry Brigade guarded the division's right flank. All three
infantry brigades had crossed the Wadi by 10 a.m. but its steep
banks were a serious obstacle to the artillery which did not
manage to get across until three hours later. This delay was
serious because the following wheeled transport, including the

field ambulances, were not able to complete their crossing until after darkness had fallen. By the time the few field ambulances had crossed the Wadi they were already receiving wounded from the battlefield. The medical staff were too busy treating the wounded to move any closer to the scene of the fighting and so take part in evacuation of the casualties.

At 11 a.m. the Turkish artillery opened up on the leading 21st Brigade and its advance troops (1/9th Gurkhas) came under heavy rifle and machine-gun fire. In pursuance of their task which was to pin down the enemy's left while the 19th and 35th Brigades and the Cavalry Brigade still further to the right manœuvred against the Turkish rear, the 21st suddenly deployed to the right of their advance guard. The 41st Dogras came up on the right of the 9th Gurkhas with the gaps being filled by 9th Bhopal Infantry. The Bhopals and Dogras managed to get within 400 yards of the Turkish line which was hurriedly digging in. The Black Watch on the right of the 41st came under heavy artillery fire at 600 yards' range and dug themselves in. The 6th Jats came up on their right.

The position at 2.30 p.m. was: the 19th and 21st Brigades were facing due south and were closely engaged with the enemy who were bringing up reserves to meet the attack; the 19th were within 300 yards of the enemy; Younghusband's artillery was in action from behind the 21st; the 35th Brigade was in reserve about a thousand yards to the rear of the 21st. The 28th Punjabis on the right of the 19th Brigade and the 1/5th Buffs to the left had managed to enter the Turkish trenches in front of them but were driven out again.

At 4.40 p.m. the 28th Brigade was observed advancing from Sheikh Saad. Supported by artillery the brigade advanced quickly with determination but encountered heavy hostile fire from the Wadi and was driven back. It attacked again and was once more repulsed with heavy losses. The ground in front of the 28th was as smooth as a billiard table. Every hundred metres the Turks had placed sticks to act as range markers. These were very effective. In a final rush the 56th Rifles and 53rd Sikhs reached a shallow irregular ditch some fifty yards from the Wadi but their losses were so heavy that they could not progress any further and were at last forced to retreat. Eventually these troops and the Leicesters were merged in an irregular firing line about 200 to 300 yards from the Wadi. The 51st Sikhs were thrown into the battle but having lost their commanding officer became disorganised and were unable to join up with the advance troops. The fight became completely stationary under heavy machine-gun cross-fire.

As darkness fell, there being no further hope of success, the remnants of the 28th Brigade were withdrawn after having suffered 648 casualties. Thus both the British flanking and frontal attacks had been checked. A night attack was not thought possible because of the disorganisation caused by the heavy casualties.

The night of 13th–14th was intensely cold with heavy rain. At 7 a.m. Younghusband received reports that the enemy had slunk away in the dark and were now entrenched between the Suwaikiya marshes and the Tigris presenting a narrow, heavily entrenched front of less than a mile. Once more the Turks had slipped out of the British grasp after inflicting severe losses. The total British casualties were 1,113 killed and wounded. Turkish losses were estimated at about 2,000. There was more rain throughout the day and evening which turned the ground into clinging, clogging mud. The fate of the British wounded was entirely similar to that of those at Sheikh Saad.

On 14 January Townshend's wireless operators intercepted further messages which gave the impression that the Turks were retiring and that Kemball's 28th Brigade was in pursuit. At 11.45 a.m. Aylmer informed Townshend that the battle had been of an obstinate and indecisive nature but the enemy 'seemed to be in retreat as large masses were seen moving westwards'. Another message said that the action had been close and continuous until nightfall; Kemball had attacked the enemy's front with the 28th Brigade but had been repulsed and had withdrawn to the east (left) bank of the Wadi.

15 January dawned wet and windy. As the day passed the garrison of Kut, having believed that they would be relieved by that day, were downcast. On regimental orders there was a farewell message from Sir John Nixon. It read:

It is with feelings of deepest regret and sorrow that owing to ill-health I am reluctantly compelled to wish you good-bye. We have now been together for over a period of nine months and during that time you have won many a hard fight under conditions that I can safely say are without parallel and as was expected of you have worthily upheld the honour of our King and country. You have also had the high honour of receiving on more than one occasion the congratulations of His Majesty the King himself. My deepest sympathy goes out to the many gallant comrades we have unfortunately lost and I sincerely hope that the wounded will continue to progress towards a final and speedy recovery. It has been the source of unbounding gratification to me that I have had the honour of commanding for such a period a body of troops on active service who are second to none and whom I can hand over to my successor with confidence assured that they will continue to maintain the high state of efficiency they are now in. I thank every one of you for all the help you have given me on all occasions and for your unswerving loyalty. Good-bye and God be with you.[14]

On 16 January Aylmer telegraphed the new Army Commander, Sir Percy Lake, that as Townshend had seen guns and infantry going back to the main Turkish camp at Shumran, Aylmer was of the opinion that the enemy's intention was to delay the Relief Force in the defile at the Wadi while crossing large numbers of troops to the right bank by the boat bridge at Shumran so as to outflank the Relief Force at Es Sinn. To counter this move Aylmer was throwing a bridge across the Tigris just above the Wadi and was passing the entire 7th Division to the right bank. If the enemy did not advance Aylmer intended to attempt to outflank the Turks at the defile. Aylmer repeated this message to Townshend.

Townshend received the discouraging news on 17 January that Aylmer's advance was being delayed by 'atrocious weather' which had interrupted the construction of his bridge. Aylmer said that his losses so far amounted to over 6,000 killed which was in excess of the reinforcements that had joined him since

his advance from Ali Gharbi. The Relief Force had been reduced to 9,000 combatants. The real seriousness of the situation
was brought home to Townshend by a copy of a telegram from
Aylmer to Lake. It read:

The situation must be fully faced. The enemy is blocking the
entrance of the Wadi-Nakhailat [Suwaikiya] defile with
very strong works and, judging from his dispositions within
them, they have been designed to resist a heavy bombardment from across river as well as attack in front. His bivouac
shelters seem to indicate I shall have opposed to me his whole
52nd Division and two regiments of the 35th and 38th
Divisions. But of course I cannot be certain of this. Emplacements for nineteen guns have been seen, eleven of which
are designed to fire across river. Behind in [the] defile there
is a single line of entrenchments through 'Y' of Sannaiyat,
between marsh and river, probably one and a half miles long.
Behind again is the Es Sinn position. It is impossible to take
the first position by *coup de main* from this side [of the river]
alone, without losing half my force. It was my intention to
cross the Third Division and Cavalry Brigade to right bank,
directly the bridge is finished, and thus enfilade enemy's
position. Even by this means I do not think our progress as
an entire force can be anything but very slow. Information
indicates that [Turkish] reinforcements may have begun to
arrive at Kut, and these may very soon amount to a ·very
considerable number. On the right bank below Kut, at present
there do not seem, at outside, more than 2,000 men, and rain
is rendering Hai crossing [for the Turks] very difficult for
transport. The best plan seems to me for Townshend to cross
the river during the night, with such able-bodied men as he
has got, in the *mahailas* and other river transport available,
and march well round Es Sinn on the right bank. I would
cross one division and Cavalry Brigade at the same time and
march to meet him and bring him back here. The opportunity
is now favourable and may cease directly enemy send troops
down right bank, which may be very soon. On 20 December
Townshend informed me he had fifty *mahailas*, besides other

8   A man of the 114th Mahrattas, 34th Infantry Brigade,
17th Division, about to throw a Mills hand-grenade from a
trench

9 Shells bursting in the distance during the siege. The
British Military Cemetery is in the foreground

10 British graves at Kut

craft. If these still exist it should be about sufficient for his
purpose although he would have to leave sick and men
unable to march, and to destroy most of his guns and material.
If Townshend thinks this possible, I shall issue orders for
him to do so.[15]

Aylmer concluded his message by asking Townshend to wire
his views on the feasibility of the proposals immediately
'remembering that opportunity may not recur'. Before Townshend had had a chance to do so he received a copy of Lake's
reply to Aylmer which saved him the trouble. Lake's telegram
was uncompromising. It read:

I do not in any way agree with your appreciation of the
situation, or that same calls for Townshend to take extreme
step you propose. Only circumstances that could in my
opinion justify this course would be a demoralisation of your
force which I have no reason to suspect. You have been
opposed from Sheikh Saad by 35th, 38th and 52nd Divisions,
some Gendarmerie and Cavalry, totalling rather over 15,000,
with at the outside forty-one guns and you have twice
defeated them [Sheikh Saad and Wadi]. Townshend has been
contained by 45th and 51st Divisions totalling possibly
8,000 with seventeen guns. Townshend has reported strong
columns, estimated at one division and twelve guns, retiring
to main camp west of Kut. Enemy have further suffered losses
estimated by you at 4,500 at Sheikh Saad and 2,000 at Wadi.
You should have between you and Kut no more than
5,000 and possibly twenty-seven guns. The total of your
losses should almost have been made good by reinforcing
units—your bridge gives you freedom of manœuvre. The
course you originally proposed, namely to employ part of
your force on right bank, should not only promise success
but afford you opportunity of inflicting severe blow on enemy
and effecting speedy relief of Townshend. I cannot believe
that [Turkish] position in front of you can equal in strength
those attacked and captured by us in the past, which had
been in preparation for four months. The course you propose
for Townshend in your telegram under reply would be

F

disastrous from every point of view to Townshend's force, to your force, to the whole of the forces in Mesopotamia, and to the Empire, and I cannot sanction it. There is no reason to suppose enemy has yet been reinforced by a sixth division, and the possibility of it arriving only emphasises necessity for prompt action. Both acknowledge.[16]

Townshend telegrammed Aylmer that he supposed the Relief Force would now advance up the right bank as it was not likely that the Turks would attempt an offensive down the left bank as long as Kut was held blocking the passage of the enemy's river transport. He took the opportunity to remind the Relief Force commander that he had informed him earlier that it was impossible for the Kut force to cross to the right bank with either rapidity or secrecy or at all unless Aylmer arrived with his troops on the bank opposite to give him cover.

A miserable Aylmer telegrammed Lake with a copy to Townshend. The message read:

I understand your telegram to mean that you desire me to get to Kut in such a way as to hold that place together with Townshend, at least until his force can be moved entirely. That is that you do not wish Townshend's breaking out to form any part of my plan. If this is so, the plan suggested by Townshend is opposed to your views, and in my opinion less likely to succeed than what I suggested, as my remaining opposite Kut while Townshend took several days to get across river would lead to Turks assaulting the place when half denuded of troops. The only way to relieve Townshend without the necessity of his breaking out is for me to force the defile and join hands with him by left bank. This I shall attempt to do by the means already indicated, namely, cross the river with part of my force, enfilade enemy, then assault his position. I have only just succeeded in completing bridge owing to extreme difficulty of getting it up from Sheikh Saad and reconstructing it here on account of storm and torrents of rain, the quantity of material [available], and only one company of Sappers and Miners. The country around is a sea of mud and animals can hardly move. I am using my utmost endeavours to carry out plan, but it must be recognised that conditions have been extraordinarily unfavourable. A comparison between works in front of me and those elsewhere is difficult, but these cannot be turned [outflanked] except in a modified manner by enfilade fire from opposite bank. I have just now heard that the bridge is breaking again.[17]

At this juncture, as he explained in his autobiography, Townshend decided to inform Aylmer of his plans for the Kut garrison if the attempts at relief were unsuccessful. Townshend told Aylmer that he considered that any attempt to break out at night with, say, 3,000 men was foredoomed to failure as this would be immediately detected by the ever-vigilant Turks and destruction would surely follow when daylight came. This method of escape would also mean the abandonment of his wounded, guns and supplies. Instead, Townshend said, he would fight from trench to trench and house to house until all his ammunition was exhausted. He said that only when all hope had gone was any general justified in making terms with the enemy and then only 'on fair conditions'. He cited as an example the terms that the British allowed Junot's force in Portugal in 1808 when the French force was transported back to France in British ships. Townshend continued:

As long as I hold Kut the enemy cannot take offensive against us towards Amara, as his steamers and barges are absolutely necessary. If you cannot relieve me and cannot contain yourself where you are, you will have to retreat; the weather here has been very bad, the rain last night has been heavy and the trenches have two feet of water in them— in many cases more—causing much discomfort and hardship for the men. I think this is the end of the wet weather; the inhabitants say so.[18]

Townshend incautiously repeated this message to Lake who immediately construed it as another manifestation of revolt against his authority. It became Townshend's turn for the disciplinary ruler. Lake cabled:

It would appear you contemplate the practical evacuation of Kut with abandonment of stores and guns after relieving column has reached there. This is by no means the intention of the Army Commander. On the arrival of Aylmer's column [at Kut] our force should be in superior strength to enemy and neither Kut nor guns nor stores must be abandoned. If Aylmer's force is so disposed along Hai to south, with portion of it north on your right flank, and it is unable at first to clear enemy from your front, there would appear to be no difficulty to combine force, maintaining position while remainder of reinforcements concentrate at Es Sinn or east of same. By first week February all columns now marching [from Basra] should reach Sheikh Saad, including drafts to complete 6th Division to service strength. [Tigris] Force will then total four full divisions except for two brigades of artillery, and we should be able to assume offensive with a view to clearing front and securing permanent position further west of Kut. Consider and advise Aylmer, repeating here, what dispositions of corps on arrival [at Kut] would fit in best with above plans.[19]

Townshend hurriedly telegrammed Lake and told him that he had contemplated the abandonment of Kut only because Aylmer had suggested it. Personally, he said, he had never wished to abandon Kut and considered it his duty to hold the Turkish forces there and give the reinforcements then arriving in Mesopotamia time to concentrate at Amara and Ali Gharbi. Townshend said that although he had bargained to be relieved in a month he nevertheless was 'delighted' to hear that Kut was not to be abandoned.

Far below the level of the pistolery between Lake and his divisional commanders the suffering of those in the Kut trenches was extreme. Not only was the weather bitterly cold but a half-gale pelted the rain at the Kut defenders. The rain drove into the trenches, redoubts and dugouts and in some cases the men were over their waists in cold, yellow water. It became difficult to move about the trenches. Men slipped and fell and vanished under the surface of the water. They fought their way to their feet and stood shivering in sopping uniforms. The incidence of frostbite was high and led in a number of cases to gangrene of the fingers and toes. Trench rheumatism, pneumonia, pleurisy and sore throats became common. In one day (20 January) thirty Indian soldiers collapsed with exposure and cold. Three of these drowned in the liquid mud before they were noticed. A favoured method of gaining some respite from the wet was to find a seat on a comparatively firm ledge of mud and withdraw one's feet out of the cold water. An added refinement was to construct an umbrella out of a greatcoat and rifle. Care had to be exercised that the coat did not protrude above the top of the parapet to provide a mark for the Turkish snipers. The stamina and fortitude of these Anatolians was almost beyond belief. Despite the awful weather these men still lay out all day in waterlogged shellholes waiting for something to fire at.

Because of the shortage of fuel for fires the wooden seats of the coffee shops, window frames and bazaar doors were requisitioned and went to make up the troops' daily half a pound ration of firewood. The ration was made up of wood chips, liquorice wood and furze bush which produced a little heat for a short time. On all regimental orders was the instruction: 'No troops and followers are permitted to cut brushwood or trees, etc. The quantity being very limited it must be taken into Government stock for issue as fuel.'[20]

On the same orders there was a strict injunction that graves for the dead must be dug at least five feet deep. The torrential rain had revealed that this had not been adhered to and here and there a stiff arm or leg showed above the waterlogged surface of the graveyard.

The plight of the sick and wounded in the matting roofed bazaars was acute. Because of the large number of patients many lay in puddles of water on the floors. Bedding became soaked and there was no means of drying the blankets.

In Kut town itself gangs of exhausted men worked in shifts in an attempt to keep the roads and alleys passable so that supplies and ammunition kept in the storehouses in the town could be removed when required. Despite their efforts they became

quagmires. The streets possessed little natural slope and the
water—and mud—stayed where it was. Small wells were dug
at the wider parts of the roads and in corners not frequented by
the transport carts. Arab labourers were provided with empty
kerosene tins and kept hard at work bailing the muddy water
lying in the roads into these 'wells'. The soft covering of the
road thus exposed was then scraped away until the original
brick sole was uncovered probably for the first time for centuries. The stench that arose during the scraping operations
defied description. As was explained earlier the roads were
covered with more than honest mud. One witness wrote: 'Even
the Arabs sometimes covered their faces with their headcloths.'[21] The Arab was considered to be no miner's canary
when it came to detecting smells. The lascar crews of the
launches which had remained behind in Kut were impressed for
this unwholesome task. The appearance of these men with their
strange uniforms around the streets of Kut caused no small
curiosity among the Indian soldiers. A British sergeant helpfully informed them that the lascars were convicts specially
sent up from Basra for the job. The Indians seemed to believe
this story for in future they gave them a wide berth.

Despite the heavy rain the Turks launched an unsuccessful
infantry attack against Woolpress village after a heavy rifle
and artillery bombardment. The enemy left twenty-one dead.
They attacked the village again the following morning this
time with the infantry carrying bundles of brushwood to throw
across and bridge the barbed wire but again they were beaten
off. A Turkish mine was exploded about a hundred yards from
the fort and the enemy infantry attempted to rush into the
crater caused by the explosion. They were driven back by rifle
and machine-gun fire. One wounded Turkish soldier was
captured after the latter attack. He was described in the diary
of a medical officer, who treated his wounds:

He was a fine-looking hefty fellow, phlegmatic and stoical
like the rest of his kind. In general they are men of splendid
physique, broad and burly, and of splendid vitality. In this
particular their allies, the Arabs, vie with them. They take a

lot of killing and when wounded recover from wounds and answer readily to the surgeon's efforts. The Turk would make a fine soldier if properly led.[22]

The doctor's closing remark was by no means an original military conclusion and it was possible that he might have recalled that similar views had already been expressed by first a French and then a German general about the fighting potential of the British private soldier and his want of adequate leadership. The wounded Turkish soldier nevertheless informed his captors, to their surprise, that Nur-ud-Din was no longer in command of the Turkish forces in Mesopotamia. His successor was the young and highly popular Halil Pasha. 'Now you are killed,' said the Turk entirely without rancour.

A visit to the Punjabis' roof gave a depressing view of the swollen Tigris and the gathering floods. Because of the height of the river the steamers at Shumran stood out boldly above the Turkish camp. Most of the quagmire roads of Kut had become untraversable and desperate measures were being employed to keep at least the main ones open. Demolition parties went round knocking down walls and used the material to fill the worst of the holes. It began to dawn on the garrison that if conditions were intolerable in a static camp like Kut, what must they be like for the mobile Relief Force?

VIII

HANNA

Under cover of darkness on 18 and 19 January Younghusband's
19th and 35th Brigades, with the 21st in support, moved
forward and dug themselves in about a thousand yards from
the Turkish first line at Hanna, so called after the adjacent
marshes (Umm al Hanna). The enemy trenches extended across
the entire width of the defile from the river bank to the marshes
—a distance of 1,350 yards. There was a second line a few
hundred yards to the rear. The rain beat down on the digging
British troops and the ground became churned into a muddy
morass making movement difficult. The rain ceased on the
morning of the 19th but the low leaden clouds warned that this
would only be a temporary respite. The British force was
reinforced by the 1st Manchesters who had just arrived in
Mesopotamia.

The bad weather prevented aerial reconnaissance and it was
difficult for Aylmer to estimate the numbers of the enemy
troops which opposed him, but Arab agents and reports from
Townshend indicated that large bodies of Turks were moving
downstream towards the enemy positions. The rain held off
again on the 20th but the ground had not dried out sufficiently
to permit of the rapid movement required for a frontal attack
of this nature. Nevertheless, Aylmer decided that an attack
would be launched the following morning (21st). To postpone
it any longer would merely enable the Turks further to reinforce and strengthen their hold on Hanna. The artillery would
bombard the Turkish first line for ten minutes during which the
7th Division was to advance to within 200 yards of the Turkish
line. The bombardment would then lift to the second line. At
this point the attack was to be pressed home against the half
of the line nearest the river.

Owing to the usual morning mist the 'zero' hour for the artillery bombardment was put back from dawn to 7.45 a.m. because of the impossibility of accurate ranging. Under cover of the bombardment the 35th Brigade advanced as planned but encountered heavy and accurate rifle and machine-gun fire, suffering considerable losses. At 7.55 a.m., as planned, the artillery lifted to the second line and the 35th dashed into the assault. They vanished into the smoke of battle. At 10.45 a.m. Aylmer heard from Younghusband that the Black Watch had managed to break into an enemy redoubt but had been driven out again. Just before noon it began to rain, with winds gusting up to gale force. At 11.45 a.m. Aylmer, hearing nothing but realising by now that the British attack must have been checked gave orders that the positions thus won were to be held and that a further attack would be launched at 1 p.m. after another ten minutes' artillery bombardment.

The attack commenced as ordered but the men, soaked and numbed by the biting gale and rain, encountered knee-deep mud. They were unable to move forward at any speed and the enemy fire took a heavy toll of the floundering troops. It was impossible to continue and at 1.15 p.m. Younghusband reported that he could not make any further progress.

Younghusband was visited by Aylmer's senior staff officer. The divisional commander told the visitor that in his opinion the condition of the ground and that of his frozen and soaked men put a further attack that day out of the question. The men's rifles were clogged with mud and had become temporarily useless. Younghusband thought it would be preferable to withdraw to the original positions held on the 19th, reorganise and try again when conditions improved. Having aired his views and assuming that as they had been listened to by Aylmer's senior staff officer this gave automatic assent, Younghusband gave orders for his saturated troops to withdraw.

When Aylmer received a copy of the orders for retreat he 'totally disapproved'.[1] He cancelled them immediately and sent word to Younghusband that the positions now held must be maintained and consolidated and he was to make preparation for an attack the next day. Younghusband countermanded his orders but it was too late. The new orders either did not reach their destinations or arrived after the withdrawals had been carried out. He informed Aylmer of this state of affairs and suggested that any future orders should be based on the fact that the withdrawals had already been made. Aylmer sent staff officers to all the brigades to ascertain their losses and the condition of the troops. The brigade commanders were unanimous in the opinion that an attack the following day was out of the question.

The men, physically exhausted, passed a miserable night in the waterlogged muddy trenches. The wounded again suffered acutely. As many as possible had been collected during the withdrawal but the heavy rain and approaching darkness made them hard to find. Some wounded were too close to the enemy trenches to be collected.

Early the following day arrangements were made with the Turks for a six-hour armistice to allow the wounded to be collected and brought in and the dead to be buried. It was found that already many had died from exposure. Because of the mud it took much hard labour and considerable time to transfer the wounded from the battlefield to the river transport to the rear. It took an able-bodied man four hours to walk the two miles to the ships and return. The transport carts and stretcher bearers took five times as long. Men were found to have drowned in the shellholes. A man with a shattered leg was miraculously found alive. He had spent the night trying to reach the lip of the crater only to slither back into the cold water again. Even when the ships were reached it was found that the medical arrangements were completely inadequate. Most of the splints and wound dressing had been used up at the battles for Sheikh Saad and the Wadi and had not been replenished.

Edmund Candler, an official 'eye witness', visited the scene of the battle and described the litter of broken wheels and debris of war as a twentieth-century battle with eighteenth-century medical arrangements. He was so appalled that he cabled home for medical supplies. Knowing the stringent censorship he referred to the shortage of 'medical comforts'. He later found that even this had been suppressed.

After the battle Aylmer put the strength of the enemy which
had opposed him at Hanna at 9,000 infantry and twenty-three
guns. He estimated their casualties to be 2,000 which seemed to
have become a stock figure. British casualties were 2,741.
Some battalions lost between fifty and ninety per cent of their
strength.

A telegram from Aylmer to Lake on 22 January, repeated to
Townshend, revealed all. It read:

From detailed statements taken from six prisoners, including
an officer, which follows, it will be seen that the force in
front of me yesterday consisted of whole of 52nd and combined 35th and 38th Division, plus two battalions of 52nd
[should be 51st] plus twenty-six guns. Drafts [reinforce-
ments] having been lately received by units. Allowing for
previous losses this [Turkish] force would admittedly amount
to at least 9,000 infantry. I am quite certain that Townshend
has observed most carefully, but, if all troops reported by
him as marching westwards during last fortnight be taken as
additionals and deducted from enemy in front of me, I
should have had to fight about 5,000 yesterday, not allowing
for losses. My *parlementaire* today, who was towards front
position, himself saw two regimental and one artillery commanders, and Halil Bey's name was given as being in command. He is reported to have superseded Nur-ud-Din. My
losses are very heavy indeed. I cannot ascertain numbers in
all cases but the 19th Brigade alone lost over 1,000 [troops]
and twenty-seven officers. The troops are not at present in a
state to assault, even if [the enemy positions are] only held
by 3,000 men; they have done most nobly all that is possible
in the face of the severest conditions. I cannot call on them
to do what is impossible in their present state. I will naturally
do what I can to ascertain the remaining strength of the
enemy in front of me. I will arrange armistice up to 6 p.m.
today, and a certain number of wounded have been brought
in and dead buried, but the Turks have taken into their lines
the wounded immediately in front of their trenches and were
most active in doing so.[2]

Townshend cabled Lake the following day that he considered, because of the arrival of Turkish reinforcements, the situation must be faced that relief might become impossible. He said that 15 January—the expected date of relief—had now passed and pointed out that in fact he had relied on being relieved by the 10th. As Aylmer had 'shot his bolt'[3] for the present, Townshend said he had come to the conclusion that he was faced with three alternatives, A, B, or C, which he offered to Lake for consideration. These were:

A. He might extricate some 4,000 of his force by making a sortie by the right bank at night, striking across the twenty-five miles of desert to Sheikh Saad. Aylmer would be asked to meet him half way. Townshend's force would consist of himself and 'those of most service to the state, engineers, sappers, gunners, signallers, flying men, British infantry, Indian infantry, cavalry and a proportion of medical personnel'. The sick, wounded and all those too weak to march would be left behind at Kut under a brigadier-general who would then make terms with the enemy. All guns would be destroyed and the *Sumana* and two barges would endeavour to run the gauntlet downstream. The moonless nights between 28 January and 3 February would be suitable for this sortie.

B. Townshend and the entire garrison would hold Kut until his ammunition and food were exhausted on the 'defence of Saragossa or Genoa principle'.[4]

C. Townshend might preserve his whole force by negotiating with the Turks by offering Kut in exchange for the release of his force. These negotiations should be conducted immediately while there was still food left to argue with, said Townshend. He wistfully cited the example of Junot and his 20,000 troops who in 1808 was even taken back to France by the British in return for the surrender of Lisbon.

Lake replied immediately that he still hoped to effect the relief of Kut but he said that he would be in a better position to express a stronger opinion on 28 January when he had reached

Aylmer's headquarters. He thought, however, that proposals B and C would be unnecessary and indeed out of the question but Townshend should prepare to put proposal A into effect but the matter must be kept strictly secret from the troops of the garrison. He asked Townshend to consider proposal A in the light of co-operation with Aylmer's force which might be able to advance so as to confine the Turks on the left bank.

Aylmer, however, expressed his opinion of the chances of reaching Kut in a telegram of the same date. It read:

I know Army Commander disagrees with me, but I must again affirm my opinion, as previously expressed, and as confirmed by recent experiences, I am not in a position to reach Kut to effect entire relief of Townshend. I believe, even after reinforcements now on their way arrive, we shall have very little chance of success. I have now only 9,000 infantry left and have just suffered reverse. I am very doubtful of morale of a good many of the Indian troops, especially I have now the gravest suspicion of self-mutilation amongst them. It is my deliberate opinion, formed after the gravest consideration, that the best course would be to adopt Townshend's plan, as suggested by me originally, and vetoed by Army Commander [then Nixon]. If this plan A is now sanctioned, I require earliest possible information, as I must cancel arrangements now under way for sending down all available ships which I must retain in order to carry out plan A and effect my own retirement when this is done. Details only would be arranged between Townshend and myself. All ships now being sent down with wounded should be returned instantly with troops to Sheikh Saad, or later to Ali Gharbi, so as to assist difficult task of my retirement from this position, where I am in actual touch with enemy and have a most difficult road to follow on both banks owing to recent floods. Reference Townshend's telegram of today, I have already expressed my opinion. The columns seen by him do not necessarily indicate deductions from force in front of us. They are much [more] likely reliefs, Townshend not being shown troops going other way.[5]

But Townshend was already having second thoughts. He thus communicated his appraisal to Lake and Aylmer on 25 January:

I have carefully thought out the situation, and wish to sum up my ideas and give you my views and the conclusions I have come to.

Paragraph 1 (a). Not only is breaking out a pure question of chance, a spin of the coin, owing to having to cross river undetected at night, but in case of success I can only extricate 3,000 odd combatants, leaving 5,000 behind, exclusive of wounded, sick and all guns.

(b) By thus doing, Kut falls at once, and this last the Turks immediately take the offensive down the Tigris, for so long as I resist at Kut they cannot get their ships, munitions, stores, etc. past me.

(c) You [Aylmer] could not remain where you are or you would share my fate. You would have to retreat in a hostile country and I doubt if you could remain in Amara, while Nasiriya would most likely be surrounded and fall.

(d) Thus we lose all territory we gained in last year's campaign and it becomes disastrous and inglorious. It is for (b), (c) and (d) above that I arrested my retirement from Ctesiphon and made a stand at Kut. It was my own decision.

(e) While I hold Kut the Russians from Kas-i-Shirin can seriously menace Baghdad.

Paragraph 2. I have now placed all food in the town under Colonel Annersley, my Assistant Director of Supplies, collected all foodstuffs and rationed inhabitants. I now find we can last for eighty-four days. As regards food, great stores of barley have been discovered. Besides this I have 3,000 animals to feed on.

Paragraph 3. As regards the want of morale of a good part of your Indian troops, I have the same here in modified form; it is my handful of Norfolks, Dorsets, Oxfords who are my sheet anchor here. We do not want interior drafts of recruits from India such as my battalions were filled up with after the battle of Kut al Amara, in September last. Melliss,

Delamain, Hamilton and Hoghton will bear me out in this.
One or two good all-British divisions are what we want. Now
is the time to demand good white troops from overseas—an
army corps to save and hold Mesopotamia, if Government
considers it worth holding, and we shed much blood to gain
this far.

Paragraph 4. I repeat I think the Turks will not have the
heart to leave their safe trenches and overwhelm me in my
trenches and houses. They would lose terribly at that game,
and have lost heavily when they tried to do so.

Paragraph 5. The [seasonal] floods will arrive, I suppose,
in February; this will compel the Turks to recede and the
side with most gunboats obtains the sea-power, which en-
abled me to take Amara last June.

Paragraph 6. The more I think out the situation, the more
convinced I am that the best and highest role I can play is to
follow the example of Osman Pasha at Plevna, where his
defence held up the Russian advance and saved Constantinople. In the same way the defence of Kut will save the whole
Basra province. It will give the Army Commander time to
get solid reinforcements and render the campaign a glorious
one instead of letting it end in disaster.[6]

Aylmer telegraphed Lake and said that Townshend's latest
reappraisal certainly threw a completely new light on the
situation. He said that had he known that the food supplies at
Kut were capable for sustaining the garrison and inhabitants
for eighty-four days he would have 'certainly modified much
that I have unsuccessfully tried to do'.[7] Under the circumstances, Aylmer said, he would no longer resort to plan 'A'.

On 26 January Townshend observed a large force of enemy
troops, estimated at a division, making its way down the right
bank in the direction of a point on the Hai where some *mahailas*
were moored with the obvious intention of crossing the channel
and proceeding to the right bank positions at Es Sinn. While
informing Aylmer of these troops movements, Townshend took
the opportunity of replying to the Relief Force commander's
blatant accusation that he had exaggerated the seriousness of

the position at Kut thus causing unnecessary loss of life while the Force was attempting an early relief of Kut. Townshend said he had not mentioned that he had rations for eighty-four days before then because there appeared no necessity to do so until the doubt that Kut would be relieved in time had arisen. Aylmer had himself said that Kut was to be relieved by 10 January because after this date further Turkish reinforcements might make this impossible. As Aylmer had stated this himself, Townshend could not see how the Relief Force commander's course of action could have been modified by the knowledge of the reserves of food at Kut. Townshend commented tartly: 'The business of a relieving force is to relieve a besieged garrison, not to prolong a siege.'[8] In his telegram to Aylmer, Townshend continued:

> The Arab population is 6,000, distinctly hostile to us and for the Turks. Such numbers in our midst are a positive danger, and I have to keep a considerable force of military police to watch them day and night. I have searched houses for arms. I did not want to search for food until obliged, as will be easily understood. I knew there was much food in the town, but not as much as we discovered.

Townshend realised that now he could no longer put off telling his garrison of the failure of the Relief Force. On 26 January he issued the following communiqué to his troops:

> The relief force under General Aylmer has been unsuccessful in its efforts to dislodge the Turks entrenched on the left bank of the river, some fourteen miles below the position at Es Sinn, where we defeated the Turks in September last, when their strength was greater than it is now. Our relieving force suffered severe loss and had very bad weather to contend against. There are entrenched close to the Turkish position. More reinforcements are on their way up river and I confidently expect to be relieved during the first half of the month of February. I desire all ranks to know why I decided to make a stand at Kut during our retirement from Ctesiphon. It was because so long as we hold Kut the Turks cannot get

their ships, barges, stores and munitions past this place, and so cannot move down to attack Amara. Thus we are holding up the whole of the Turkish advance. It also gives time for our reinforcements to come upriver from Basra and so restore success to our arms; it gives time for our allies, the Russians, who are now overrunning Persia to move towards Baghdad. I had a personal message from General Baratoff, commanding the Russian Expeditionary Force in Persia, the other day, telling me of his admiration of what you men of the Sixth Division and troops attached have done in the past few months, and telling me of his own progress on the road from Kermanshah to Baghdad. By standing at Kut I maintain the territory we have won in the past year at the expense of much blood, commencing with your glorious victory at Shaiba, and thus we maintain the campaign as a glorious one instead of letting disaster pursue its course down to Amara and perhaps beyond. I have ample food for eighty-four days, and that is not counting the 3,000 animals which can be eaten. When I defended Chitral some twenty years ago, we lived well on atta and horseflesh, but, I repeat, I expect confidently to be relieved in the first half of the month of February. Our duty stands out plain and simple. It is our duty to our Empire, to our beloved King and Country, to stand here and hold up the Turkish advance as we are doing now, and with the help of all, heart and soul with me together, we will make this defence to be remembered in history as a glorious one. All England and India are watching us now and are proud of the splendid courage and devotion you have shown. Let us all remember the glorious defence of Plevna, for that is what is in my mind. I am absolutely calm and confident as to the result. The Turk, although good behind a trench, is of little value in the attack. They have tried it once, and their losses in one night in their attempt on the fort were 2,000 alone. They have also had very heavy losses from General Aylmer's musketry and guns, and I have no doubt they have had enough. I want to tell you now that, when I was ordered to advance on Ctesiphon, I officially demanded an army corps, or at least two divisions, to perform the task

successfully. Having pointed out the grave danger of attempting to do this with one division only, I had done my duty.
You know the result, and whether I was right or not; and
your name will go down in history as the heroes of Ctesiphon;
for heroes you proved yourselves in that battle. Perhaps by
right I should not have told you of the above, but I feel I owe
it to all of you to speak straightly and openly and take you
into my confidence. God knows I felt our heavy losses, and
the suffering of my poor brave wounded, and I shall remember it as long as I live. I may truly say that no General
I know of has been·more loyally obeyed and served than I
have been in command of the Sixth Division. These words
are long, I am afraid, but I speak straight from the heart,
and you see I have thrown all officialdom overboard. We will
succeed; mark my words. Save your ammunition as if it were
gold.[9]

Townshend was confident that his communiqué had fully
conveyed the bad news but at the same time 'animated' the
defence by taking the troops into his confidence. In his memoirs
he mentions that he was congratulated by the officers commanding the Kut brigades and received messages from the Indian
troops assuring him of their 'absolute devotion'. There was
doubt that Townshend was congratulated on his communiqué
by several officers but there was also no doubt that his words
caused considerable alarm among certain sections of his troops.
Was it then the right time to confide to his troops that Ctesiphon had been a blunder; a battle forced on the Sixth Division
at the instance of senior officers in Whitehall or at Delhi despite Townshend's protestations that his force was inadequate?
The reference to 'ample food for eighty-four days' did not
inspire confidence in the Relief Force. Whether the Turkish
soldiers lacked staunchness in the attack was debatable—few
apart from Townshend and other senior officers in Mesopotamia
thought so—but to be reminded that the enemy excelled in
defence was a psychological error. Would this characteristic
not prove to be the most harmful to any further attempts to
break through to relieve Kut? The reference to reserves of food

in the form of horseflesh raised severe qualms amongst most of
the Indian troops. At this stage Townshend does not even seem
to have considered that the majority of his force were strictly
forbidden by their religion from eating meat of certain kinds—
including horseflesh.

But the promise of relief by the first half of February did
raise hope. Although confidence in the Relief Force had waned
when the sound of gunfire downstream had died away there
was very little doubt that relief was inevitable and whether it
would be soon or later was the only questionable part of it.
The garrison had other problems on its mind at the time.
Because of the heavy rain the Tigris was rising rapidly—almost
four inches a day. Dams were built across the trenches in many
places in anticipation of flooding. At 6.30 a.m. on 21 January
the Tigris had overflowed its banks and burst into the British
first line trenches and the greater proportion of the North-West
Section were soon neck deep in water. As the British troops
were driven from their trenches by the rising water the Turkish
troops opposite opened fire and shot down the men as they slipped
and staggered across the waterlogged ground towards the middle
line carrying boxes of ammunition and equipment. But at
8 a.m. the Turks in turn were flushed out of their trenches by
the rising Tigris and the British troops took advantage of this
for revenge. By 10 a.m. the North-West Section of the British
first line had been completely evacuated with the exception of
the four redoubts. Apart from these the opposing forces were
now about a thousand yards apart. Great swamps now precluded any possibility of a serious Turkish infantry assault.
Because of the distance between the front lines sniping activity
on this side of Kut became less severe and there was comparatively little shelling. With the likelihood of assault thus dimi-
nished the main preoccupations of the garrison became the rising
flood waters and the weather. It was still bitterly cold, with
high winds and frequent heavy rainstorms. At night, on two
occasions, eight degrees of frost were registered. In the mornings
thin films of ice covered the water in the trenches. The miserable troops mused that the misty frozen swamps of winter and
the brazen 120 degrees heat of summer made the climate of

Mesopotamia somewhat trying. But the decreased enemy activity on the north side made it possible for the officers at least to re-experience what it was like to leave their trenches and wander about in the open. Some paused in the middle of their strolls and gazed towards the snow-covered summits of the Pusht-i-Kuh. It reminded many of Safaid Koh, north of the Khyber; others insisted that the view was more reminiscent of the long white wall of the Himalayas as seen from the Indian hills. Officers, some of whom had not met since the start of the siege, discussed everything and nothing. The lull in enemy activity provided opportunities for the auctioning of dead officers' effects. These were always sad affairs.

To prevent Kut and its defences from becoming inundated during the imminent seasonal floods, a vast scheme for their encirclement with a mud wall or 'bund' was put in hand. It was considered that a four-foot high 'bund' along the front of the middle line trenches linked with another 'bund' two to three feet high along the raised river bank would be necessary. To the north it was pretty safe but the construction work along the river bank had to be conducted at night because of the activities of snipers and gunners who with increasing frequency swept the 'bund' constructors with bullets and shrapnel. At dusk each day about 300 Arabs collected near a Kut thoroughfare called Spink Road. They were divided into parties under a Royal Engineer 'headman', issued with picks and shovels and marched off to work on the 'bunds'. The amount of work completed each night depended on the weight of the Turkish rifle and shell fire. One shell was enough to scatter a working party irretrievably. An Engineer officer commented: 'They were paid one rupee (1s. 4d.) for four hours work. Good pay considering casualties were comparatively few.'[10]

When the 'bunds' were completed they were carefully patrolled at regular intervals and holes, shell and rat, repaired immediately.

The Turks were engaged in similar work with the same kind of interruption from the British rifles and artillery. The enemy, however, had a considerable advantage as their 'bunds' could be built a long way from the river bank making the task of obstruction or destruction difficult. In addition the Turks were still digging trenches furiously and it became obvious to all at Kut that these earthworks were intended more for keeping the British in Kut rather than for protection.

With the complete exhaustion of fresh meat at the end of January the slaughter of the heavy battery bullocks and horses for food began. The British troops each received a daily ration of half a pound of beef, alternating with a pound of horse-flesh. This arrangement lasted for a fortnight after which horse-flesh only was available for issue. But despite strong encourage-ment and later, threats of disciplinary action, the Indian soldiers stuck to their religious principles and categorically refused to accept horseflesh as part of their ration. This, oddly enough, came as a profound shock to Townshend who immed-iately construed this as just one more manifestation of the un-co-operative attitude of that race. It had always been considered by the Indian Army authorities that Mohammedan troops would eat horseflesh if required to do so by extreme circum-stances. It was thought that all that would be required was a promise of a dispensation from their religious leaders in India. This revulsion at the mere thought of eating horseflesh seems to have been dismissed lightly by many of the senior British officers of the Indian Army, with all the usual characteristics born of a religion which has no such dietary scruples. This refusal had no immediate effect on the fighting quality of the Indian troops and seems to have been ignored until it was too late. From the beginning of February as the other rations declined the Mohammedans began slowly to suffer from the effects of malnutrition. Their daily ration was eight ounces of both rice and atta and two ounces of potato meal.

The British troops too were beginning to feel a certain amount of hardship. Fresh vegetables were no longer obtainable and their ration was one pound of horseflesh, three ounces of jam, two ounces of dates, three ounces of butter or cheese, three ounces of potato meal and a third of an ounce of tea.

The small supplies of food held by the officers' messes and by individual officers at first tended to lessen the effect of the reduced rations. All officers had their own tin of jam clearly labelled with the owner's name. At meal times a mess table would be littered with cigarette tins, similarly labelled, containing butter, sugar and other 'goodies'. These were closely guarded by their owners who in time developed to what amounted to an hysteria about their safety. Also the officers— and the troops with money—could at first supplement their ration with food purchased from the Arabs such as coffee beans, lentils and 'kebaabs'—small, thin, sweet pancakes made of flour, ghee (clarified butter) and sugar.

Because of the shortage of wood those billeted in the houses in Kut had to decide whether to burn their doors to cook their food or starve and remain moderately warm. They always chose the former course. There was a certain amount of coal-dust still to be had. This was mixed with mud and crude oil and moulded into 'coal balls', which gave off a guttering flame from improvised braziers. The earlier experiments in the use of crude oil for cooking purposes caused some amusement for those not actually engaged in them. The hospital kitchens, where the first attempt to use crude oil was made, looked like ships' stokeholds with their occupants resembling stokers. Eventually the Royal Engineers, temporarily relieved of their 'jam pot' bomb manufacturing operations, found a solution which although it had its faults made the use of oil for cooking a safe and practical proposition. The successful oven was an inclined tin trough covered by another sheet of tin perforated with holes over which were placed the cooking pots. A tall tin or zinc chimney at the lower end of the trough took the fumes and black smoke outside the kitchens.

Cigarettes made of Virginia tobacco, apart from private hoards, were unobtainable, as were the stocks of local tobacco, unless in the form of dust. Paper tubes pinched at one end were constructed and partly filled with grains of Arab tobacco dust. When ignited these cigarettes threw out showers of sparks and puffs of smoke and were reminiscent of pyrotechnics. It was found that glowing fragments of tobacco and khaki drill uniforms combined well to produce personal conflagrations.

Captain Sandes' 'Bridging Train' was now hard at work preparing means of crossing the Tigris or the Hai to be used if the Relief Force approached Kut by the right bank. The bridge for the Hai—the channel was approximately 150 yards wide when in flood—would consist, it was decided, of twenty-four giant floating baulks of timber which were available but the problem was the shortage of planking with which to build a smooth roadway across these 'pontoons'.

Like many of Townshend's schemes this involved Sandes in trouble with the local populace. Arab front doors, it was suggested, would fit the bill admirably. The burghers of Kut watched with undisguised suspicion as the entrances to their houses were examined by squads of Engineers. They rubbed their forefingers thoughtfully on the white-painted numbers that appeared on the doors. Then Sandes' men struck. A dozen doors were removed to build a trial bridge in the palm grove to the east of the town. Test runs with 15-pounder guns, limbers and horses charging across the structure were made and the trial bridge was pronounced a success. All the preordained doors, numbering about 200, were removed to the utter disgust and anger of their owners. Curses and even blows rained about the ears of the soldiery as they went about their task. But worse was to come. The squads reappeared in the town and removed the iron railings from the doorless residences to be cut up into dog-spikes to hold the door roadway together.

Sandes' party then prepared the 'flying bridges' that would be required to cross the 500 yard wide Tigris itself. These would be rafts of two small *mahailas* lashed gunwale to gunwale which could be winched back and forwards across the river on cables. The 'Bridging Train' accordingly busied itself making two large wooden drums on which was to be wound all the two-inch and one-inch steel cable available in Kut. Other workers prepared pulleys, belaying posts, travellers and other paraphernalia for the bridge while the Arabs clutched their remaining property in despair.

As the Turks had vacated their first line it was considered that this presented an opportunity to fill in their saps. A large party of Oxfords and Sirmur Sappers crept out from the fort under the cover of darkness. As the party squelched across the open ground and through the barbed wire there came the sickly,

sweet smell of decomposition. The dead lay everywhere; some
had obviously been there since the attack on the fort some six
weeks before. The party filled in the saps but found nothing
could be done to the Turkish main trenches which were eight
feet wide and six feet deep. The success of this operation
prompted another sortie into the abandoned Turkish positions,
this time to see if any useful information could be picked up.
At 4 p.m. in the afternoon Lieutenant Naylor of the Oxfords
and two volunteers eased their way on their stomachs across
no-man's-land to the Turkish front line trenches. A dank smell
warned them that the trench was flooded and the patrol was
obliged to keep above ground. By using the cover of the raised
parapets of the numerous fire and communication trenches the
three penetrated to a point some 500 yards from the fort. The
small party, however, learned very little except the massive-
ness of the Turkish defences. There was a cry and a bullet
ploughed into the sodden earth near where the men were lying.
A Turkish picquet (sentry) was shouting and pointing with his
arm straight at them. The British patrol took to its heels,
springing with difficulty across the wet ground then wallowing
knee deep in the mud with the bullets cracking and fizzing
about them. A small party of Turkish infantry appeared from
the west and threatened to cut off their line of retreat—a
change of direction and then they were home. The Turks
established a picquet and sniper's post 300 yards from the fort
to prevent a repetition of this exploit.

The heavy rain had now ceased and the Tigris began to drop
as quickly as it had risen. Townshend, who had been contemplating the abandonment of the fort because the floods had
threatened to completely isolate it from the other defences,
decided that now this would be no longer necessary. He exchanged this concern for another. The major-general was
becoming convinced that Arab spies, in the pay of the Turk,
were swimming the Tigris and were preparing an insurrection
by the native inhabitants. Guards over the ammunition magazines in Kut town were doubled and an after-dark curfew
imposed.

But with the cessation of the rain the morning and evening

'hates' began again and so did the sniping on the northern front. The enemy artillery commenced its new season with a brief and ineffectual pummelling of the *Sumana* obviously with the intention of putting her out of commission. The steamer and the launches were the lifeline between Woolpress and the town. Each night the vessels plied between the banks of the Tigris carrying stores and sick and wounded. As the craft began to move from their Kut moorings this was the signal for a rifle barrage from the snipers near the mouth of the Hai. The noisy engines of the motor boats particularly drew bullets like magnets until one of the stranded R.F.C. pilots, Captain Winfield-Smith, devised silencers out of felt.

With the return of sniping on the northern front all regimental orders carried the following injunction:

All tins for the purpose of drawing water and other sanitary purposes must be painted a dull colour or covered with sacking or some other material. Bhisties are forbidden to draw water with tins that are not painted or covered as the tins glister in the sun and draw the attention of the enemy snipers.[11]

A British private, already a patient at the hospital, was seated in a patch of sunlight picking lice from his blanket when a sniper's bullet struck a near-by wall, ricocheted and wounded him in the leg. He was very depressed and said that he had had no luck in the war. He had lost two brothers in France and this was the third time he had been wounded. Alas, the sad man was shortly to join his brothers.

On 2 February a Relief Force aeroplane flew over and dropped some British newspapers. One of them gave the Turkish account of the battle of Ctesiphon and described how Nixon had fled to Basra with his army. Greater annoyance, however, came after reading a report in a British 'picture paper' which said that it had just heard that Townshend had 'retired to a position at Kut—a coaling station on the River Tigris'. The report clearly indicated that the British public was completely unaware that Kut had been surrounded by the Turks for several weeks. The garrison felt 'very hurt'.

That evening there was a brisk 'hate' and a Reuter message that England was being raided by zeppelins. Characteristically the troops began to worry more about their families in England than about their own plight.

Townshend received a message from Basra:

Following gracious message had been received from H.E. the Viceroy. Begins:

Please transmit following message from me to General Townshend. The bravery and endurance with which you and the troops under your command have resisted the attacks of the enemy have excited admiration of all, and I am confident resistance will be maintained until help reaches you in the near future. India thinks of you and your troops all the time.[12]

That day too Townshend issued another communiqué with the intention of heartening his troops. It announced that the 13th British Division was earmarked for Mesopotamia and was to commence embarkation for Egypt on 10 February. This started a bout of dismal speculation by the men crowding the noticeboards. How long would it take to get the division from Basra to the fighting fronts? The most optimistic estimators thought this would take at least a month. Others shook their heads and trudged away in silence.

Townshend also was having qualms about the import of Lake's telegram. From the division's number Townshend knew that it was one of the newly-raised 'Kitchener's Army' divisions composed of 'war gifts' as the regular soldiers derisively called their amateur comrades. The major-general read in one of the copies of *The Times* dropped by the aroplane that this division had been severely mauled at Gallipoli where it had received some 4,000 casualties in one action therefore it was certainly not likely to be at full strength. The telegram containing the division's embarkation date did not even approximate when the troops would arrive at the front.

A medical officer conducting the daily sick parade gazed wearily at the long line of Sikhs, Dogras, Pathans and Rajputs shuffling past his desk. Because of their refusal to eat horseflesh they were suffering from malnutrition. He was, however, puzzled by some other symptoms. To prescribe treatment for a condition which he neither recognised nor could put a name to, would be unethical but the officer decided, he would have to mention the disease, whatever it was, in his daily report to Colonel Hehir. The doctor examined a Rajput sepoy (private) closely. He noted his bleeding gums. Another had a cut which showed no signs of healing. A naik (corporal) had scratches which looked no better than when the officer had seen him four days previously. This last man also had red blotches on his skin. He was observing the first symptoms of the disease which had decimated the fleets of Drake and Anson during their protracted voyages. It was scurvy.

Townshend was enraged when news of the outbreak was given to him. Earlier it had been reported that the Afridis of the 24th Punjabis had been deterring other Indian troops from eating horseflesh. He telegraphed Aylmer, repeating to Lake, that there had been an outbreak of scurvy and he urgently requested that the men's religious leaders should be told to order their followers to eat horseflesh.

On 12 February Lake cabled Aylmer, repeating to Townshend, news of the 13th Division which completely altered the Relief Force commander's plans to wait for the new troops before making another attempt to relieve Kut. General Headquarters warned, that it would be unsafe to assume that either the 13th Division or another division from India, which had been promised, would reach the front in time to take part in any relief operations. Lake said that this was due to the falling behind of deliveries of river craft from England. Because of this it was unlikely that the 13th Division would be able to reach Aylmer much before the end of March although some Indian units without the bulky equipment of the British division would be pushed upstream as soon as possible after arrival in Mesopotamia. In the telegram Lake also gave reasons for and against delaying the advance to Kut. Under the heading 'In Favour of Postponement' the Army Commander had listed: *a.* that Aylmer would be reinforced by eighteen guns and 450 British infantry who were now on the march from Basra; *b.* 3,500 replacements for the Indian troops lost in the battles of Sheikh Saad, Wadi and Hanna were now at Baghdad and would be shortly sent up to him. Another 2,000 replacements were expected to arrive at Basra on 18 February; c. about 1,000 British infantry replacements, 500 cavalry and field artillery replacements were due to arrive from England on 14 February. Most of these could be with Aylmer by the 25th; d. the advance units of the 13th Division would be arriving at Basra between 25 February and the end of the month. These would be pushed up to Aylmer immediately; postponement would give more time to arrange for Russian pressure towards Kermanshah although 'there is no reason to anticipate anything very effective in this direction at present'.

Under 'Against Postponement' were: a. from the latest information on enemy reinforcements in addition to the 2nd, 35th, 38th, 45th, 51st and 52nd Divisions already in Mesopotamia it was likely that a further division with twelve guns could arrive at Kut by the middle of February and another with similar artillery strength by the end of the month; b. further delay would give the enemy time to strengthen his defences, particularly those on the right bank of the river, especially if it became known that Aylmer's main concentration of troops was on that bank; c. delay might also give the enemy time to improve his communications across the Tigris below Kut and across the Hai.

Lake skilfully added that he did not want to sway Aylmer's decision either way as he felt the Relief Force commander's local knowledge of the situation must also be taken into account. He concluded by saying that he agreed with Aylmer that unless he was given a favourable opportunity for an advance up the right bank 'the only alternative is to wait maximum reinforcements that can arrive within Townshend's limit of holding out'.[13]

Townshend was exasperated. He wrote in his diary: 'Where now is the promised relief in two months?'[14] He wired Lake confessing that he was extremely worried by the news of impending Turkish reinforcements and that he had altered his views in regard to Aylmer waiting for reinforcements from

England or India before advancing. Townshend said that he thought that two more Turkish divisions, suitably installed, would prevent the relief of Kut. Aylmer should make another attempt as soon as possible.

Townshend received a copy of a long awaited telegram from the Chief of General Staff at Delhi. It read:

Please inform Townshend that he can quote the Immam Jumma Musjud, Delhi, as saying there is no objection to Musalmans eating horse in stress of war providing it is halaled [cutting the throat of a bird or animal to drain it of blood]. Leading Pandit, Delhi, says there is no objection to eating horse. Both authorities are willing to give statements to this effect. We will get you similar authorities from leading Granthis as soon as possible.[15]

This information was immediately displayed on all notice boards at Kut and Townshend complacently awaited the meat eating to commence. Below it, by way of encouragement, were placed the following notices:

Two sepoys deserted to the enemy on the 12th and 13th of this month. The G.O.C. Sixth Division has telegraphed to the Army Commander asking that these men may be proclaimed in their district of Campbellpur as outlaws and that their property, if any, should be confiscated by Government. All are reminded that these men who have shown themselves despicable traitors to the Sovereign and their Country will be outcasts from their native land for ever and without money and means of livelihood will become as slaves to the Turks.[16]

C.O. regrets to observe that when the regiment (48th Pioneers) is out as close reserve, the trenches are fouled. In future to prevent such fouling, two sentries will be detailed, one sentry facing towards the enemy and one sentry to maintain the cleanliness of the trench.[17]

At 9.15 a.m. on the morning of 13 February the weather was cold but fine. The hum of an aeroplane engine was heard. It had a different sound from the normal Relief Force aeroplanes and billets, dugouts and other skulking points were hastily vacated by the troops, in order to catch a glimpse of the latest development in aviation. A dark-coloured aircraft, flying at not more than 3,000 feet, was observed crossing Kut from the north-west. There was whining noise, faint at first but rapidly growing louder and louder and pulsating in a curious way. Then there was a violent explosion and a column of black smoke arose from the town near the river bank. Three more explosions followed at short intervals. Kut was being bombed from the air.

A fusillade of rifle bullets followed the progress of the slowly circling aeroplane but it flew away unscathed. Three times that day the aroplane returned and dropped four bombs each visit. The bombing was to become a regular daily event. 'Fritz' as the pilot was called, was joined by 'Franz' and later still by 'Abdul'.

At first the air raids were considered to be little more than a nuisance. Shell case 'alarm gongs' were mounted at the fort, in the trenches and in the town. Observers on the rooftops could spot the development of an aerial attack without difficulty. As soon as an enemy aeroplane was seen to rise from its airfield some four miles away on the left bank just below Shumran the gongs would be sounded. The aeroplane rose in slow spirals, crossing to the right bank as it gained altitude, a tiny speck in the distant sky. In a few minutes the Fokker would start to come downstream, usually on a slanting course, growing larger, the engine sounding louder as it approached Kut. There was the muffled roar of the British field guns and the wake of the aircraft was dotted with puffs of white and black smoke. Then the magpie chatter of the machine-guns would be heard. 'Fritz' would continue on his way, apparently oblivious of the fire, fly along 'C' or 'D' road, bank into a turn and then race back across the town. He would drop his four bombs in rapid succession. There would be the roar of the explosions and the columns of black smoke. His work done for the day, 'Fritz' would return to the north-west.

The 30-pounder bombs dropped by the German aircraft were invariably detonated by the roofs of mud huts so those taking shelter on the ground floor of a double storey building were more or less safe except for falling debris.

A series of cautionary, admonitory and informatory notices appeared in regimental orders. One read:

> Sentries must report the approach of aircraft at once. On the approach of aircraft men should at once get under cover and remain there until the machine has passed. Company commanders must see that all ranks remain inside their dugouts till the machine has passed. Only troops in the North-West Section and the fort may bring rifles to bear.[18]

A complaint from the Relief Force reconnaissance pilots caused the following notice to appear:

> All our aeroplanes are now marked with red bull's eyes, white inner, black outer. Diameter of outer is five feet. Black patches on the bottoms of planes have been removed. On sighting an aeroplane news will at once be conveyed to a British officer who will at once send the following signal '0–0–0–aeroplane-ends'.[19]

The medical staff were kept busy for a day or two painting large red crosses on sheets of canvas which were pegged to the hospital roofs in the hope that these would divert the attentions of enemy airmen elsewhere. More tangible anti-aircraft defences were prepared. Six Maxim machine-guns, complete with tripods, were mounted on large wooden barrels which could freely pivot about on an axle mounted in a wooden stand. The guns were located on roofs and the system worked fairly well, the Maxim gun tripod allowing the gun to be elevated to the vertical if required, while the rotating barrel provided a 360 degree sweep. An anti-aircraft gun was improvised from a 13-pounder field-gun. A large circular pit with a deeper trench running around its periphery was dug. The gun, minus wheels, was then fixed to the top of the post, its trail resting on the bottom of the pit. This system gave the gun the required increase in elevation but it could only traverse over an angle of ninety degrees.

It was suspected that two hits with shrapnel were scored on the enemy aircraft but no serious damage was ever inflicted. It was learned later that a bullet from one of the barrel-mounted

Maxims inflicted a leg wound to one of the pilots but he was able to land safely at Shumran. The anti-aircraft machine-gun fire always drew the attention of the Turkish snipers who let fly at the roofs in the hope of hitting the gunners.

The aerial bombing coincided with a recrudescence of enemy activity. The shelling 'hates', including the night bombardments were intensified.

Mules were now being slaughtered for food and Kut gourmets agreed that, if properly prepared, the meat was superior to horseflesh. The grain confiscated from the Arabs was ground into flour at two mills driven by 16 horse-power Ruston diesel engines installed in the old Turkish bath building. These were carefully guarded against sabotage. Despite the notice concerning the consumption of horseflesh the Indian troops were still refusing to eat it. By the middle of the month 150 cases of scurvy had been detected and the numbers were increasing at a rate of five new cases a day. Other diseases which had reached serious proportions were gastro-enteritis, dysentery, diarrhoea and pneumonia. The lice reached hitherto unheard of proportions.

Cheers, rifle fire and bugling from the Turkish trenches marked the German success at Verdun. The garrison of Kut, temporarily at a loss to explain this latest display of Ottoman joy, humorously attributed it to either an inspection by von der Goltz, a Turkish pay-day or the news of the death of the Turkish War Minister, Enver Pasha.

The Tigris began to climb its banks once more. This was no temporary rain flood but one of the two annual inundations caused by the melting snow at the sources of the river. The painstakingly prepared 'bunds' which surrounded Kut, however, proved equal to the task and all that was immediately required was vigilance against damage to them by shells or rats.

The officers found a way to supplement their diet. Towards the end of the month thousands of starlings and sparrows began to gather in the palm groves at sunset. They clustered and swayed in the palm fronds making a hideous din. Sportsmen with shotguns issued forth at the said hour and had no diffi-

culty in bringing down a mixed shower of birds which were
collected by the Indian orderlies. The record was thirty-seven
with two barrels. The starlings were considered good eating
when roasted. The sparrows, spurned at first, were later found
to be palatable. For some unexplained reason it was essential
to behead the starling soon after shooting or the flesh took on a
bitter taste. Just before dark a regular fusillade could be heard,
particularly in the south palm grove. Townshend on his
evening walk was struck on the cheek by a spent pellet and
orders were issued confining the starling shoots to certain areas.

Townshend's thoughts were distracted from friendly shotgun
pellets and what he suspected was a newly-arrived Turkish
battery of quick-firing guns which was pumping shells into Kut,
by a personal message from King George V. It read:

> I, together with all your fellow countrymen, continue to
> follow with admiration the gallant fighting of the troops
> under your command against great odds. Every possible
> effort is being made to support your splendid resistance.[20]

Townshend was very much impressed by this message. He
passed it on to his troops and replied via Basra to the Secretary
of State for India:

> It is hard for me to express by words how profoundly touched
> and inspirited all ranks of my command have been by His
> Majesty's message. On behalf of my command—that is to
> say Royal Naval Detachment, the Sixth Division, all ranks
> of the British and Indian Units composing it, and of the
> troops attached, including Territorials—I hope you will
> convey to His Majesty that the knowledge that we have
> gained the praise of our beloved Sovereign and our fellow
> countrymen will be our sheet anchor in this defence.[21]

More good news was on its way. The following day Townshend received by radio a message from General Baratoff now
at Kazvin. It read:

> General Townshend. I am happy to share with the gallant
> English army corps in Mesopotamia the joy of the capture of
> Erzerum by our army.[22]

G

Townshend was flattered by this direct despatch from the Russian general which ignored Lake at Basra. He immediately replied as follows:

> General Baratoff, Kazvin. Thanks for your message. We are all delighted by the capture of Erzerum, which plays a part of the highest political strategical importance in the Turkish Empire. Congratulations from myself and my comrades here to the brave Russians.[23]

And even better. Aylmer informed Townshend that he had decided not to wait for reinforcements and was going to attack before the middle of March when the floods would not have reached sufficient height to hamper operations. Five brigades would mount a surprise assault on the Dujaila Redoubt, a vast earthwork, on the Turkish right flank on the right bank. The two other brigades would mount a feint attack on the Es Sinn position on the other side of the river. Aylmer said he needed just a few more fine days to dry up the country so his right columns could move across country with ease. The Relief Force commander might wait a short time to see if two additional brigades that he had been promised would arrive. But of this he was extremely doubtful. He would discount the expected British and Indian divisions in his plans for the attack as it seemed that they would not now be able to arrive before high Tigris.

The news of Aylmer's plans leaked out and the garrison began to bubble with excitement. The cherished visions of Cossacks at the gates of Baghdad and Aylmer shaking hands with Townshend were expected to shortly become a reality. Even the swarms of beetles, slugs and the scorpions which had now appeared in the dugouts did little to dampen this enthusiasm.

Late at night on 21 February the hopes of the garrison were brought to the peak of expectation, Townshend called his troops to a state of 'complete readiness'. At first faint and then louder the booming of Relief Force guns came floating up the river. The excitement destroyed sleep. The guns rumbled throughout the night and when dawn came the men stood in groups watching the eastern horizon. At 9 a.m. the gunfire ceased; all became completely still. Three more heavy bombardments were heard during the day. At 11 a.m. a Relief Force aeroplane appeared over Kut, dropped a message and flew away again. At 3 p.m. the aircraft reappeared. The troops waited expectantly but at 5 p.m. the word came to fall out and the troops reverted, as some wag put it, to a state of 'partial unreadiness'.[24]

As it grew dark the camp fires of the Turks could be seen at Es Sinn, apparently undisturbed. The reason for the state of 'complete readiness' was never explained to the troops but Aylmer had told Townshend that he believed that it might have been possible by heavy bombardment to induce the enemy to vacate their Es Sinn positions. If this had been the case the Relief Force would have set off in pursuit. Townshend had been asked to hold his troops ready to take the offensive against the Turks if they had retreated past Kut or to attack reinforcements going eastwards from Shumran towards Hanna. The Turks had stoically refused to leave their trenches. Townshend said later that the only effect of the bombardment had been to make them dig in deeper.

Townshend confided to his diary that he was seriously concerned about the morale of his Indian troops. The previous evening four more Punjabis had taken advantage of the destruction downstream to desert. That day a sepoy had shot and killed the jemadar adjutant of the 119th Infantry while attempting to do likewise. The Indian private was condemned to death and shot at sunset. The majority of the Indian troops were still refusing horseflesh. The news of the dispensation from the religious leaders in India had not made the slightest difference. The hospital at the end of No. 1 Avenue presented a dismal sight with the weak and listless Indians lying in the open on their blankets.

Kerosene oil was now becoming scarce and only issued to officers' messes and then only in small quantities. The troops were supplied with the foul-smelling crude oil which dimmed what little light it gave off with wreaths of smoke. Eggs and milk, even for the hospital, became non-existent. Food could no longer be purchased from the Arabs.

The troops watched the flooding Tigris creep over its bank towards the mud 'bunds'. But they refused to allow their spirits to be lowered. Relief could not be far off now. They occupied their time with repairing the 'bunds', killing rats and yarning.

The officers resorted to their gramophones. The most popular records were those of Harry Lauder and, oddly enough, the 'Marseillaise'. The expiration of the last bottles of whisky might have accounted for the success of the former but the desire to hear the French national anthem was beyond reason.

Two Relief Force aircraft passed over Kut and explosions and fountains of earth could be seen in the direction of the Turkish positions near Shumran. Townshend had asked for 'reprisal raids' to be made after the bombing of Kut. The raid had a cheering effect on the garrison although they were never able to find out what success it achieved.

The fort, once more virtually isolated by the rising river, was a dismal place. Inside was a maze of trenches and dugouts, sandbags and loopholes, wooden beams and corrugated iron sheeting. The walls were battered and torn, the north-east bastion remained unrepaired. The wall and the trenches behind them were still not separable into their component parts. Strands of barbed wire tore at legs and the corrugated iron sheets were riddled with bullet holes, eloquent of the defence at Christmas. Looking cautiously through a periscope the casual visitor would discover the answer to the faint but persistent odour which hung over the fort. The remains of the Turkish attack were still hanging on the barbed wire. Perched on them were sparrows and starlings which pecked curiously amongst the decay. Some of the bodies had fallen from the wire and were lying on the scarp where the entanglement stood. Where they lay one could see the first green shoots of spring. Any visitor from the town who saw the birds busily at work returned to Kut and gave away his remaining shot-gun cartridges and frequented the dusk-dimmed palm groves no more.

Tobacco of any description had given out and cigarettes of dried lime leaves became the usual smoke. The garrison's numerous cats warranted closer inspection. They began to lose the gloss from their coats and then the coats themselves. Hunger made these animals bold and to leave one's scanty food ration unguarded, even for a few seconds, was to invite disaster.

Townshend received another radio message from General Baratoff which announced that in order to shorten the distance between him and Kut he was moving his expeditionary force on Kermanshah. He said that on 9 February his force had occupied the strongly fortified Bidesdourka passes and now his cavalry were in pursuit of the enemy who were retreating on Kermanshah. The Russian general then gave an impressive and involved list of war booty, even down to hand grenades and lengths of telephone cable. Townshend was mystified by the tone of the message and attention to detail until at last realising its significance he hurriedly passed it on to Lake asking the Army Commander to put Baratoff right on whom was actually in command in Mesopotamia.

On 29 February Aylmer informed Townshend of the final details of his forthcoming attack, which he said would take place in eight or nine days. Under cover of darkness six brigades were to advance from Aylmer's forward position at Umm al Uruk and march south until they were due east of the Turkish Sinn Abtar–Dujaila Redoubt flank. The six brigades would then launch a surprise attack at dawn; two brigades at the Sinn Abtar–Dujaila sector; two brigades would march round the enemy's flank and take the Turkish reserves in the rear; two brigades would follow behind, acting as reserves, or possibly be ready to take on any Turkish reinforcements from Shumran which might approach across the Hai bridge.

Aylmer continued:

The method of your co-operation must depend on local conditions, as you must be the best judge; but the following points are for your consideration; Your heavy guns to fire on hostile forces trying to cross the Hai bridge; lighter guns to fire on any hostile troops offering good target within your effective range thus limiting area in which Turks can manœuvre on right bank; the crossing of a bridge (from Kut) by *mahailas*, if you have a favourable opportunity, then direct co-operation in battle. Sortie to north of Kut if enemy withdraws so many of his troops as to give you favourable opportunity.[25]

Townshend replied that he would endeavour to co-operate with Aylmer's plan to the extent of two brigades and four field-gun batteries but he would only begin to put his troops across the river when he could see the Relief Force's outflanking brigade coming around to the south of the Dujaila Redoubt. To attempt to do so before this would be to invite disaster. He reasoned:

> If I cross at night there is no concealment in the terrain of the right bank and I should be overwhelmed on that bank before you could arrive. My engineers declare that it will take three hours to fix up the flying bridge, and a further two hours for a smaller *mahaila* flying bridge [this was in fact a dummy to mislead the Turks as to the actual crossing point]. Divisional Engineer Commander says that not more than 150 men an hour could be crossed by the flying bridges.[26]

Townshend said he would concentrate twenty-one guns to sweep the zone to the south of Kut and he would ascertain if his big guns could destroy the Hai bridge. He did in fact order his guns to try a few trial shots at the Turkish bridge which fell short and merely prompted the Turks to move their bridge further down the Hai out of range of the Kut guns.

Towards the end of February two unofficial sweepstakes were organised on when the first Relief Force boat would pass Kut. was organised by a Royal Engineer lieutenant; the other by Townshend's aide-de-camp. There was much demand for the tickets bearing the dates 10 or 12 March. Such was the overall response that dummy tickets were introduced to make up the number. One dummy was marked 'Mosul'—the probable destination of the Kut garrison if not relieved. This ticket was drawn by Major-General Melliss to much amusement.

A telegram from Indian Army headquarters was displayed on all notice boards which pointed out that according to Hindu laws horseflesh was not one of the kinds of flesh forbidden. It then gave a list of the holy books in which the sacrifice and eating of the horse was mentioned. If the telegrams made any sense to the Indians they did not show it. Very few were eating horseflesh and the others showed little signs of wanting to. Some of the abstainers became so weak that they were unable to carry their equipment. They began to employ Arabs to carry their rifles. This practice was subsequently forbidden. Scurvy was on the increase, even amongst the Gurkhas who had had no objection to eating horseflesh. This was attributed to the complete absence of any fresh vegetables. Because of scurvy, pneumonia, tuberculosis and wounds that remained unhealed, there were now approximately a dozen deaths a day. The average daily ration for the British soldier was now eight ounces horsemeat, twelve ounces bread, two ounces cheese or dates. There was no sugar left in Kut and the craving for it was intense. In response to a request a Relief Force aeroplane dropped four and three-quarter pounds of saccharine, but this quantity was considered too small for a general issue and its use was confined to the hospitals. Because of the sufferings through hunger of the Indian troops a further request was made to Ali Gharbi for drugs. Two pounds of opium pills were dropped by aeroplane and were issued to regimental medical officers who distributed them as they saw fit. This helped to ameliorate the more severe stomach pains.

From the beginning of the siege until the end of February there had been 2,977 casualties of which 846 had been either killed instantly or had died of wounds. Another 443 had died of disease or starvation and thirty more had deserted or were otherwise missing.

On 28 February the siege-worn officers held a 'dinner' to celebrate the 16th anniversary of Relief of Ladysmith (see Appendix G).

IX
DUJAILA

March came in traditionally with the roar of enemy artillery and aeroplane bombs. One bomb destroyed an Arab house killing or maiming the eight occupants. As the neighbours crowded around the bloodied mud bricks a second bomb dropped on the same spot claiming another seventeen victims. Scurvy was having a serious effect on wounds which had stopped healing altogether and bled easily when dressed. Because of this the amputation of limbs was resorted to with increasing frequency. The amputees surprisingly survived the ordeal well. A number of Indian hospital patients grew rapidly weaker and succumbed to exhaustion through starvation.

The snipers became active once again to the north and the crack and whine of bullets kept the soldiers undergound. The thrice wounded soldier, now discharged from hospital, was sitting on the bottom step of a dugout talking to his pals. A bullet twanged against a door post, found its way inside and struck the soldier in the chest. Dying and half-conscious the luckless man murmured; 'It's no blooming use—they're set on having me and they've got me all right this time.'[1]

A new instrument was added to the Turkish artillery orchestra—the ancient mortar which the 6th Division troops had captured and then abandoned at 'High Wall'. The mortar was sited just upstream of Woolpress village from where it lobbed its extraordinary projectiles into the northern palm groves. This freak cannon, known affectionately as 'Flatulent Fanny' to the officers and 'Farting Fanny' to the rank and file, had a highly ornamented brass barrel with a bore of thirteen and a half inches. It threw a spherical projectile weighing twenty pounds, the walls of which were brass and about three-

quarters of an inch thick. This sphere was filled with black
powder and fitted with a time fuse which was ignited by the
charge which sped it from the mortar. The great missile
thumped into the palm grove and lay there fizzing for about
ten seconds giving ample time for everyone to get out of the
way and then it would explode with a tremendous bang, up-
root a palm tree or two and scatter its brass case broadcast
over the area. If it did nothing else the mortar provided
the garrison with mementos of the siege in the shape of fragments which were highly polished in the workshops, dugouts
and elsewhere. Competition for the pieces was fierce for the
mortar was rarely fired more than once a day. Its gunner was
nicknamed the 'Arquebusier-in-Chief.'

During the heavy Turkish bombardments and consequent
British artillery reply the roofs of Kut were crowded with
sightseers. The sight well repaid the risk. The enemy gun
positions belched flame and smoke. The British guns roared in
reply dotting the landscape with little white puffs of smoke
from which the shrapnel rained down. The naval ratings
manning the 4·7-inch naval guns mounted in horse transport
boats moored out in the river were much admired as they were
completely unprotected from enemy fire except for the gun
shields and a few thin gauge steel plates proof against rifle
bullets only. It was considered only a matter of time before the
Turkish artillery could score a direct hit. Occasionally a near-by
mahaila would be struck by a shell and sink below the surface
of the river with a gurgle, resting on the bottom with its mast
showing above the surface.

'Fritz', 'Franz' and 'Abdul' had implemented a system of
rotation whereby there was always one aircraft over Kut
during daylight. They would drop about forty bombs a day
between them. These were normally 30-pounders but occasional
larger 70-pounder bombs were dropped. Air attack casualties
were light but the loud detonations plus the chatter and bang
of Kut's ineffectual anti-aircraft weapons often reduced the
Arabs to panic.

The reason for the intensive shelling and bombing at the
beginning of March was never explained. No infantry attacks

were made and as the Kut garrison normally lived below ground few casualties were inflicted.

As the attempt to destroy the enemy's bridge of boats across the Hai channel by gunfire had failed much thought was expended on how this could be achieved. It was necessary for all the Turkish traffic down the right bank to cross this bridge and it would be a severe blow if it was destroyed. The Royal Engineers received inspiration from the behaviour of a rusty kerosene can as it floated downstream. Just as it reached the mouth of the Hai it swerved from the centre of the river and bobbled down the channel. The Engineers wondered if a floating mine would behave similarly. A number of kerosene cans launched from the Kut bank sailed smartly past the channel and it was then discovered that the cans had to be in position at midstream before the mouth of the channel was reached. If the cans were launched from Woolpress they were invariably sucked up the channel. The ever vigilant Turks watched these experiments with interest and proved their marksmanship by repeatedly hitting one of the channel-bound cans until it sank. This proved something else. If a mine was to succeed it must not look even vaguely like one so it was ordained that the mine should look like a derelict packing case. Such a box was procured and rendered water tight with tar and a 150-lb. charge of dynamite secured inside. The charge would be detonated electrically by the current of the two dry cell batteries connected to a mechanism removed from an alarm clock. An additional feature—two contacts made from beaten out silver rupees—provided for the unexpected. If the mine was swamped when it struck the bridge, the clockwork circuit would be short circuited and the mine would explode. Otherwise the dynamite charge would be detonated four hours after the packing case was launched. The mine was completed and placed aside to await a strategic moment.

Occasionally the rumble of artillery could be heard from downstream. The bursts of gunfire were attributed by the Kut garrison to Aylmer ranging his guns ready for the main attack. Those who could gain access to the rooftops stared in the direction of the enemy positions in the hope of catching the first

signs of the attack which would bring the end of their beleaguerment. The Turkish snipers sent bullets clattering among
the mud brick walls in the hope of killing a few of the watchers
but this did little to dampen their ardour. As wind of the proposed assault spread throughout the garrison those with
sweepstake tickets dated after 10 March began to wonder if
they had been too pessimistic in their speculations as the date
of relief. The excitement rose to fever pitch when the troops
who were to take part in the supporting sortie to the right bank
were withdrawn from their stations at the fort and elsewhere.
This excitement was tempered with a severe shock on the
morning of the 6th.

An observer staring through his telescope at the river bank
near the main Turkish camp at Shumran noticed that a few
more ships had arrived from upstream. An increase in the numbers of the ships was not hard to discern owing to the rising
river level which lifted the hulls of the steamers above the
surrounding flat land. The officer watched the derricks aboard
one of the ships as they lifted and carried the cargo to the river
bank. There was the usual impedimenta of war; field-guns,
crates of ammunition, rope nets full of stores, but silhouetted
against the brown plain was a cylinder, about five feet in length,
probably metal. It hung there swaying on the crane rope
momentarily before descending from view. Then there was
another, and then another. The observer turned this queer
cargo over in his mind and wondered what they were. Con-
tainers for fuel oil possibly? The cylinders could mean poison
gas. He picked up his telephone and contacted Townshend's
headquarters. This information confirmed Townshend's fear
that the Germans had provided the Turks with this horrible
weapon. He promptly issued respirators to the defenders of
the North-East and North-West defensive sectors. A small
supply of crude flannel respirators had been sent to Kut at
about the time when Townshend was commencing his advance
from Aziziya. The Turks never did use poison gas although it
was confirmed later that these cylinders were what the observer
suspected. Possibly the weather-cocking winds constantly veer-
ing and backing would have made the weapon too dangerous

for the enemy's own troops. Nevertheless the knowledge that the Turks had the means to launch such an attack added another worry to those of the Kut garrison.

Townshend then, characteristically, turned his attention to a matter which was to him of supreme importance. He completed his despatches to Lake covering his operations at Ctesiphon and the subsequent retreat. Townshend pointed out to the Army Commander that the sooner these were published in the *London Gazette* the better for the morale of his troops. Townshend said that throughout his force there was the belief that Mesopotamia had been forgotten and that the officers were suffering professionally as a consequence. Their colleagues in other theatres had an advantage inasmuch as the reports of their battles were published promptly and their endeavours quickly rewarded. Townshend had heard that several major-generals with neither his experience nor service had been promoted over his head. His subordinates had also suffered in this respect. Naval operations in Mesopotamia, however, had not suffered similarly. Lieutenant Tudway, for example, had already received the Distinguished Service Order for his part in the retirement to Kut.

A wire from Aylmer informed Townshend that due to bad weather the forthcoming operations were being delayed for twenty-four hours and the attack was now scheduled for the morning of 8 March. The major-general bridled at this delay. He was convinced that three *mahaila* crews which had disappeared from the town had deserted to the Turks with information of the projected advance, of the flying bridges and the planned sortie to the right bank in co-operation with Aylmer's force. Some Turkish troops were seen to be digging and occupying a line of trenches at precisely the spot where it had been proposed to land the British party.

On the night of 7 March those selected to take part in the sorties moved into position, the flying bridges were made ready and the whole garrison called to arms. All walking wounded were armed and posted about the town to quell any disturbance or insurrection if they should arise. Townshend was a stickler for using convalescents in this way. Napoleon had thought of

the idea and according to Townshend this should always be
resorted to as a matter of military economy. The convalescents
did not object as anything was better than the interminable
waiting for something to happen.

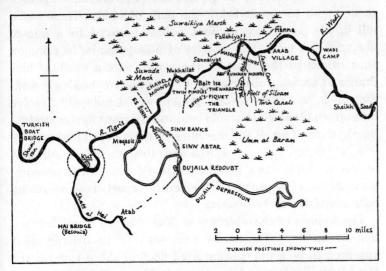

Operations between January and end of April 1916

The early hours of 8 March passed in expectation. At 4 a.m.
a tremendous explosion shattered the silence. Earlier a party
of Engineers had crossed to Woolpress village and working
up to their waists in the water had launched the packing
case mine on its journey to destroy the Turkish bridge of
boats across the Shatt al Hai. At first all had gone well.
The four-hour mechanism had ticked lustily as the packing
case had swung away from the bank and vanished into the
gloom. Then the mine had stuck fast on a submerged sandbank at the mouth of the Hai, ticked away the remaining
hours and minutes and then exploded. Apart from terrifying
a few Turkish sentries at the mouth of the channel the plan
had failed.

The sound of the explosion had barely died away when the
rumble of guns from the direction of Es Sinn began. The
garrison watched the tremendous bombardment light up the

sky and flash off the snow on Pusht-i-Kuh. An early morning
mist hung over the ground near the Es Sinn position. The mist
slowly lifted revealing a wonderful sight. Shrapnel shells were
bursting in salvos along the entire horizon to the south of the
Es Sinn position and great geysers of earth from high-explosive
shells began to sprout below the puffs of smoke. There was a
lull in the bombardment, then a haze followed by a mirage
obscured the view. The mirages of Mesopotamia, in common
with others in that part of the world, were a constant hin-
drance to accurate observation. Columns or troops slowly wen-
ding their way over the flat ground would suddenly dissolve
into brown blobs which would contort into giant figures stretching skywards. Camels and marching men developed long spindly
legs, expanded into tall spires and then vanished. All that
remained visible was a bubbling haze. Because of this phenom-
enon flocks of sheep were frequently reported as marching
columns of men and *vice versa*.

The feelings of the watchers at Kut changed from anticipation to anxiety. The Turks were seen to be driving what
appeared to be a mirage-contorted flock of sheep towards the
Hai bridge. The hours dragged on. At 11 a.m. the Kut garrison
began to feel that something was amiss. Eyes straining to
catch the fervently hoped-for spectacle of khaki uniforms
approaching in the distance grew tired and the ennui began to
set in again. At 12.30 p.m. Townshend heard from Aylmer
that the enemy were sending reinforcements from Fort Maqasis
to the Dujaila Redoubt and there they were putting up a
stubborn resistance. He said that an aeroplane had reported
that about 1,000 Turks were crossing from the left to the right
bank of the river at Maqasis and that another 1,500 were
moving from Shumran towards the Hai bridge. He asked why
Townshend had not reported these later reinforcements and
what steps the major-general was taking to co-operate. Townshend replied that he had been watching Shumran carefully
and no such reinforcements had been sighted. Three squadrons
of cavalry and about 200 infantry had however been seen
moving eastwards down the left bank. He aded that as
arranged he would only begin to co-operate by putting his

troops across to the right bank when he saw some signs of Aylmer's troops at Dujaila.

At 5 p.m. a second message from Aylmer said that up to that time he had failed to take the Dujaila Redoubt but that he was launching another attack immediately. Townshend's observers reported that the mirage and haze were beginning to dissolve and that Turkish troops could be seen moving in front of the ridge at Es Sinn and marching towards Maqasis. British shells could be seen bursting near the troops and also the flashes of the replying Turkish guns. At 5.45 a.m. a faint flashing, suspected of being a heliograph trying to call up the Kut garrison, was seen for a moment near the top of the Dujaila Redoubt. Frantic efforts were made to try to establish contact but the distant flashes died away. Townshend, who had heard nothing further from Aylmer, concluded that the attack on the Dujaila Redoubt had been successful. He had to wait until 11 p.m. before he received a further message from the Relief Force commander. It read:

> Enemy lost heavily today and it is doubtful whether they will be able to maintain their positions. Will let you know tomorrow proposed plan, which will include British division has now arrived.[2]

Townshend was left in some doubt as to whether the Dujaila Redoubt was still in enemy hands but the news that the long-awaited 13th Division had somehow miraculously managed to arrive was extremely heartening and promised success. Townshend was unable to get confirmation of the message by radio as the calls were not being answered.

The night passed quietly and without incident. At dawn gunfire could be heard to the east. At 9.30 a.m. a British aeroplane dropped a message. It read:

> Today's operation terminated in a gallant but unsuccessful attempt to storm Dujaila Redoubt. Troops pushed home and carried out the operation with great gallantry, but the enemy was able to mass reinforcements, which arrived from left bank at Maqasis and from Shumran, and we were unable to

break through. Unless enemy retires from his present position on the right bank, which does not seem probable, we shall be unable to maintain ourselves in present position owing to lack of water, and unless the enemy evacuates the Es Sinn position tonight we shall be obliged to withdraw to our previous position at Wadi. Casualties today have been heavy.[3]

Townshend was deeply dismayed by this tragic news. He was also aware that the message contained more than a faint suggestion that the defeat had been contributed to by heavy enemy reinforcements which he himself had not seen, or had done nothing to prevent. Townshend was also puzzled. Where then was the British 13th Division referred to in last night's message and why was Aylmer not replying to his repeated wireless enquiries for more news?

Two aeroplane messages gave the answer. The first told him that the information about the arrival of the British division had been bogus because it was suspected that the Turks had managed to crack the British cypher and were acting with foreknowledge of the moves of the Relief Force. The second message sounded the death knell. It read:

We have been unable to break through to relieve you today and may have to withdraw to Wadi tomorrow, but hope to make another attempt before long to relieve you at an early date. Please wire movements of enemy who in any case have suffered most severely as their repeated counter-attacks have been repulsed with heavy loss.[4]

Townshend seemed to have developed the art of what might be described as a portmanteau telegram which carried congratulations mingled with other views and even downright criticism. Aylmer's eyebrows must have risen when he read the second sentence of the major-general's reply. The message read:

I hope you will convey the gratitude of myself and my command and sympathy to you and your force for their gallant effort to relieve us. I should like to make it clear to you, as I told you on 8 March that the only reserves that went east from Shumran and Es Sinn on the right bank were a regiment of cavalry which I saw leaving Shumran myself

and watched it cross Hai bridge, and 200 infantry along the
left bank, counted by the observers at the fort as they
passed well in sight. That you did not execute the projected
manœuvre round the south of Dujaila with four of the six
brigades which I had to see before I committed my sortie to
crossing the Tigris was due, I suppose, to your aerial reconnaissance report of the approach of reserves from Shumran.
Many mistakes are made by young officers observing from
aircraft at a great height; in this country it is difficult to
to judge numbers between men and cattle in the field, even
by experienced officers—let alone the extra height of 4,000
feet up. Such a mistake delayed me one day during my
advance on Ctesiphon, as Kemball can tell you. Up to
11.30 a.m. on 8 March, practically no reserves from Shumran
passed the Hai on the right bank or our fort on the left bank,
going east, and at that hour thick haze enshrouded the whole
country like a sea-fog. But had they left Shumran after
11.30 a.m. they could not have possibly reached your field
of battle in time to take any part of it. I am now going to kill
off animals to enable us to continue our task of holding the
Turkish advance at Kut. By killing off 1,000 animals at once
and reducing British troops' loaf from twelve to ten ounces,
and Indian troops' to ten ounces flour meal [for chapaties]
and four ounces barley for parching per diem, I can make my
present stock of barley last until roughly 7 April. As I told
you, however, I am entirely dependent on my mills, the
stones and engines of which keep giving trouble and anxiety
and require careful nursing by that able officer Winfield-
Smith, Royal Flying Corps, who manages all this for me.
British troops will have to exist entirely on bread and horsemeat and Indian troops on meal, parched barley and ghee,
all other articles of rations will be finished, even on a reduced scale, by 15 March. Of these 1,000 I am killing, I may
say that if put down in India now they would require six
months rest before being able to do a hard day's work. I
propose keeping about 1,300 animals, of which 900 will be
required for meat up to 7 April, but those remaining alive
will be incapable of work. My troops are ready to live on

short rations, but they will become weak, and desertion among the Indian troops will increase. I hope that the next effort will be with such a maximum force as will make an absolute certainty of success. This suspense is hard to bear; it breaks down the health and depresses. To all men and all people uncertainty is intolerable. Twice now I have promised the men that relief was at hand. I ought to be relieved before 7 April, unless there is some truth in the Turkish peace proposals mentioned in Reuter's [telegrams], in which case our relief may possibly settle itself in this way. Perhaps Baratoff may be induced to press his advance on Khanaqin and seriously menace Baghdad, by which he should relieve me automatically. I suppose he has difficulty in the way of transport; still he should be called on to help. [5]

On the same day Townshend received a telegram from Field-Marshal Viscount French. It read: 'Watching your work with great interest. Best Wishes.' [6]

After this avuncular pat on the head Townshend turned to his next task. Another blindfolded Turkish envoy had been ushered through the lines with a message. It read:

Your Excellency.
The English forces which are to relieve you were compelled to retreat after giving battle at Falahieh and suffering 7,000 casualties. After this retreat General Aylmer, who was a month and a half making preparations, yesterday, when he thought he was strong enough, resumed the offensive with the 5th, 6th, 8th and 12th Brigades of infantry and one cavalry brigade on the right bank of the Tigris as you saw. But he was again compelled to retreat with 4,000 casualties, and I am left with adequate forces. For your part you have heroically fulfilled your military duty. From henceforth I see no likelihood that you will be relieved. According to your deserters I believe you are without food and that diseases are prevalent among your troops. You are free to continue your resistance at Kut, or to surrender to my forces which are growing larger and larger. Receive, General, the assurances of our highest considerations.

Halil, Commanding Turkish Forces in Iraq, Governor of
Baghdad.[7]

Townshend replied that although he thanked Halil Pasha for
his courtesy his opinion of the situation was to the contrary.
There was much chance of relief and he could not countenance
surrender. By the way, Townshend asked, had the Turkish
commander heard that Turkish troops were in a state of mutiny
at Smyrna and that there were riots in Constantinople over the
fall of Erzerum?

Having thus dealt with the Turkish commander-in-chief
Townshend now had to face the painful task of telling his
anxiously awaiting troops that relief was not yet at hand. He introduced his communiqué by telling them that once again he
was going to take his rank and file into his confidence and he
quoted the two aeroplane messages from Aylmer in their en-
tirety. He then continued:

I know you will all be disappointed by this news. We have
now stood a three months' siege in a manner which has called
upon you the praise of our beloved King and our fellow
countrymen in England, Ireland, Scotland and India, and
all this too after your brilliant battles of Kut al Amara and
Ctesiphon, and your retirement to Kut, all of which feats of
arms are now famous. Since 5 December, you have passed
three months of cruel uncertainty and to all men uncertainty
is intolerable. As I say, on top of all this comes the second
failure to relieve us. I ask you to give a little sympathy to
me, who have commanded you in those battles referred to;
and who, have come to the Division as a stranger, now love
my command with a depth of feeling I have never known in
my life before. When I mention myself I would couple the
names of the Generals under me, whose names are distinguished in the Army as leaders of men. I am speaking to
you as I did before, straight from the heart and, as I say, I
ask your sympathy for my feelings, having promised you
relief on certain dates on the promise of those ordered to
relieve us. Not their fault, no doubt—do not think that I
blame them. They are giving their lives freely and deserve

our gratitude and admiration. I want you to help me again as
before. I have asked General Aylmer for the next attempt,
which must be made before the end of this month, to bring
such numbers as will break down all resistance and leave no
doubt of the issue. Large forces are reaching out, including
an English Division of 17,000, the leading brigade of which
must have reached Wadi by now, i.e. General Aylmer's
Headquarters. In order to hold out I am killing a large
number of horses so as to reduce the quantity of grain eaten
every day and I have had to reduce your rations. It is necessary to do this in order to keep our flag flying. I am determined to hold out and I know you are with me in this heart
and soul.[8]

What Townshend did not know and, therefore, could not
tell his troops was that this latest relief attempt had come within an ace of success. At 6 a.m. on the morning of 8 March the
advance guard of the Relief Force, the 26th Punjabis, had
arrived at a point from where the Dujaila Redoubt could be
clearly seen. Intelligence sources had discovered that often this
impressive-looking earthwork was not manned owing to a
shortage of water. The Punjabis had examined the redoubt with
care. Nothing stirred. The redoubt was empty. Here at last was
a vital chink in the enemy's armour. When this fact was
reported to Kemball he was sceptical. Too often it had been
reported that Turkish positions were empty only to be found
later, very much to the attacking side's cost, that they were
fully manned. He ordered the Punjabis to fall back. Although
the night march across country had been made in fine clear
conditions, delays had made it impossible to deliver the attack
at dawn as planned. The Relief Force arrived in full daylight,
the alarm was raised and the Turks poured into their trenches
and into the Dujaila Redoubt which, in fact had been unoccupied. The same old frontal attack in broad daylight against a
fully prepared enemy had taken place with the result that
3,474 casualties were incurred and in the end the whole force
was pursued back to Wadi. The attack did, however, have one
hitherto unprecedented feature. All the wounded who managed

to survive the trip back to Wadi in the transport carts found sufficient medical treatment and accommodation waiting for them.

Townshend informed Aylmer and Lake of the contents of Halil Pasha's letter and of his reply. He said that the approach of the Tigris flood season expected about 16 March might suggest a determined Turkish effort to take Kut by storm and he informed the Army Commander that he had reinforced Woolpress village with another company of Norfolks. Having got this off his chest Townshend came to the real substance of his message. Townshend asked whether, while Aylmer prepared his force for the third attempt at relief, it would not be advantageous if he opened negotiations with Halil Pasha on the grounds that he would agree to evacute Kut if the garrison, complete with arms and equipment, were allowed to pass through the Turkish lines to join Aylmer? The major-general said he could see nothing dishonourable in coming to such terms as the now badly battered Kut, not anything like the size of those villages captured and recaptured daily in the great battle for Verdun, had served its purpose. The original idea had been to hold up the Turkish counter-offensive at Kut so as to prevent the recapture of Amara and Nasiriya and the loss of the whole Basra province. This had now been accomplished. The Turks now dared not attack the Relief Force and the coming floods utterly precluded any further Turkish advance or attempt to recapture the lost province The whole province of Basra was now in British hands, said Townshend, and it might be recalled that the occupation of Kut had not been in the original scheme of things and consequently it had never been proclaimed British territory. Townshend said that he thought that Halil Pasha would agree to exchange the lives of the garrison for Kut. He said that the Turkish commander had hinted that the right climate existed for such negotiations by expressing his opinion of the quality of the defence. If either Halil or von der Goltz refused negotiations on these terms then no harm would have been done and the resistance would be continued until all the food was exhausted. Townshend said that he had enough food for about another month but by putting his troops

on 'starvation rations' he supposed he could hold out until
17 April. Townshend concluded:

> At the last moment if he still commands a disciplined body of
> men who are in good heart, a general may perhaps cut his
> way out and join the neighbouring army in the field. In
> doing so, if he can carry off two-thirds of the garrison that
> remains to him, the operation is well worth trying. But as I
> said before, when invited to break out, the difference between
> theory and practice in this case is that we have an impassable
> river on three sides and on the land side the terrain is flooded.
> In addition there is a network of deep entrenchments, galleries
> and communication ways that would trouble a cat to pick
> his way through. Moreover, we are in Mesopotamia—an
> Arab country, a country in which every man's hand, and rifle,
> is against you. If I could get out with 300 men only it would
> be great luck.[9]

On 11 March Lake cabled Townshend to say that he realised
to the full, and sympathised most deeply with, the disappointment that Townshend and his command felt at the failure of
the recent attempt at relief, but they must rest assured that
the effort would not be abandoned and that maximum numbers
would be employed in the next attempt. If Townshend thought
that this was a reply to his proposals he was mistaken for two
days later Lake countered with a cable of a much different tone.
The Army-Commander did not approve of Townshend's proposal to open negotiations with Halil Pasha but nevertheless
he had forwarded a copy of the major-general's cable to
Beauchamp Duff in India, and to Whitehall. Lake said that
even if the most pessimistic view of the possibilities of the
Relief Force was taken, it did not seem likely that any advantage would be gained from starting negotiations with Halil
Pasha at that juncture. Lake continued that if the Relief
Force's next attempt should fail the effect would undoubtedly
cancel out any terms that the Turks might have agreed to.
Moreover it was inevitable that the Turks would make no secret
of the fact that Townshend had asked for terms and this would
have a serious effect amongst Britain's allies—present and

potential. If Halil Pasha had indicated that he wanted to come to terms it would only be because he was anxious to transfer his troops to other battlefields.

The following day Townshend received the news that Aylmer had been relieved of his command. His successor would be his immediate subordinate officer Major-General Gorringe. An aeroplane dropped an anguished personal letter from the deposed Relief Force commander which concluded:

> It all looks very easy when one sits in an armchair at the War Office. I heartily pray that you will gain your reward in speedy relief. Give my best wishes to Delamain, Mellis and Hamilton. Good-bye and God bless you all, and may you be more fortunate than myself.[10]

The gloom of the garrison at the failure of the Relief Force was profound. Now there was no sound of gunfire downstream and as if to intensify the agony the spell of fine weather which had lasted since the beginning of March came to an end. Heavy downpours once more turned the remaining unflooded country into a quagmire.

The British officers and troops now received a ten-ounce loaf of bread daily which was made from a mixture of wheat and barley flour. It was very coarse and very heavy. The Indians were given their ten ounce ration in the form of flour so that they could follow their usual custom of making chapaties. The British troops, and the few Indian troops who had overcome their religious principles, were also issued with one pound of horseflesh. For the rank and file this was boiled into a stew. There was now an addition to this diet which helped to a minor degree to combat the ravages of scurvy. The brown plain, traditionally the site of the Garden of Eden, gave forth its biblical promise. At first a fine hair-like grass had appeared and then weeds of great variety. Scavenging parties using sun helmets and caps as collection baskets scoured the town's palm groves and gardens for the precious greenstuff. It was either eaten raw or added to the daily horsemeat stew.

Growing alongside the edible weeds such as wild mustard, wild carrot, clover, thistles and dandelions, however, were others of a mildly or even deadly poisonous nature. Large numbers of troops began to suffer from severe stomach cramps, attacks of diarrhoea and other illnesses. The consumption of innocent-looking but highly dangerous weeds which turned out to be stanesacre, spurge, wild cannabis indica, and datera, sometimes resulted in death. Regimental officers received strict instructions that the collection of herbage must be confined to four-man parties under an N.C.O. who had received instructions on which weeds were safe and which were not. Displays of edible and poisonous weeds were established in all regimental offices. Although these measures largely eliminated the dangers the poisonous weeds still remained a hazard to health until the end of the siege.

The Turkish snipers were not slow to take advantage of these 'grazing parties'. Individuals whose craving for greenstuff was too great to be controlled became victims as they crawled out into no-man's-land under the cover of darkness. Regimental orders warned that the relatives or dependants of any men killed while disobeying the orders covering the collection of herbage would suffer as they would automatically be deprived of any pension rights. Further regulations became necessary when troops in control of horses and mules allowed them to graze freely to such an extent that wandering animals threatened to strip Kut and its immediate surroundings bare of greenstuff in a short time. On 16 March the following order appeared on all notice boards; it gives several clues to the many devious schemes the officers employed to obtain food for their animals:

Owing to the supply of grass in the Kut defensive area being limited and likely soon to be exhausted if cut indiscriminately all individuals who send their own parties out to cut grass must take steps to ensure that no more than six pounds per horse is gathered.

1. The hanging of clothes on or the removal of fences round vegetable gardens is forbidden.
2. Thieving of vegetables will be severely punished.
3. An immediate report should be sent to O.C. Fire Brigade

by any officer or man who notices any loose horse or mule straying near the gardens.[11]

The news that Aylmer had been superseded by Gorringe was received generally with approval. This was not because those in Kut believed that Gorringe was in any way superior to Aylmer, who was still held in high esteem, but simply because it was believed that any change might bring some improvement.

The struggle to keep the rising flood waters at bay was beginning to take its toll of the remaining energy of the slowly starving men. The troops tired quickly and the length of shifts of those employed on heightening or repairing 'bunds' or damming trenches to prevent complete inundation had to be curtailed. Men moving about after dark were ordered to walk on the 'bunds' in order to firm them down and thus save this having to be done by working parties. A rumour that the Turks were training rats to burrow through the 'bunds', and thus unleash streams of flood water into the trenches, was not entirely disbelieved by the more simple-minded. These rodents certainly seemed to have the uncanny knack of making holes where they did most damage.

Townshend was continually worried by deserting Indian troops. He issued an informative note on regimental orders. It read:

The Officer Commanding Relief Force reports that Turkish troops are deserting to him because they do not get sufficient rations. General Townshend considers the sepoys will like to know that while they are on short rations which cannot be avoided our enemy, who has lines of communication and the whole country to draw on, does not give them sufficient food.

The major-general was also extremely annoyed when news of the sweepstakes reached his ears. Those who had been too pessimistic in their forecasts of the probable date of relief lived in fear of being detected. Some even cancelled their tickets. Townshend also discovered that some officers were actually offering odds against the possibility of relief. One of these was 'carpeted' and told that he was acting in a manner likely to cause alarm and despondency amongst the troops. Others, when assured that the major-general was on their track, called off their bets.

The rain ceased suddenly and warm sun began to shine down on Kut. The most salubrious place in the whole peninsula was the middle (now because of the floods first line) trenches. Here, away from the stale air and smells of the town and the sniper's bullets and shells from across the river unemployed officers sat on the firestep with their backs against the parapet basking in the spring sunshine. In front of them was a carpet of fresh green young grass. They heard the snipers' bullets whizz overhead and idly watched them land a hundred yards or so behind the trench and saw the burst of shells in the town revelling in the pleasure of being, for a short time, a spectator. They heard the gentle lap-lap of the tiney wavelets of flood water against the trench's protective 'bund'. Through a loop-hole would be seen the great expanse of flood from the 'bund' to a group of sandhills some 1,000 yards away.

With the return of fine weather, however, came the Fokkers. On 18 March after a heavy shelling the three enemy aircraft returned. It was a bad day. A bomb dropped on the middle of the British hospital in the upper part of the bazaar. Owing to the lack of 'ward' space the covered road through the bazaar had two lines of beds running down its entire length. At the time of the bombing soldiers were in the wards visiting their mates. The bomb struck a wall and exploded. Three men were killed instantly and thirty injured of which twelve died within the next twenty-four hours.

That night the sleepers were roused by the sound of an approaching aeroplane. Henceforth night bombing became a regular practice, weather and other operations permitting. Although the garrison cursed the enemy pilots there was considerable admiration for their skill as night flying was then rather novel. The bombing was resumed the following morning and by ill luck—the garrison refused to believe that it was deliberate—more bombs dropped in or around the hospitals. Fortunately there were few casualties.

The shelling too was intensified. The Turks made another

determined bid to sink the *Sumana*. During the hours of darkness an 18-pounder quick-firing gun (captured from the British
a year before) was moved close to the bank of the Tigris opposite the lower pump house where the steamer was moored.
Screened by an early morning mist the gun opened fire at almost
point-blank range. A shell pierced the steamer's funnel, another
tore the roof off her bridge, a third removed part of her superstructure and killed a naval rating. The answering British
artillery silenced the gun. The *Sumana* was not seriously damaged but the keen interest in her destruction prompted elabor-
ate defensive measures for her future protection. *Mahailas*
were moored immediately ahead and astern of the steamer
and a steel barge was moved into position alongside her on
which a wall of sand-filled kerosene cans was erected.

A terrific bombardment was opened up on Kut on the morning of 22 March by an estimated thirty enemy guns. The
British guns replied; the roars of the two 5-inch and three 4·7-
inch guns upstream were punctuated at intervals by the sharp
barking of the two field-guns and the 12-pounder in the town.
From the direction of the Brick Kilns came a continuous
thunder. The bombardment ceased after three and a half hours
only to resume at mid-afternoon and continue until 7 p.m. There
was silence until 10.30 p.m. when the enemy artillery opened
up again and continued its bombardment throughout the night.
The bombardment, which continued until dawn, merely succeeded in driving the garrison into the damp but deep dugouts.
Very few of the siege-hardened troops lost much sleep over it.

The engineers utilised the morning's lull to build a brick wall
around the wireless shed located in the south end of Kut town.
This vital installation was extremely vulnerable, both to shots
aimed at its fifty feet high *mahaila* mast aerial and to 'overs'
from guns firing at the *Sumana*. While the work was proceeding a message was received from one of Gorringe's aircraft.
Earlier in the month the rooftop observers had discerned that
the Turks were digging emplacements for two large naval guns
to the north of Kut. It was feared that the guns would be able
to fire 6-inch high-explosive shells. Just one shell of this variety
would be disastrous if fired into Kut. The Turks had now

completed their work and the two guns were manned and their crews appeared to be waiting for ammunition. Townshend had asked for the aircraft to help the British 5-inch guns by the Brick Kilns to range accurately. Seven rounds at a range of over 7,000 yards were fired as the aircraft circled overhead reporting the result. The first shell struck one enemy emplacement, killing the gun crew, another blew the second gun off its mounting rendering it useless. The British guns then switched back to the first gun and this time destroyed it. The chagrin of the Turks was utter and complete. They had brought the unwieldy weapons more than 1,500 miles across mountain and desert only to have them wrecked before one shot was fired. The destruction of the Turkish naval guns undoubtedly saved Kut.

On the same day a vigorous Arab rumour spread through the town that the Turks were preparing to make an infantry assault on Kut across the river. This rumour was so persistent that Townshend called his troops to the ready but nothing occurred and later that night after many hours watching the Turkish bank for signs of aggression the garrison was stood down.

On 26 March the Tigris reached a height of two feet above the highest level experienced during the January rain floods and six inches higher than any previous level that the Arabs could remember. The water advanced over the previously unflooded areas at about a yard an hour. It was a very anxious time for the garrison as there was no telling how far the water might rise.

To worsen matters high winds began to whip the surface of the swollen Tigris into waves which scoured the banks and 'bunds' and repair parties were kept hard at work keeping the water defences intact. Fortunately the Turks were also experiencing this problem and the workers on both sides of the river became far too busy to worry each other with rifle fire.

The river reached maximum height on 26 March and remained like this for three days before beginning to drop, leaving the land flooded. As far as the eye could see the water stretched in all directions broken only by raised strips which marked the Turkish roads. Along them on both sides of Kut strings of animal transport and men plodded between the high ground at Shumran and the Es Sinn ridge. Caravans of loaded camels glided by. Oddly enough the British had been extremely reluctant to adopt these extremely reliable and useful beasts. This was almost certainly due to the almost grotesque belief that camels by nature found it impossible to stand on wet muddy ground because they were incapable of preventing their legs from sliding outwards, thus causing them to split. If any further proof was needed that this was nonsense the British could now see these animals scudding efficiently over ground which would be almost impossible for even mules to traverse.

Although the floods were keeping the Turks fully occupied one of the few enemy shells fired during this respite succeeded where others had failed. Shell fragments smashed the *Sumana*'s steam pressure valve thus putting the long-suffering vessel out of action. A futile request for a valve was wired downstream but fortunately the Kut Engineers were able to make a replacement and three days later the *Sumana*, with the customary bullets clanging against her steel plates, was able to continue her nocturnal journeys between Kut and Woolpress village.

And so March began to draw to its close. The Indians who were still refusing to eat horseflesh moped around habitually chewing grass and looking little better than skeletons. The British troops who themselves gained little nourishment from the horse stew turned away when one of these creatures was seen approaching. To look at him was painful, to refuse to give him some bread was heart-breaking. A few handed the Indians their bread rations and contemplated twenty-four hours on nothing but a plate of horsemeat stew. The Indians were existing at this time on a ration of one ounce ginger, one and a half ounces dhal, ten ounces barley meal, four ounces unhusked whole barley, a half ounce tumeric.

The craving for something sweet to eat overcame almost every other culinary consideration. The few officers who still possessed the remains of a bottle of whisky advertised with a view to exchanging the spirits for a part of a tin of jam. No food could be purchased for cash. An officer, after dividing his eight-ounce loaf of bread into four equal parts, would arrange his meals as follows. Breakfast; quarter of bread, a small piece of fried horse and one cup of tea. Lunch; the same as breakfast but without the tea. Tea; quarter of bread, one cup of tea. Dinner; quarter of bread, horse soup, horse-meat in some form, perhaps a small quantity of potato meal, weed 'spinach', one cup of tea.

The fat officers developed graceful figures; the lean ones became finely drawn.

Life in the trenches was still a miserable existence despite the warmer weather. The men still stood, slept and ate in muddy water. By the end of the month the decomposed bodies at the fort were still creating such a stench that every night for a week a fatigue party crept out and dragged the remains into a near-by drainage ditch. As the bodies disintegrated at a touch this was neither an easy nor a pleasant job. Altogether ninety-seven bodies were disposed of in this way with consequent improvement in the surrounding air.

On the last day of March Townshend received a telegram from Gorringe. The new Relief Force commander informed him:

> Preparations for your relief are well forward, and you may be assured that I shall not be a day later than is absolutely necessary. According to Baghdad records and all information, the last flood is the maximum we are likely to have. Another one of possibly equal height at 10–15th of next month.[12]

On this day the wind changed to the south-east bringing heavy clouds. Down came the rain and once more the streets of Kut became almost impassable. At 10 p.m. lightning of extraordinary brillance lit the great banks of black cloud and the rain increased to a deluge. The wind howled, shaking walls and tearing masonry from the houses.

X

SANNAIYAT

Early in the morning of 1 April 1916 a major of the Oxford
Light Infantry lay in bed, with his head well under the blankets,
attempting not to hear the violent weather that buffeted his
matting covered window. On hearing a knock at the door and
the rattle of a cup and saucer he instantly remembered that it
was a 'tea morning' and was wide awake in an instant. His
Indian servant placed the tray on the small table beside the bed
and stood back. What was wrong with the dratted fellow this
morning? The officer leant out of bed, picked up the teapot and
commenced to pour. A trickle of sawdust dropped from the
spout into the cup. The major could hardly credit his senses.
The Indian announced calmly: 'It is April the Fool's Day,
Sahib.'[1] He bowed and left the room. The officer was convinced
that the Indian had been actuated by a sense of duty.

Townshend received a telegram from Lake on 2 April. There
is no possibility that it had arrived a day late. Lake asked the
major-general how he proposed to ferry his men across the
Tigris if the need did arise, but supposed that he had prepared
for this contingency by constructing rafts of inflated skins.
These, of course, would have been readily available from the
animals butchered for food.

Townshend replied patiently that there still seemed to be
some misunderstanding about the difficulties of crossing the
Tigris although his previous telegrams had explained them fully.
The major-general reiterated that as the Turks had now installed
guns on the right bank in order to smash any attempt at a crossing he would have to wait for the Relief Force to put in some
appearance before he attempted to do so. Townshend said that
the Relief Force must win through on its own and not rely on
any aid from Kut. Butler neither asked for nor received any

aid from White at Ladysmith and White did not have a 500 yard-wide river flowing at five knots on three sides of him with the fourth side enclosed by a triple line of enemy redoubts and entrenchments. Townshend continued:

> Nor do I think that Gorringe, with 29,000 men and 108 guns, which strength gives him a maximum force of 24,000 men and ample gun-power, will require assistance from me to win through a division and a half, or possibly, two weak divisions of enemy, holding a front of fourteen miles, which extent should on principle require three army corps to hold. My force has now been besieged for some four months; the Indian troops are weak and dejected on the total ration of ten ounces of unclean barley meal, and depressed by the two unsuccessful attempts of the Relief Force to relieve Kut. Had the Relief Force arrived in January, we could have co-operated with vigour; but now it is very different, and it is the same in every case in history of a beleaguered force. If Gorringe comes by the left bank, I will attack the enemy in his entrenchments opposite the fort—and we will have to wade through floods to do it. At any rate, Gorringe can be assured I shall do the utmost in my power to co-operate on either bank. I have never contemplated using the skins of the butchered animals for rafts, as I still possess three barges and a dozen *mahailas*, and only one tow for the lot—a steam launch. The skin rafts cannot be moved without falling to pieces and are no use in a strong current. There is no straw or brushwood to stuff the skins, no wood for platforms for the rafts, all the available woodwork has been used to make two flying bridges and trestles for bridging the Hai, in accordance with Aylmer's wishes.[2]

On the morning of the 4th Gorringe wired Townshend, repeating to Lake, as follows:

> My plans for the final stage of operations must necessarily depend on measure of success in the first stage, which commences tomorrow, on the state of the river and floods, and on enemy's dispositions, all of which factors cannot be ascer-

11   A Graves Registration Officer locating a grave in the
old trenches

12 Townshend and his staff at Kut in September 1915 before the advance
to Ctesiphon
Left to Right: Captain Clifton (Townshend's A.D.C.), Major E. E. Forbes
(D.A.D. Transport), Colonel Annesley (A.D.S. & T.), Colonel U. W. Evans
(G.S.O.1), Colonel P. Hehir (A.D.M.S.), Major-General C. V. F. Townshend,
C.B., D.S.O. (G.O.C.), Captain W. F. C. Gilchrist (D.A., Q.M.G.), Colonel
W. W. Chitty (A.A. & Q.M.G.), Lt.-Colonel N. S. Maude (acting C.R.A.),
Lt.-Colonel H. O. Parr, Lt.-Colonel F. A. Wilson (D.C.R.E.)

tained at present. I quite appreciate that your co-operation
must be in the first instance passive, but you are the rock on
which I hope to split the Turkish forces, and your co-operation
by gunfire, etc. on his ferry at Maqasis, and by containing
enemy on left bank in the last day's operations will assist us
greatly. I will keep you fully informed of our progress.[3]

The Turks, obsessed by the idea of sinking the *Sumana*,
resorted to a new measure. On the Turkish side of the river, just
south of the bend, was a shallow ditch about 1,500 yards from
the river where the Turks would position a gun during the night.
Frequently throughout the day the enemy gun detachment
would leave their dugout at the end of the ditch and crawl along
on their hands and knees towards their weapon. Keeping well
down the gunners would load the gun; one man would sight it at
the *Sumana* by cautiously raising his head above the level of the
ditch. The crew would then crawl back along the ditch trailing a
long lanyard connected to the gun's firing handle. A quick jerk
was all that was necessary to send a shell screaming towards the
British steamer. This ditch-crawling required courage. The
observing officer on the Rajput roof would invariably spot the
gun's latest position from the tops of the wheels which protruded
above the ditch. When the observer suspected that the gun was
being loaded and trained he would make a quick phone call to
the Brick Kilns and the 5-inch howitzers would open up. The
ditch would be enveloped in black smoke and debris. Unless the
watcher actually caught sight of an enemy artilleryman at the
gun, which was seldom the case, he had to rely completely on
intuition. This method was never successful. All sorts of strate-
gems were tried to catch the Turks at their gun but these too
were unsuccessful. The Turks learned to confuse the issue by
loading and training the gun during the day and firing at night
when they suspected that the *Sumana*'s crew were aboard preparing for a trip to Woolpress. On one occasion the gun was
destroyed when it received a direct hit but it was replaced that
night and ready for action the following morning.

On 3 April three survivors of the Siege of Ladysmith held a
dinner to mournfully celebrate the surpassing of the South

H

African town's record of beleaguerment of 120 days. But otherwise the garrison ate their stew without ceremony and contemplated relief which strong rumour held would be on the morrow. Then the news spread that because of bad weather the assault on the Turkish position at Hanna was being postponed for twenty-four hours.

Just before dawn on the 5th the bombardment commenced downstream. The continuous detonation of bursting shells shook the Kut billets and the whole atmosphere pulsated with the concussions. The Kut garrison was called to arms and the watchers on the roofs stared towards the east. In the grey of early morning the flashes of guns could be seen but as it grew lighter the struggle—some fifteen miles away—was obscured by a dense mist. The rolling gunfire continued until 6.15 a.m. when it ceased. Then the news spread like wildfire. Gorringe's troops, including the newly-arrived division, had captured the Turkish positions at Hanna. Townshend was jubilant in the confirmation of his view. The British troops had been all that was needed to drive the Turks back. In fact it had been easier than that. The 13th Division, under Major-General F. S. Maude, had attacked the Hanna positions at 4.55 a.m. and captured the Turkish first and second lines with trifling losses and little opposition. There had been a slight delay to wait for the guns to lift and then the attack had swept forward into the Turkish third lines. They were found to be empty. The British 13th Division started off in pursuit of the fleeing Turks.

The cheers echoed around the Kut trenches. A young subaltern sobbed unashamedly. The mist slowly cleared and the gunfire downstream began to thunder and roll in a great sea of sound. Turkish reinforcements could be seen grouped to the rear of the Es Sinn positions while away to the east the powder-puffs of the shrapnel could be seen together with the tall smoke fountains of exploding lyddite which sprang up and died away before the light breeze. As darkness began to fall, the whole horizon to the east glowed and sparkled. The flashes of the guns and the flame from the exploding shells which burst in salvoes of sixes lit up the entire plain like a great firework display. Coloured lights directed to the rear of the Turkish positions

flickered out urgent messages; one red light—enemy advancing;
two red lights—reinforcements wanted; one green light—more
ammunition required. Star shells crackled and banged; Very
lights soared into the sky. At 8 p.m. the barrage died away and
all was silent. The Kut garrison was more than satisfied with the
day's operations and there were great expectations for the
morrow. Long after midnight the unemployed part of the garrison rested their arms on the rooftop walls and talked about
England and India.

Dawn broke and the gunfire commenced once more but it did
not seem to be so intense as the previous day's furore nor did it
appear to be any closer. Some of the cheerful expectation had
bubbled away during the night and the troops were restless and
irritable. At the back of everyone's mind was the dread of
another disappointment.

Kut was quiet except for some desultory Turkish sniping.
Everywhere stalked the spectre of famine, desolation and ruin.
A working party was pulling down the gabled roof of the lower
bazaar for wood to feed the *Sumana*'s boilers. It took one ton to
raise the steam pressure to the required fifty pounds per square
inch. The steamer's engineers were experimenting to see if the
furnace could be adapted to burn the crude oil. In the Turkish
baths the mills were still. There was nothing left for them to
grind. The palms in the little mud yards had notices saying that
the trees were 'sacred' to the Arabs and therefore must not be
destroyed for firewood or damaged. There was no noise now
from the Royal Engineers workshop. The Tigris was the only
thing that showed life. The wooden tide gauges indicated that
the second seasonal flood was already on its way—and that it
was coming quickly.

Townshend received a wire from Lake saying that the Army
Commander had heard from the British liaison officer with
Baratoff that the Russian general had been ordered to advance
on Khanaqin with all his available troops and with all possible
speed. This message rather mystified Townshend as he had been
under the impression that Baratoff's advance on the Persian
city had commenced some three weeks before. His major concern was, however, with what was happening downstream. He

had heard nothing since Gorringe had told him that he had taken five lines of trenches at Hanna. Townshend wired to the Relief Force commander for news, adding that he had seen a Turkish 40-pounder gun, drawn by bullocks, going east after having apparently crossed the Hai bridge. The Kut observers reported that Maqasis ferry seemed to be in use. This ferry was the old 'Bridging Train' barge which had gone adrift at Christmas. Townshend ordered his 5-inch guns to open fire on the ferry to discourage this activity. The range was extreme—over 10,000 yards.

There was still no news from Gorringe and in desperation Townshend wired Lake:

Can you give me any news of Gorringe? I have not heard from him since 8.30 yesterday morning, when he wired me that he had carried the first five lines of the Hanna position. It is now 4.30 p.m. and I have heard nothing. No news I suppose is good news but it makes my people uneasy. I do not want to bother Gorringe in the midst of work, but he should not keep one like this without news.[4]

Later that day Townshend wired Gorringe informing him of the artillery action he was taking against the ferry at Fort Maqasis. He said that he intended to fire at the ferry at intervals throughout the night, provided this met with the Relief Force commander's approval. He pressed for news of the advance. Still later after hearing nothing he wired again, repeating the message of Lake:

I have not heard from you for thirty-six hours. The river has risen three feet two and a half inches in the last twenty-four hours. At the fort the flood is an inch higher than the last flood level and the intervening ground between the enemy's trenches and ours is flooded. In the North-West section of defence there are fifteen inches of water in the reserve communication trenches; everyone is being put on flood protection works.[5]

To add to the difficulty unfavourable atmospheric conditions made it difficult to transmit and receive messages. At 4 p.m. the

Kut wireless room was unable to understand a message after receiving what was believed to be the Kut call sign. And as luck would have it the Kut wireless expert, Lieutenant Green, was wounded by a shell fragment while trying to make adjustments to the *mahaila* mast aerial. At 10 p.m., however, a message from Gorringe was picked up. It referred only to Townshend's message about shelling the Maqasis ferry at night and merely said: 'Not at present. Better reserve fire for later.'[6] And that was all.

Townshend fumed but although he was without messages from Gorringe his chaplain thought he might have received one from a Higher Authority. The Rev. Mr. Spooner put his head round the major-general's office door and told him that the date was propitious. He showed Townshend the collect for the week —the 4th Sunday in Lent, which read, 'Grant, we beseech Thee, Almighty God, that we who for our evil deeds deserve to be punished, by the comfort of Thy grace may mercifully be relieved; through our Lord and Saviour Jesus Christ, Amen'.[7]

There was also a telegram from Reuter's. Townshend read that Lord Beresford had asked in the House of Lords if Townshend had been consulted before the order to advance on Baghdad had been given; if Townshend had less than a division when he had started the advance and should he have not had three; and was Nixon or Townshend responsible for the order for the advance? Lord Islington had replied that he was unable to answer the first question; that nothing was known of any representation addressed to Nixon from Townshend with reference to the advance; and that the advance was authorised by the Imperial Government on the advice of Nixon and the Government of India. Lord Crewe, supplementing Islington's statement, said that there had not been one instance in the war where the naval or military commander had been asked to undertake operations with forces which he had previously declared were insufficient. He added that he made this statement without reserve. Townshend could have wished for a better time to be informed of Crewe's gratuitous statement.

At 11 p.m. on 9 April at last there was news of the attack from Gorringe. The cable read:

This morning we again attacked the Sannaiyat trenches, but failed to win through. We are consolidating our positions as close as we can to the enemy's trenches and pressing on all preparations for digging still closer with the intention of attacking again. We have been hampered by heavy floods on the right bank stretching from the river both east and west of the Abu Roman mounds down to the Umm al Brahm [a marsh]; this, however, is being remedied. Sannaiyat is held by the enemy in strength. Aeroplane states that Bait Isa was held, also Sinn banks and Dujaila, cavalry camp at Atab. These latter operate daily along the Jumeilat ridge and there is a position there.[8]

The long-awaited telegram from the Relief Force commander had not even told half the real story. The attack on the strong Turkish line at Sannaiyat had been scheduled for just before dawn on the 6th but because of delays for various reasons the young inexperienced soldiers of the 13th Division had not reached their assault positions until well after the first streaks of dawn were in the eastern sky. There was a further difficulty. Kemball hazarded a guess that the Turkish trenches were about a mile ahead. The actual distance was nearer twice that estimate. Despite the hour (it was now thirty-five minutes after the scheduled time of the attack), despite the imminence of daylight and the uncertainty about the distance to be covered, Young-husband told Kemball to commence the attack.

This was a terrible decision. To order infantry forward over a mile of open country in broad daylight to deliver a frontal attack against a strongly entrenched enemy was inviting disaster. The Turks held their fire until the advancing British infantry were within 700 yards and then hit them with what has been described as a 'solid sheet of lead'.[9] The advance dragged itself forward for 200 yards more and then crumpled to the ground. If this was not enough the wind suddenly changed and blew the water off the nearby Suwaikiya marsh into shell holes, drowning many of the British wounded crouching there. In this one attack 1,168 were killed and wounded.

On the morning of the 9th another attack over 650 yards was

launched. It commenced at 4.40 a.m. this time to be on the safe side. Despite heavy losses—1,807 killed and wounded—the British had managed to dig themselves in some 400 yards short of the Turkish line.

Townshend wired Lake that he had no confidence in any plans which included 'consolidating positions' as this would entirely suit the enemy's purpose. He said that the Turks would do likewise and had proved that they were much faster and better at it than the British. He added:

I have ordered the reduction of all rations, British and Indian, still further to five ounces of barley meal. I can no longer favour the Indian troops in the matter of meal. There is the horse meat, which their religious leaders in India have authorised them to eat, and, by their not having taken advantage of this, they have weakened my power of resistance by one month at least, so I have no sympathy for them in that direction. This reduction of ration should enable me to hold on to 21 April, I think, but I will inform you later on. Would you tell me if reinforcements are on their way to fill up the gaps in the [Tigris] Corps, and if they are close enough at hand to turn the scale? Our 'bunds' are holding the water out. If Kut falls we shall require food sent up at once under armistice; the Turks will have no spare food for us.[10]

On 10 April Townshend published the following communiqué to his troops:

The result of the attack of the Relief Force on the Turks entrenched at the Sannaiyat position is that the Relief Force has not yet won its way through, but is entrenched close up to the Turks, in some places some 200 to 300 yards distant. General Gorringe wired me last night that he was consolidating his positions as close to the enemy's trenches as he can get, with the intention of attacking again. He had some difficulty with the flood which he had remedied. I have no other details. However, you will see that I must not run any risk over the date calculated to which our rations would last— namely 15 April. As you will understand well, digging means delays, though General Gorringe does not say so. I am compelled therefore to appeal to you all to make a determined effort to eke out our scanty means so that I can hold out for certain until our comrades arrive, and I know I shall not appeal to you in vain. I have then to reduce our rations to five ounces of meal for all ranks, British and Indian. In this way I can hold out until 21 April, if it becomes necessary, and it is my duty to take all precautions in my power. I am very sorry that I can no longer favour the Indian soldiers in the matter of meal, but there is no possibility of doing so now. It must be remembered that there is plenty of horse-flesh which they have been authorised by their religious leaders to eat, and I have to recall with sorrow that by not taking advantage of this wise and just dispensation, they have weakened my power of resistance by one month. In my communiqué to you of 26 January. I told you that our duty stood out plain and simple; it was to stand here and hold up the Turkish advance on the Tigris, working heart and soul together. I expressed the hope that we would make this defence to be remembered in history as a glorious one, and I asked you in this connection to remember the defence of Plevna, which was longer than that of even Ladysmith. Well! You have nobly carried out your mission; you have nobly answered the trust and appeal I made to you. The whole British Empire, let me tell you, is ringing now with our defence of Kut. You will be proud to say one day; 'I was one of the garrison of Kut!' As for Plevna and Ladysmith, we have outlasted them also. Whatever happens now we have all done our duty. As I said in my report of the defence of this place, which has now been telegraphed to Headquarters—I said it was not possible to mention in desdespatches everyone, but I could safely say that every individual in this force had done his duty to his King and country. I was absolutely calm and confident, as I told you on 26 January, of the ultimate result; and I am confident now. I ask you all, comrades of all ranks, British and Indian, to help me now in this food question in the manner I have mentioned'.[11]

Townshend reported that in response to his appeal 5,135

Indian soldiers, including camp followers, were eating horse-flesh by the next day. He must have considered that a more forceful approach was necessary for on the following day he issued another one. It read:

In continuation of my communiqué to all troops, dated 10 April, and with special reference to the attached note of the A.D.M.S. in which he emphasises the vital importance of every Indian of the force at once eating horseflesh for the preservation of his strength and even life during the next few days—I again issue an appeal to every man of you to stand by your King, your ruler [a considerable number of the Indian troops were enlisted in the independent states of India] and the Government that protects you, by taking heed of the warning note of the A.D.M.S. You have already received permission and every encouragement from your ruling princes and your religious leaders also to eat flesh in the dire emergency. Five thousand, one hundred and thirty-five of you now see your duty plain and clear, and are already eating horseflesh to preserve their health and strength. As General Officer Commanding this force I wish it to be clearly understood that I shall replace all non-meat eaters who become too feeble to do their duty efficiently as officers or non-commissioned officers, by other men who eat meat and remain strong. In the case of all officers and men who fail in their duty to the state, I shall cause a list of their names to be prepared and lay those names before the Government of India for such action as the Government may think fit.[12]

The attached report from Hehir read as follows:

The Indian troops and followers are now in a state of semi-starvation. The reduction of the grain ration to five ounces per man, which has of necessity been commenced, will reduce them to a state of great debility and emaciation, and very seriously militate against their utility as a defence force. In expressing this opinion I would lay great stress on the fact that the quantity of grain mentioned forms their entire ration. I would consider that the universal use of horse-flesh by

Indians would materially keep down the death and sickness rates, ameliorate a vast amount of human suffering, assist in preventing the progress of the effects of starvation, and maintain a large share in such a physical state as will enable them to carry on their duties.[13]

It was difficult to discover whether hunger or the appeal to loyalty or the threat to promote meat-eaters in place of the abstainers had the most effect but Townshend reported by nightfall 7,954 Indians and followers were consuming horseflesh. Two days later this number had risen to 9,329. But it was a hollow victory for Townshend. The mischief was already done. No amount of horseflesh eating could possibly affect the declining physical state of the Indians.

Townshend received a telegram from Lake which went a long way to confirm what he already feared. The Army Commander said that there could be no doubt that Gorringe would be able 'in time'[14] to force his way through to Kut but as a consequence of the latest failure it was doubtful if this could be effected by 15 April. Lake proposed two alternative plans:

1. Townshend should evict the Arab population from Kut retaining only those that were of any use to him. In this way a supply of food would be made available which could sustain the garrison to such times as relief could be effected. Or, 2. Ships carrying food would attempt to run the blockade under the Turkish guns at night.

Lake was not optimistic about the possibility of success of the latter plan. He said that the Royal Navy considered this a hazardous enterprise as the navigational difficulties of the Tigris confined any such attempts to moonlight nights, thus eliminating any surprise element. The Tigris was now in full spate and the five-knot current would reduce the progress of ships fighting their way upstream to a crawl. Lake thought his plan would have better chances of success if the Relief Force could advance to Sannaiyat thus reducing the distance by river that the ships would have to travel. Lake asked Townshend how long his garrison could hold out if the plan to evict the Arabs was adopted.

Townshend was astonished by Lake's proposal to evict the Arabs. He recalled that he himself thought this a good idea only to be persuaded out of it on humanitarian grounds. He replied that this plan would have disastrous consequences. The Turks realised only too well that the longer they kept the Arabs inside Kut the more they would be hastening its fall and naturally, they would prevent any attempts to evict the Arabs with all the means in their power. Isolated attempts to escape from Kut had been made by Arabs who had swum the Tigris, but these had met with instant retribution. Four nights previously a wounded Arab had arrived on the British bank in a state of terror. According to the man's story he was the sole survivor of a party of some twenty male Arabs which had successfully crossed to the Turkish bank on goatskin rafts only to be rounded up and shot. Townshend said that the native population could not be put out of Kut by the landward side as the waterlogged ground and flooded trenches were an impenetrable barrier. The Arab women and children would never be able to cross the river on goatskins and if the 6,000 Arabs were packed into the thirty *mahailas* that were still afloat the Turkish artillery would make short work of them. The news of this massacre would soon get about Mesopotamia and be used as an example to show how worthless were the British promises of protection. The political consequences of such an act would be severe. Even if the Arabs were somehow thrown out of Kut the advantages would be minimal. Since the commencement of the siege he had managed to extract from the town, by barter and straightforward confiscation, some 900 tons of wheat, 1,500 tons of barley and a large quantity of ghee but now the military were having to feed well over half the population from its own slender resources. Townshend said that his appeals to the Indians to induce them to eat horseflesh had been successful but even so he could only hold out until 20 April. There was no possibility of extending this date. The major-general was also gloomy about the prospect of food ships running the gauntlet, for even if they managed to fight their way upstream they would be under bombardment from the time they arrived at Kut until the time they left.

In a later telegram to Lake, Townshend added that if the food ships did not arrive until 21 April he believed that a large number of the Indians who were still refusing horseflesh would die. He said that already this was a daily occurrence.

Security at Kut had never been efficient and somehow news of Lake's 'in time' telegram got about. The garrison was completely downcast. 'In what time?' asked the hungry men. The daily diet of a pound and a quarter of horseflesh, four thick slices of bread and dandelion leaf 'spinach' was at best depressing. It was a matter of some surprise that one could eat that quantity of horseflesh without severe gastric troubles. They attributed this to the fact that if the body was starving it could assimilate an excess of any sort of healthy food. The large quantities of meat stilled the pangs of hunger for a short time but they returned long before the next meal was due. The almost completely carnivorous diet did however produce some peculiar effects. Cramp of the hands and feet was common and at night came peculiarly startling dreams from which the sleeper scrambled breathlessly bathed in sweat. The flea plague was abating slightly only for the torment to be taken over by the sharp-stinging sandfly. Keatings' powder stolen from the officers' messes was in great demand. The supply of this was limited to commissioned ranks. The sandfly attacks grew so intense that sleep was only possible if the soldiers wore socks over their hands and cocooned themselves in their blankets. It was found that cigarettes, now made of a mixture of dried lime and tea leaves and shavings of ginger, gave off a choking vapour which kept the sandflies at bay for the duration of the smoke.

A comparison of the troops' normal rations and those issued at Kut at this time is revealing (also see Appendix A) and was as follows:

BRITISH TROOPS

	Normal Field Service Ration	Kut (mid-April)
Bread	1¼ lb.	4 oz.
Fresh meat	1¼ lb	1 lb. (horse or mule)
Potatoes and vegetables	½ lb.	Nil (weeds)

	Normal Field Service Ration	Kut (mid-April)
Bacon	3 oz. (or butter 1½ oz. twice a week)	Nil
Tea	⅝ oz.	Nil
Sugar	3 oz.	Nil
Salt	½ oz.	Nil
Jam	4 oz.	Nil
Cheese	3 oz.	Nil
Ginger	Nil	⅓ oz.

INDIAN TROOPS

Atta (wheat meal)	1½ oz.	4 oz. barley meal
Ghee	2 oz.	½ oz.
Dhall	4 oz.	Nil
Meat	4 oz.	9 oz. (horse or mule)
Gur	1 oz.	
Potatoes	2 oz.	
Tea	⅓ oz.	
Ginger	⅓ oz.	⅛ oz.
Chillies	⅙ oz.	(mixture)
Turmeric	⅙ oz.	
Garlic	⅙ oz.	
Salt	½ oz.	

The prices paid at this time at an auction of a deceased officer's effects were:

A box of one hundred cigarettes; 100 rupees (£6 13s. 4d.); one half-pound tin of 'doubtful' butter; 12 rupees (15s. 6d.); a small shaving mirror 32 rupees (£2 2s. 8d.); one pound of coarse sugar: 20 rupees (£1 5s. 4d.); one *oke* (2¾ lb.) of Arab tobacco (normal price 6d.): 34 rupees (£3 12s. 0d.). Also 50 rupees (£3 6s. 8d.) were offered for a bottle of Johnny Walker Whisky but the bid was refused and the spirits presented to the hospitals. When the box of cigarettes was handed to its new owner a messmate asked casually: 'I say have you got such a thing as a cigarette about you?' The answer was a strong negative.

On the night of 11 April General Hoghton was taken ill and died within a few hours. This formerly physically robust officer had been in poor health for some time. His sudden death was attributed to the accidental consumption of one of the poisonous weeds. He was buried on the afternoon of the 13th in the little cemetery to the north of Kut. The mourners at the small grave-side ceremony became aware of the rising wind which rattled the near-by palm fronds. They heard the faint booming of guns from downstream but the four and a half months of siege had pro-duced a dull, bruised feeling in which neither hope nor complete acceptance of failure played a part. At the commencement of the siege the prospect of ever having to open the gates of Kut to the enemy had been unthinkable but now almost everyone was thinking of it. Although defeat was never spoken of it was now apparent that it was much more than a possibility. One still tended to joke about one's declining physical stature yet, as one officer described it, it was a time of misery; a long-drawn-out agony of suspense and disappointment, and not a little suffering. But no one ever joked about the Indians as they shambled listlessly about, hollow-eyed with pinched cheeks.

There was very little doubt in the minds of those at Kut that those downstream were doing everything possible to relieve Kut but the Arabs—those barometers of British success and failure —were uncompromising in their belief that collapse was inevit-able. Acquaintances among the Arab population began to avert their gaze when approached. They were silent and made no conversation. As Turkish subjects they knew what to expect if Kut fell. The Turks had acquired an unblemished reputation for inflicting retribution on all they suspected of co-operating with the British invaders. The fact that the Arabs of Kut had not risen against the garrison would provide ample excuse. The Turks had no love for the Arabs, considering them to be unreli-able and treacherous, and would not hesitate to make examples of them to encourage the rest. And was not the Turkish Com-mander-in-Chief, the almost legendary Halil Pasha, the scourge of the Armenians? A man who, if not the architect, was certainly one of the head bricklayers of the massacre of hundreds of thousands of them. Not, it was said, because they were Christians, but merely because they were Armenians—or non-Turks.

As the Rev. Spooner finished the burial service the heat went out of the sun. The rising wind settled in the south-east and the hateful rain clouds began to roll across the sky. On his return from Hoghton's funeral Townshend was handed a telegram from Gorringe which informed him that the Relief Force Commander had been forced to postpone further relief operations to allow the ground to dry out after heavy rain. Townshend confided to his diary the suspicion that the Turks seemed to have control over the weather.

XI

AIR DROP

Even the lowliest sepoy could reason that the rain, which had now turned into a steady drizzle, would delay relief operations but Townshend was one of the few in Kut who could fully appreciate the serious effect of this latest spell of bad weather. He had just been informed that someone at Lake's headquarters had thought of a revolutionary scheme for getting food to Kut. The aeroplanes of the Relief Force would attempt to drop supplies from the air. From the first Townshend appears to have considered that the plan was foredoomed to failure and although he never stated a specific reason for his misgivings it is more than likely that the major-general's love of orthodoxy and the very fact that there was no military precedent for reprovisioning a besieged town from the air made the plan suspect. Nevertheless when asked what his minimum daily requirements were Townshend replied that 5,000 pounds of supplies dropped each day would provide a ration of six ounces for his 13,840 troops and followers and the 3,700 indigent Arabs. He said that flour, sugar, chocolate, salt and ghee were the most urgently required items.

Major Broke-Smith, the officer commanding the aviation service, had told Gorringe that if each of his serviceable aeroplanes could make three trips each day it might be possible to deliver this amount but the weather would have to be favourable. The major's concern about the weather was more than usual even for these early flying days. The fourteen aircraft at his disposal were by no means the cream of the Royal Flying Corps but because of the imperative demands of the more important theatres of war he had to be thankful for what he could get.

The original commander of the expedition to Mesopotamia, Sir Arthur Barrat, had soon seen the need for aeroplanes. In

January 1915 he had reported that the country with its annual
flooding would limit his ability to make reconnaissances to 'a
dangerous extent'.[1] The Indian Government agreed but the few
flying officers that the Indian Army possessed had been sent to
Egypt and requests for their return were ignored. The Government then turned to Australia and New Zealand for help. New
Zealand was only able to offer one flying officer but Australia
was willing to supply the nucleus of a flying corps—four
trained pilots, about fifty mechanics and other ground staff and
a complete mobile workshop with mule transport. The detachment duly arrived in Mesopotamia and established itself at
Tanouma across the Tigris from Basra. Britain's contribution,
apart from Broke-Smith, was two complete Maurice Farmans.
By the end of May 1915 two more Maurice Farmans were
shipped from Egypt but this time the despatching authority had
not seen fit to send the engines. Now the air service had grown
to eight B.E.2c's, one Voisin, one Henri Farman and four Short
seaplanes. The possession of the more or less obsolescent B.E.2c's
instead of the aircraft's successor, the D.H.2, was by no means a
disadvantage. On the Western Front the former was remembered as 'Stability Jane' but her replacement was rapidly
earning the sobriquet 'The Spinning Incinerator'.

Broke-Smith's mechanics set about fitting food racks to the aircraft. The B.E.2c's carried a fifty-pound bag, lying fore and aft,
on each lower wing, resting against the fuselage. Underneath the
aircraft, lying between the wheel chasis struts where the bomb
rack was normally fitted, were two twenty-five-pound bags.
These were slung over a metal bar, pivoted at one end and
secured by a removable pin at the other. The pilot could withdraw the pin and release the load from inside his cockpit. The
Voisin, Henri Farman and the Short seaplanes each carried a
250-pound load secured below the fuselage by a similar arrangement.

As the pilots waited for the weather to change at their airfield
at Ali Gharbi they had their own misgivings about the air drop.
The weight of the supplies made it necessary for the aircraft to
be flown without observers and their defensive Lewis machine-
guns, making an encounter with the enemy force of three fast

heavily-armed Fokkers extremely undesirable. The only defensive weapon allowed the pilot was a revolver.

15 April 1916 dawned perfectly. The rain had ceased and the clouds had sped away to the north-east. Just a faint breeze ruffled the palms at Kut. The convalescent British and Indian troops at the *serai* dozed on their blankets and picked lice. The active soldiers stood in their water-filled trenches in bare feet. A row of drying boots and socks appeared along the parapets of the fire trenches. The men leaned listlessly against the earth walls, searching for lice, seldom speaking. Even the sergeants seemed to have lost heart. A thousand yards away across the flooded land the Turks were silent too. The Anatolians had completed their digging and were dozing in the sun. In just over four months they had dug thirty-one miles of trenches around Kut.

At first there was a single rifle shot, then a crackle and then an avalanche of fire from the Turkish entrenchments. Whistles shrilled in the British trenches, the men knocked their drying clothing from the parapets into the muddy water. It was thought the long-awaited enemy infantry assault had come at last. The British and Indian soldiers stared through their loopholes. The long-silent Turkish artillery opened up with vigour. Strangely, something seemed wrong; few shells were falling in or near Kut. Then over the tumult came the drone of aircraft engines. Studding the blue sky was Broke-Smith's crazy squadron.

The patients at the *serai*, ignoring the few shots from the equally amazed transfluvial snipers, shouted in glee and pointed skywards. From the leading aeroplane, a Farman, came a tiny speck, turning over and over, getting larger and larger. A faint white plume of flour followed its descent. The bag landed with a 'whump' near the Brick Kilns. The air drop had begun. On the first day 3,350 pounds of supplies thudded into Kut but the furious Turkish cannonade kept the aircraft at 6,000 feet, making accurate drops difficult. The following day only 1,333 pounds were collected. To the chagrin of the hungry watchers many sacks of supplies dropped into the Tigris, on the Turkish side of the river and even as far away as the Turkish lines. The troops, unable to appreciate the difficulty of obtaining accuracy from that height with the pilots having to operate the makeshift release equipment and fly the aircraft at the same time, complained bitterly. The main target of their abuse was the naval pilots in the Short aeroplanes who seemed to make a large number of 'boss shots' as the inaccurate drops were called. Messages of doubtful origin began to be received at the Relief Force headquarters. 'Was the Relief Force on the right river?' one asked. Another requested: 'H.M. Navy to drop us something instead of the Turks.'[2]

Townshend, however, was in no mood for banter. Despite the absence of enemy aircraft the air drop was falling well behind expectations. He telegraphed Gorringe, repeating to Lake as follows: 'This puts a new light on the question. If they cannot put in 5,000 pounds a day, I see nothing for it but that a steamer should run the blockade with say fifty tons of supplies, which would give a reserve of twelve days' food at an eight ounce ration, including town people.' He added that the Turks would now perceive what desperate straits for food Kut was in, and knowing that the air drop was proving to be unsuccessful, their thoughts might bring them to suspect that an attempt might be made to run the blockade by food steamers and take steps to prevent this by placing their guns in strategic positions and even blocking the river with booms.

Townshend's fear, however, were not entirely confined to the difficulties of food ships coming upstream. In fact a few days previously he had proposed to Lake that an attempt to run the blockade in the other direction might offer most promise. He cabled Lake accordingly:

Secret. Personal. May I have an answer to my proposal in my telegram of 10 April, re the *Sumana* running the blockade with 600 or 700 of the most useful men to the state? I want to know if the Government thinks I should break out with that party or remain behind with the Division and sick and wounded to go into captivity. There is no precedent to go on except the commander of a besieged garrison plays the correct role when he tries to break out, and this attempt of running the blockade would be a most hazardous one. To break out

with the bulk of my force is, as I have explained before, with
an impassable swift river of 500 yards' breadth on three sides,
and on the land side a lake with submerged trenches and network of trenches beyond manned by the Turks, utterly
impossible. My second-in-command, Sir Charles Melliss,
volunteers to stay behind. I have every hope that the Relief
Force will ram its way through, but after what has happened
before, I think it will be a close thing, and I am anxious about
food business. Everything should be understood as there will
be no time in the end.[3]

Townshend, however, had decided not to wait for Lake's
formal approval before going ahead with his plans for the break
out. The work was already in hand. He had first to tackle the
problem of security. Townshend knew that he stood little chance
of preparing the *Sumana* for her desperate venture without first
exciting considerable speculation among the troops and then,
inevitably, the Arabs. Absolute secrecy as to his intentions was
essential if a panic was to be avoided. A whisper that Kut was
to be partially abandoned would cause the inhabitants to stampede. This could be controlled but by then the damage would
have been done. The Arabs already in the pay of the Turks, and
the many others who wished to gain or regain favour with their
former masters, would lose no time in informing them of their suspicions thus rendering the plan impracticable. It was possible that
the Indians might mutiny if they became aware of a plan which in
effect would confirm Turkish allegations that the British did not
hesitate to desert their brothers-in-arms when the going got
tough. Some strong reaction might even be expected from the
British troops, especially the sick and wounded, if it became
known that the majority were to be abandoned to the Turks.
How then could the secret be kept until the last possible
moment? Townshend, thus prevented from telling his troops the
whole truth, decided on a compromise. He would only tell them
part of it. Townshend told those who were not privy to the real
story that there had been reports that the Turks were making
intensive efforts to build a floating bridge at Es Sinn. Such a
bridge, connecting as it would the two parts of the enemy's

positions, would greatly facilitate the transfer of reinforcements from one side of the river to the other. The bridge, most likely constructed from pontoons captured from the British, must be destroyed—the only way to do it was to ram it with the *Sumana*. On the next moonless night the *Sumana*, with a steel barge secured to either side, was to slip off downstream. The barges were to be fitted with projecting prows made of wooden beams which would cut through the floating roadway. On board, in addition to the crew commanded by Lieutenant Tudway, would be Captain Sandes with ten Engineers, and an infantry officer with twenty men. If the *Sumana* and her barges failed to breach the bridge by ramming, the twenty infantrymen were to leap on to the structure and run along it in either direction and destroy it with 'jam pot' bombs. Meanwhile the Engineers would endeavour to cut the *Sumana* and her barges free. The steamer would then proceed downstream to Gorringe. The infantrymen left on the floating wreckage of the bridge would be issued with lifebelts. They would dive into the water—those already thrown into it by the violent struggles of the *Sumana* would obviously be saved this trouble—and swim after the steamer.

It was a terrible plan. Undoubtedly if a bridge of *gissaras* or another obstruction had been thrown across the river Townshend would have used this method of cutting his way through. The only part of the plan that had not been mentioned was that Townshend and 700 chosen men would be aboard the steamer during her bridge-destroying mission. Captain Sandes and his Engineers, the infantry officer and his 'bombers' would be hardly likely to freely discuss their preparations or their briefing, neither would those who were being ordered to dive into a five-knot current in pitch dark and swim after the steamer in the hope of being picked up. By then the fully-alarmed Turkish artillery would be in action and surely the ship would not hang around waiting for swimming men. They were facing almost certain death or capture as it was and they would hardly be likely to aggravate their plight by talking about it.

Captain Sandes completed the building of the cutting superstructure on the bows of one of the barges but already he was beginning to wonder if his starving men were fatiguing themselves unnecessarily. After all it was only an unconfirmed report that the Turks were building a bridge at Es Sinn. The experienced Sandes knew that the swift-flowing river would make the task an immensely difficult one. He doubted if the enemy even had a sufficient number of *gissaras* or material for such a structure. He made his doubts known to Townshend through his superior and recommended that an aeroplane reconnaissance be made over the area to find out if the reports were true.

Townshend's plan, however received a setback. On the morning of 17 April he received an answering telegram from Lake:

> In the event of relief in time proving to be impracticable and should the attempt to run supplies to you fail, Army Commander is prepared to sanction the proposal contained in your telegraph of the 10th instant—namely that the *Sumana* shall try to run the blockade, taking as many officers and other ranks as possible whose services are of most use to the state. Army Commander, however, makes this one exception, that he considers you yourself bound to remain behind in command of the garrison, though he would deeply regret the loss of your services. In other respects he leaves the composition of the party entirely to you. It is obvious that should so much as a whisper of this project get about it would have the worst possible effect on the Indian troops. As stated above, the project is not to be put into effect except at the last extremity, and then only on receipt of a direct order from the Army Commander'.[4]

The project was never mentioned again. There is no doubt that if it had been put into operation the 700 men would have been butchered. However, Sandes was told that an aeroplane reconnaissance had revealed that his suspicions had been borne out by the fact and that no bridge was being built at Es Sinn. He was told to forget about the completion of the other barge.

Since dawn that morning the guns downstream had been growling. Later the rattle of rifle and machine-gun fire could be heard distinctly from the direction of Bait Isa, on the right bank and only six or seven miles from Kut, and the garrison was called to arms. That the Relief Force was so close was considerably heartening. Some men in the trenches even raised a cheer.

At noon there was a wild stampede by the Arabs. Rifle butts, boots and bayonets had to be used to subdue them. The reason for this outburst was not obvious but it was suspected that the Arabs had mistaken a small party of wounded Turks limping towards Shumran for advancing infantry. Later it was discovered that the Arabs had heard about Townshend's plan for a breakout. During the siege the Arabs established an almost untarnished record for ferreting out information. Earlier, when goods had been available for sale, the prices had been an accurate guide to how the Relief Force was faring. A sudden rise in prices always meant a Turkish victory and a British setback.

The artillery downstream murmured all day rising to a continuous roar in the evening. As darkness fell the glorious firework display could be clearly seen. The bursting shells lit the near horizon; the red and green signal lights of the Turks blinked unceasingly until 4 a.m. on the 18th when the firing began to decrease and then died away leaving the garrison wondering.

Because of the heat the smells of Kut had now become appalling. The river front, a repository for all the filth imaginable, and the walls of the *serai* had served as a urinal and worse for the Indian convalescents who lay in abject huddles near by. Lying among the garbage in various states of emaciation and collapse were many Arabs. The issue of soup had been discontinued. There was barely enough for the troops; the Arabs came definitely last. They crouched in doorways along the streets that they knew were frequented by the British troops and held out supplicating hands every time they heard approaching army boots.

The Arabs who possessed enough strength began to escape from the stinking and stricken town under the cover of darkness. Parties of Arabs were seen in the open streets making rafts of inflated skins and wooden settles, kerosene tins, large jars, anything that would float or stood the slightest chance of floating their women and children to the other bank. The British warned the now terrified Arabs that if the attempts were unsuccessful

they would not be allowed to return to Kut. Townshend feared
that Turkish soldiers might steal their way into Kut in the guise
of failed escapees. And of course there was the constant fear of
spies.

The Turks mercilessly resisted these attempts at escape. They
were determined that the Arabs should remain in Kut and con-
sume the British force's remaining supplies. The enemy, as
always, believing that one picture was worth a thousand words,
sent a mutilated Arab across no-man's land into the British
lines. Both the man's hands had been severed and his tongue
removed. A note round the Arab's neck informed the horrified
British soldiers that likewise would happen to any Arab who
attempted to leave Kut. The note commanded the Arabs to
remain in Kut and await judgement and punishment when the
town capitulated.

Despite this warning the Arabs persisted in their attempts to
escape the wrath of the Turks and the Turks were as good as
their word. They murdered every man, woman or child who fell
into their hands. Night after night the loaded rafts were pushed
out into the stream. Night after night the crackle of rifles and
machine-guns told the same story. A submerged sandbank 600
yards above the fort divided the main river current in two. If
the drifting rafts managed to get into the current near the right
or far bank it was possible to make a landing opposite the fort.
The Turks and their desert Arab allies were not so thick on the
ground at this point and a landing here brought the chances of
eluding capture into the realm of possibility. But to be caught
in the left bank, or Kut side, current was disastrous. This
carried the islands of screaming Arabs close inshore by the fort
and straight into the rifle and machine-gun fire of the waiting
Turkish picquets. As soon as they realised their plight these
unfortunates cried plaintively to their friends who had gained
the right bank, but few survived. In the morning the banks at
this point were always littered with bodies and wreckage.

The air drop was falling badly behind expectations. Invariably
the elderly aircraft developed engine trouble which either kept
them on the ground or forced them to return to the airfield without completing the mission. Bad weather prevented any aircraft

taking off on the 17th—two days after the drop had commenced. A total of 140 missions were flown by the nine aircraft employed in the task and 19,000 pounds of food were dropped. The aircraft were never able to repeat the success of the first day's drop.

In the way of hungry people food became the main topic of conversation at Kut. The troops sat around in the sun and thought of little else. It seems that even these imaginings were subject to class-consciousness. The British rank and file stood in their local fish and chip shops ordering gargantuan portions of cod, eels, jellied, boiled, baked or stewed; steak and kidney puddings, roast beef and mutton, all came up for scrutiny. The officers pondered on ideal menus of real turtle soup, *filet mignon*, *pâté de foie gras*, grouse or pheasant and the like. Reality, however was a great leveller and they all got the same in the end— horseflesh, a few weeds and four ounces of bread.

The non-meat eating Indians were dying at a rate of fifteen a day. The later converts were scarcely strong enough to walk. Scurvy was still the most common complaint, followed by dysentery, malaria, pneumonia, diarrhoea, beri-beri (particularly among the British troops), bronchitis, jaundice and gastro-enteritis. The last two named diseases caused 165 deaths during the last five weeks of the siege.

The falling food sacks were kept under strict surveillance. This notice appeared on all regimental orders:

> The following are rules for the collection of parcels dropped from aircraft. Every aeroplane must be carefully watched and any man seeing one or more parcels fall will at once report to the nearest British officer who will report to the Commanding Officer. If the spot where the parcel fell is inaccessible by day a sentry is to watch the spot and the parcel picked up as soon as it is dark and taken to Divisional Headquarters. Observers are to continue to watch the aircraft until it leaves the area. On an aeroplane being sighted the N.C.O. of the Quarter Guard will detail a sentry who will keep the aeroplane under observation as long as it may remain in the area. [5]

Another order for 22 April shows clearly the sorry physical condition of the men:

In order to lighten the weight on the men to conserve as far as possible their strength:

1. On defensive duties only fifty rounds of S.A.A. [Small Arms Ammunition] will be carried instead of 150. The balance is to be stored on the spot.

2. Men moving on duty or otherwise away from their defensive positions to carry their rifles with magazines charged and no other equipment or ammunition.

Two young puppies were spirited away from Kut town, were seen later at the fort and then vanished for ever. A rather interesting drawing in the style of the Bayeux tapestry appeared in the Oxford Light Infantry Officers' mess which illustrated the fate of the animals. Someone suggested that this battalion should change its name to the 'Dogeaters'.[6]

Those with more catholic tastes resorted to nocturnal fishing expeditions. Sometimes a few insignificant mud-and-cotton-wool tasting fish were obtained by exploding small dynamite charges or detonators in the pump house sumps. This method required kingfisher-like skill. The Turkish snipers would gaze in the direction of the explosion looking for some signs of movement. If the dead fish were left too long they drifted out into the stream and away. The bang had to be followed up by a swift advance to the sump and hasty retreat before the enemy marksmen could take aim.

Attempts were made at night to catch fish by dragging the small river bays with nets but this method was hardly ever rewarded by success. Captain Sandes and three brother Engineer officers devised an equally ineffectual but far more heroic scheme. The four men slung a length of net from a *mahaila* mast, pushed it out into the river and anchored it at right angles to the bank. They then motored upstream for a short way in a small launch, lit a four pound 'jam pot' bomb, dropped it in the river, then raced at full speed towards the cover of the Woolpress bank. In about fifteen seconds a violent concussion like a blow from a sledgehammer struck the hull of the small craft making it leap upwards. The boat sped on with the sniper's bullets whanging astern. Later when all was quiet again the net was retrieved and examined for dead or stunned fish. There were none. A friendly observer reported that although the bomb had killed some fish they had come to the surface further down-stream beyond the net. The river current was obviously too swift for this method. The sudden explosion of the 'jam pot' bomb disturbed the slumberers of Kut and Woolpress and some searching enquiries were made about the disturbance the following day.

On 20 April at 8.05 a.m. Townshend received an encouraging telegram from the Army Commander which he published in the form of a communiqué:

> You can assure all ranks their relief will be effected shortly. They must not relax their gallant efforts during the next few days, and I am quite sure that you will continue to inspire them by your courageous example.[7]

Early on the morning of the 22nd heavy artillery fire was heard but this time it came from further east. High-explosive shells could be seen bursting along a line of a mile or more in the direction of Sannaiyat. The food situation had deteriorated to such a degree that it became obvious to all that the air drop could not provide the answer. The first aeroplane over Kut that morning, a B.E.2c, had dropped its load into the Tigris near the mouth of the Shatt al Hai, the second had caused a terrific splash when its sack had plunged into the river east of the town. Four hundred pounds of desperately needed food had been lost. Fortunately the enemy aeroplanes had not put in an appearance for days and it was obvious that they were busy elsewhere. The air drop had been a good idea but with this rate of wastage it had begun far too late.

At 7.50 p.m. that day Townshend received a cable from Lake:

> Much regret that the attack on Sannaiyat position this morning was repulsed. Gorringe, however, will not relax efforts.[8]

The gunfire that the garrison had heard—and seen—on the 17th had been from the successful British attack on the enemy positions at Bait Isa and the subsequent Turkish counter-attacks. The assaulting troops had swarmed into the opposing positions and captured them, killing some 300 Turks and taking sixty prisoners. Gorringe then decided to transfer his triumphant 13th Division to the left bank to explore his advantage to the full being now able to engulf the Sannaiyat positions with enfilade fire from the right bank. At about 7 p.m. the Turks launched a series of furious counter-attacks on the right bank and succeeded in breaking the centre of the British line. All night the battle raged to and fro until, at a critical moment, the 13th Division which had been hurriedly brought back came to the rescue. The original line west of Bait Asisa was not regained but by daylight the situation had been restored.

The 13th Division was once more ordered to the left bank to join the 7th Division. Gorringe was determined that a final and third attempt must be made to break the Turkish resistance at Sannaiyat. The troops arrived only to find that the Tigris had flooded its bank and joined the Suwaikiya marshes which had been driven southwards by a strong north wind. There was a continuous sheet of water, about 100 yards wide, lying on the land between the opposing forces. The following night (18th/19th) a patrol managed to find a strip of ground about 600 yards wide where the water was only a few inches deep. On 21 April orders were issued for attack the following morning. At 7 a.m. under cover of a terrific bombardment from both banks, the British troops crossed the 400 yards to the enemy trenches, sometimes wading up to their waists in water. The losses were slight. It was found that the Turkish first and second lines of trenches were flooded and had been abandoned. The attackers, now floundering up to their armpits in a quagmire, struggled towards the enemy's third line. The resisting fire rose in intensity. The Turkish troops counter-attacked and the British, except with bombs and bayonets, were practically incapable of defending themselves as the breeches of their rifles were clogged with mud. The Turks were only kept at bay by heavy machine-gun fire from both banks. Fighting with what few weapons that were still serviceable, the 19th Brigade held on, expecting reinforcements to arrive at any minute. The 28th Brigade tried to flounder through the waist-deep mud and water towards them but at 8.20 a.m. they could press forward no further and were recalled. The 19th received orders to retire. At 11.20 a.m. a truce was arranged with the Turks so that the wounded could be collected and the dead buried. British casualties were 1,283 killed and wounded.

XII
JULNAR

Townshend broke the news of the failure of the British attack on the morning of 23 April. He issued the troops with two days emergency rations, all other food apart from horseflesh being exhausted. Each ration consisted of six ounces of biscuits; some of them were sweet biscuits and were the first tasty food that the troops had received since just after Christmas. Townshend gave his artillery leave to fire at anything they thought fit. The conservation of ammunition had become a farce as the stocks of shells would last far longer than his starving troops would be able to resist. The British gunners gave the Turks hell. This may have been a bad mistake.

Townshend knew now that the end was fast approaching. He telegraphed Lake telling him so and said that nothing short of a miracle could save Kut. The extreme limit of the garrison's resistance might be extended to the 29th but Gorringe had not even taken Sannaiyat yet. The major-general asked the Army Commander to open negotiations with Halil Pasha immediately. Kut should be offered in exchange for a free withdrawal by Townshend and his force. This would be honourable for both sides. Townshend continued that the Turkish commander-in-chief would probably insist that the 6th Division should never fight again during the war. If he did, Lake should try to get the enemy commander to agree that an undertaking not to fight against the Turks would suffice thus making the division available for service in France.

Townshend's own will to resist was coming to an end. He was ill with a 'feverish ague' which he attributed to the damp from the floods which surrounded Kut. He wrote in his diary that the garrison was now 'absolutely done'.[1]

Lake, however, was not finished yet. He still had one other

card to play. This was the 900-ton, 210-ft long river steamer now
called H.M.S. *Julnar*. She had been built in 1908 by E. Rennie
and Co. of Greenwich, London, for the Euphrates and Tigris
Steam Navigation Company and was the fastest craft in Mesopotamia. For the past few days the Royal Navy had been busy
aboard the *Julnar*, now lying at Amara. Most of the inflammable woodwork in her cabins and saloons had been removed.
She had been lightened by cutting away much of her superstructure. Sheets of quarter inch thick steel plate—the heaviest
gauge in the country—had been fixed around her bridge and
engine room.

The *Julnar*'s naval crew lay about her decks in the shade of
awnings and smoked. They beat off the flies and watched the
Arab labourers as they sweated up the gangway with sacks of
supplies. The bluejackets had been informed that the steamer
was to make an extended trip up the Euphrates as part of a sortie
against the Arabs pillaging and plundering around Nasiriya.
The ratings did not believe one word of it—neither did anyone
else in Amara. It was common knowledge that her destination
was Kut.

If any doubts did exist about the *Julnar*'s destination these
were dispelled by the arrival aboard of Lieutenant-Commander
C. H. Cowley, R.N.V.R.—a Tigris river pilot of some thirty
years' standing. This elderly, dignified man had been employed
by Lynch Bros. in the Basra vilayet for so long that he was a
local celebrity. The Turks actually considered him to be a
Turkish subject. Cowley joked about this piece of fiction but the
Turks were not similarly amused. In fact they had threatened to
execute him as a traitor if he ever fell into their hands. Another
ex-employee of Lynch Bros. also came aboard. He was Engineer-
Lieutenant Lewis Reed, R.N.V.R., a ruddy-faced man who
possessed the ability to coax the last ounce out of a steam engine.

A petty-officer ordered the men out of their reverie and below.
Here they met the newly-appointed captain of the *Julnar*,
Lieutenant H. O. B. Firman, R.N., a tall, slim, quietly-spoken
young man. All married men were excused then Firman told the
ratings what they already knew; that the steamer was to
attempt to run the blockade up the Tigris with food for the

starving garrison of Kut. The 270 tons of supplies would enable
Townshend to hold out until Gorringe could make another
attempt at relief. Firman explained that once the *Julnar* had
proceeded past the British positions at Sannaiyat every field-
gun, machine-gun and rifle would try to prevent the steamer
from reaching Kut. The attempt would be made at night but the
return voyage would have to be under moonlight conditions.
Julnar would leave as soon as it got dark at 8 p.m. and she would
have to make the twenty-odd mile trip to Kut in five hours
against an adverse four or five knot current, before the moon
rose at 1.15 a.m. Then the steamer would have to return from
Kut after being unloaded. Firman concluded that he had already
excused married men and he was also prepared to do likewise to
anyone else who did not feel up to the trip or had other family
commitments and that no explanation would be required. No
one withdrew. Firman thanked the men and they were dismissed
but were told to stay aboard. He had not informed the men that
an army officer at a prisoner-of-war camp had said that the
nature of the *Julnar*'s enterprise was common knowledge
amongst his Turkish inmates. These had access to the Arabs
who in turn wandered freely between the British and Turkish
lines. The odds against the success of the trip were reckoned in
the officers' messes at Amara at a hundred to one.

Darkness was beginning to gather as *Julnar*'s twin propellers
began to thrash the dark water into yellow and she moved from
the river bank. The current was strong and she barely made
headway at first. The watchers on the river bank were silent.
Strict orders had been given that there was to be no display of
any kind. No bugles, no cheering, no shouted good-byes. The
Julnar's single, slender funnel thumped black smoke into the
darkening sky as she began to move ahead. She ran into heavy
rifle fire as soon as she passed the Turkish positions at Sannaiyat. Starshells turned the night into day. Cowley at the wheel of
his vividly lit bridge felt the steamer slacken momentarily in her
progress then surge forward. A grating noise was heard running
down the hull. The *Julnar* had scraped over the cables of a
Turkish 'flying bridge'.

Firman made sure the red light was burning strongly at the

ALIQVOT : MILITES : DE : OXENFORDE : FAME : CONSVMPTI : CATVLOS : DEVORANT.

hIC : MILITES : DE : OXENFORDE.

hIC : MATER : DOLOROSA.

KUT FRESCOES NO X.

DIVERS : MEN : OF : OXENFORDE : SORE : PRESSED : FOR : FOODE : EATE : OF : YE : YONGE : OF : DOGGES.

[By permission of Major N. V. L. Rybot, D.S.O.]

13   The Kut Fresco

14   The memorial plaque erected in the crypt of St. Paul's Cathedral.

mast head. He had been informed by Intelligence that this was a Turkish recognition signal and with luck the *Julnar* might be mistaken for a Turkish vessel when further up the river. The naval officer had been badly informed. It will be recalled that this signal actually meant 'Enemy Approaching'. After Sannaiyat the river was straight for about two miles as far as Bait Isa, then some tortuous bends, and then came Es Sinn, another stretch and then Maqasis.

Below, Reed had a problem. Up ahead the heavy guns of Fort Maqasis were waiting. Too little coal now would result in a drop of steam pressure and a slackening of speed. Too much coal would result in a 'green' fire—an excess of unignited coal—and a loss of power and the steamer would never reach Maqasis. The engineer nursed his fires as the rumpus grew outside.

About fifteen minutes before reaching the Turkish fort, the steamer ran into heavy shell fire. The Turks had lined the bank with field-guns but although shell after shell struck the *Julnar*'s remaining superstructure they did little real damage. Then a shell exploded on the bridge killing Firman instantly. The pilot was wounded in the groin by a shell splinter and thrown to the deck but, crawling, he managed to spin the wheel and put the steamer back on course. The starshells were doing their work well and Cowley had no difficulty in making out the channel. A shell crashed into the engine-room killing Reed and severely wounding two stokers but the *Julnar* was going at full speed as she approached the final bend and Fort Maqasis.

Another scraping sound came from the steamer's bows. Cowley immediately recognised this as another submerged cable but this time the *Julnar* did not break free. There was a noise like a circular saw biting metal as the propellers scored into the two-inch cable. Cowley rang the engine room telegraph for 'Full Astern', but the *Julnar* was held fast. She bumped on to a sand-bank near the right bank and under the guns of Fort Maqasis. Bathed in the daylight of starshells she became a chopping block for the Turkish artillery as the heavy guns opened fire. Cowley, bleeding profusely from his wound, tottered out on deck with a square of white rag.

That afternoon twenty-five men of the 1st Oxfords had been

I

ordered to report to the river bank just upstream of the fort. They found they were not alone. Indian troops lined the bank from the fort to the end of the middle line trenches. Engineers had rigged up a wooden roadway stretching back from the river and wooden gangways had been provided. Machine-gun emplacements covered the opposite bank and a darkened signal lamp on a stand faced downstream. The Oxfords' lieutenant was told that his job was to guard stores that were to be unloaded from a steamer. To his surprise he was then issued with a pound of atta and two ounces of chocolate per man. Another party from the 30th Brigade was told that they were to unload the steamer quickly as soon as she arrived because she had to be well on her way back downstream by daybreak.

Kut was agog with excitement. As usual word of the *Julnar* and her desperate enterprise had leaked out. As dusk approached, the watchers began to crowd the flat roofs of Kut. The last of the Relief Force food-dropping aircraft were still overhead but then they suddenly flew southwards. Just as the last rays of the setting sun were creeping away over the western horizon aeroplane engines were heard approaching from the south. Three Fokker aircraft circled over Kut for a few minutes and then landed at the Shumran airfield. The Kutites pondered on the probable fate of the air drop now.

The watchers in Kut heard the gunfire which marked the progress of the *Julnar*—faint at first then growing in intensity. They saw the starshells at Maqasis and then heard the baying of the heavy guns. Then the fire lessened and then faded entirely. The men of the working party at the fort were silent as they marched away. No words could express their feelings.

The sick Townshend, still exhausted after his night's vigil, was roused just after dawn. With a blanket about his shoulders he climbed to the roof of his headquarters once more. One look through binoculars was enough. The *Julnar*, her blackened superstructure high above the Tigris banks, was motionless. She was just within the range of the Kut heavy guns. It was the bitterest moment of Townshend's life.

XIII
NEGOTIATIONS FOR SURRENDER

The three Fokkers were waiting for the Relief Force aeroplanes when they arrived at 11 a.m. that day. Circling high into the sun they pounced on a Short seaplane. The machine-guns prattled and the old aircraft floated down behind the sandhills on the right bank. The enemy aircraft then seized on a B.E.2c. The troops in the trenches below could hear the crack of a pistol as the aircraft wheeled overhead. The pilot of the British plane, Lieutenant S. A. L. Robinson, was wounded but he managed to return to Ali Gharbi. The air drop was abandoned.

With the clatter of the one-sided aerial combat dying away in the distance, Townshend received a telegram from Lake replying to the major-general's plea of 23 April. The Army Commander said that he had cabled Whitehall for permission to commence negotiations with Halil Pasha on the lines that Townshend had suggested. He said that he himself had introduced some suggestions for gaining more favourable terms. Lake did, however, feel that if Kitchener did sanction the surrender of Kut the negotiations should be conducted by Townshend and not himself. Lake said:

> It is for consideration whether if Government sanctions the opening of negotiations, you yourself will not be in a better position to get better terms than any emissary of ours. You would, of course, be ordered by the Army Commander to open negotiations for surrender, the onus not lying with yourself.[1]

Lake added that he consulted Admiral Wemyss, commanding the naval forces in Mesopotamia and a personal friend of Townshend, who had been in entire agreement that Townshend's prestige with Halil Pasha should be used to full advantage to get the best terms. Lake asked for Townshend's views.

Townshend remained unconvinced that he was the right person to conduct the surrender negotiations and thought that Lake was in a far better position as he would be playing from strength. It seemed to the major-general that Kut had become a hot potato and that the Army Commander wanted to keep his name as much as possible out of the big type of the criticism in newspapers which would follow. Nevertheless, Townshend replied that he would conduct the negotiations if Lake insisted and that he would ask for a six-day armistice for the discussion of terms and to allow food to be sent upstream from Amara for his garrison.

At 3 a.m. the following morning Townshend was awakened by an urgent message from Lake. The Army Commander informed him that Kitchener directed Townshend to open negotiations with the Turks forthwith. The Secretary of State for War had considered the various proposals and he thought that Lake's suggestion that Townshend should offer his artillery to the Turks as an added inducement to the Turkish Commander-in-Chief to allow the Kut garrison to pass through would be limited because of the small quantity of British ammunition that would fall into their hands.

Then Kitchener made a proposal which provided the Turks with a powerful weapon of propaganda which, despite strenuous British denials, was to cause Great Britain considerable embarrassment and loss of prestige abroad. Townshend was authorised to offer Halil Pasha one million pounds in silver if it would help negotiations at all. The services of Captains, the Hon. Aubrey Herbert, M.P., and T. E. Lawrence, both of the Cairo Intelligence Service, who had now arrived in Mesopotamia, would also be available as these officers had 'special qualifications for such work'. The impact on Townshend of this blatant suggestion that bribery be used to secure his force is not known and he ignores any reference to it in his autobiography but, as will be seen, Townshend did offer Halil Pasha the money and in fact suggested to Kitchener that the offer be improved.

Somehow the news of this attempt at bribery leaked out at Basra and some staff officers gave Lawrence a cool reception when he arrived in Mesopotamia. Lawrence wrote of the affair:

Meanwhile, our Government had relented, and, for reasons not unconnected with the fall of Erzerum, sent me to Mesopotamia to see what could be done by indirect means to relieve the beleaguered garrison. The local British had the strongest objection to my coming; and two Generals of them were good enough to explain to me that my mission (which they did not really know) was dishonourable to a soldier (which I was not).[2]

Fortunately for posterity there is some degree of explanation for the statement in Kitchener's telegram that Lawrence had 'special qualifications for such work'. From this it might be surmised, with or without profit, that the British Empire was not unfamiliar with the technique of buying herself out of nasty situations. In 1932 Lawrence's biographer, Captain Sir Basil Liddell Hart, submitted a long interrogatory to Lawrence which contained the following question: 'How did you come to receive instructions for the Mespot Mission?' Lawrence replied 'I had put the Grand Duke Nicholas in touch with certain disaffected Arab officers in Erzerum. Did it through the War Office and our Military Attaché in Russia. So the War Office thought I could do the same thing over Mespot and accordingly wired out to Clayton [Lawrence's chief in Cairo].'

Lawrence's reply also goes a long way to answering the unsubstantiated accusations that Townshend himself had originated the suggestion that the one million pounds bribe be offered to Halil Pasha.

An hour later a letter for Halil Pasha was passed across the lines. Townshend informed the Turkish Commander-in-Chief that he had been authorised to negotiate the surrender of Kut and asked for a six-days' armistice and permission to receive ten days supplies of food from downstream. The major-general said that he had no food for the 19,000 military and civilian occupants of Kut, including the sick and wounded, fifteen of which were dying each day from starvation. He said that he was confidently hoping that Halil Pasha, who had already expressed his admiration for the defence of Kut, would be generous and allow the British and Indian troops which formed the garrison to proceed to Amara and then to India under parole not to engage in hostilities against the Sultan's armies for the duration of the war. Townshend continued that these terms would be honourable to both sides and such as the Austrians had allowed Masenna at the Siege of Genoa in 1800 and the British had allowed the French in 1808 in Portugal. By letting the British troops go free Halil Pasha would be doing himself and his country a service as he had neither enough food for that number of prisoners nor sufficient river transport to convey them into captivity as the garrison was far too weak and threatened with disease to march. Also as prisoners-of-war they would have to be paid by the Turks. Townshend asked for an early reply to his letter so that he could telegraph the food ships to start their journey as soon as possible. He was also afraid that pestilence might break out at any moment. He requested an early meeting with Halil Pasha to discuss the final terms of the surrender.

That evening a blindfolded Turkish bimbashi, Halil Pasha's aide-de-camp, arrived in Kut under a white flag and was taken to Townshend's headquarters. The letter he gave to Townshend was scarcely satisfactory. Halil Pasha acknowledged receipt of his communication and agreed that the garrison had carried out their duties heroically but added that they would certainly meet with the same reception as prisoners in Turkey as the troops of Osman Pasha, the hero of Plevna, had met as prisoners in Russia. He said that Townshend and his troops were assured of food, transport to Baghdad and their pay as prisoners-of-war. Halil Pasha said he was leaving at once in a motor boat and suggested that Townshend should do likewise so that they could discuss arrangements for the surrender.

Conjecture at Kut which became rife when the Turkish officer had arrived at Kut, reached a peak when this officer was conducted to the fort by Townshend's aide-de-camp, Captain A. J. Shakeshaft, and departed downstream. It could hardly escape notice that the Turk was allowed to leave Kut without his eyes bandaged.

Townshend did arrange to leave Kut to meet Halil Pasha as requested but as the *Sumana* began to get up steam she was fired on by enemy artillery. Townshend cancelled the trip and sent word across the lines explaining his predicament and asked for a meeting next morning.

27 April dawned quietly. The Turkish snipers and artillery had been given orders to cease their activity. The stillness after almost five months of bombardment was uncanny. Cautiously in ones and twos and then in hundreds the British troops wandered along the river front. The rooftops became crowded with curious spectators watching the developments at the river bank.

Lieutenant R. D. Merriman, Royal Indian Marines, in white dress uniform, stood watching Captain S. C. Winfield-Smith as he tinkered with the engine of one of the motor launches. From the launch's ensign jackstaff fluttered a white flag. Shortly after 9 a.m. Townshend, accompanied by Lieutenant-Colonel Parr (G.S.O. 1), Captain Moreland (G.S.O. 3) and Captain Shakeshaft arrived at the river bank. The sun struck sparks from the highly polished metal on the officers' uniforms. The three men, Townshend rather unsteadily, clambered into the launch and with a few preliminary blips of the engine they departed upstream.

Before leaving his headquarters Townshend had informed Lake of Halil Pasha's uncompromising attitude and said that he would propose to the Turkish Commander-in-Chief that the final details of the surrender negotiations be conducted with British headquarters.

As Townshend's launch grew smaller in the distance its white flag fluttering gaily in the breeze, the rooftop watchers saw another craft appear from upstream. Halil Pasha, tactlessly, was using one of the launches captured from the British after Ctesiphon. Eyes glued to binoculars saw the two launches meet about a mile and a half upstream from Kut. Townshend and his officers were seen to board the Turkish craft. There was a brief introduction and Townshend went below, his officers, returning to their own craft, separated. The British launch arrived back at the river bank and Townshend came ashore with his officers. Townshend looked strained but carried his head high. The officers vanished into the headquarters building.

Clusters of Arabs, carefully watched by specially placed sentries, stood about chattering ceaselessly. The British and Indian troops wandered around listlessly or sat in the courtyards and speculated on the outcome of the meeting—and the terms that Townshend might have gained from Halil Pasha. Many believed that they would become prisoners-of-war but the majority thought that they would be given their freedom after being paroled not to fight against the Turks. The hours passed without a word from Townshend, apart from an order that there was to be no firing of any description until further orders. On the previous day the troops had eaten the last of their emergency rations but they were receiving a small ration from the food dropped by the last of the aircraft.

Immediately on his return to Kut Townshend telegraphed Lake giving an account of the meeting with the Turkish general. He said that although at first Halil Pasha had been extremely cordial he had declined to hold out any hope of anything but unconditional surrender followed by captivity. Townshend had spoken persuasively and then mentioned the one million pounds. At this the Turk had shown interest and said that under those circumstances he might be able to get better terms but he would have to communicate first with the Turkish War Minister, Enver Pasha. Halil Pasha, however, had insisted that Townshend must first march his force out of Kut and camp outside his defences. He said that tents and food would be provided from the captured *Julnar* and that food ships would be allowed to come upstream. The march out, however, must begin immediately. Townshend had demurred and said he must consult his superior before any such move was even contemplated. Townshend ended his telegram with the plea that Lake take over the negotiations.

The Army Commander's reply came three hours later saying that in his view Halil Pasha's proposals amounted to unconditional surrender and if he persisted in his attitude further negotiations seemed a waste of time. If, however, Halil Pasha was prepared to reconsider the matter Townshend could offer the one million pounds, his artillery and probably an exchange of an equal number of Turkish prisoners-of-war. Agreement from Whitehall for the exchange of prisoners was being sought at that time. Lake once more refused to conduct the negotiations. He said that Townshend was near Halil Pasha and he himself was

not, so the preliminary negotiations at any rate must be left to
the major-general. Lake however, said he would send Lieutenant-Colonel W. H. Beach, R.E., head of his Intelligence section,
Herbert and Lawrence to meet Halil Pasha if their services were
required. If the Turk still insisted on the march out to camp
Townshend should destroy his guns, useful stores and possibly
block the river with the *Sumana* and the *mahailas*. Lake said
that Townshend should also insist that no reprisals were to be
taken against the Arabs at Kut or alternatively get permission
for them to go downstream.

That night Townshend issued orders for the destruction of the
artillery ammunition to begin. All gun batteries were told to
retain a small number of rounds but to dump the rest in the
Tigris. The dark hours were disturbed with a sound like a
thousand blacksmiths as the brass cases of the shells were
hammered in before they were slid down specially prepared
chutes into the Tigris. The garrison gloomily went about this
work knowing now that surrender was inevitable.

Just after daybreak Moreland and Shakeshaft were off upstream again bearing Townshend's latest proposals. They proceeded to the right bank of the river just opposite the Turkish
advance trenches where they were met by a Turkish yuzbashi
who motioned them into a tent and provided them with a breakfast of coffee, baklava and some dates. The Turk watched them
as they ate ravenously but when they began to thank him he put
one finger to his lips in the international signal for silence. He
did, however, thoughtfully aim a kick at a burly Turkish
trooper who was waiting outside the tent with horses because he
was a bit tardy in handing over the reins. The three officers rode
along the river bank for about five miles to the camp at Shumran. The Turkish officer began to show signs of uneasiness as
they approached the gangway of a large steamer, the *Busrah*
which was guarded by sentries and surrounded with a small wire
picket fence. They climbed the gangway, walked aft and entered
a small sumptuously furnished cabin. There was a strong smell of
perfume. Standing against one wall was Halil Pasha. He accepted the letter, told the officers to be seated and waved the
terrified Turkish officer away.

As Halil Pasha read the letter the two British officers had
ample time to study this man who apart from a brief glimpse the
previous day had been little more than just a name. The Turkish
Commander-in-Chief was young, unusually so for such a high
position; he looked about thirty-three. He had dark brown hair
and an olive skin and deep-set eyes. His jaw was like a trap. He
wore a simple, brown, high collared tunic without any badges of
rank. His highly polished boots jutted out from under the desk.
As he read he displayed a singular mannerism. He would
occasionally glance up and stare at the two British officers without
any expression on his face. After a considerable period he offered
them cigarettes and then returned to his reading well aware that
he was being scrutinised. A tall officer entered the cabin. He had
the same colouring and features as Halil Pasha but wore an
angry expression. He flung himself on a settee and contemplated
his highly polished riding boots. This was Krazim Bey, commander of the XVIIIth Turkish Army Corps.

Townshend's letter informed Halil Pasha of Lake's proposals
and his remarks concerning the apparent demand for unconditional surrender. It appeared to Townshend that having conducted an heroic defence on which the Turkish general had himself commented, he deserved better terms, especially from an
adversary of Halil Pasha's qualities. He asked him to reconsider
on the lines of Lake's proposals—the guns, money and exchange
of prisoners. If, however, Halil Pasha persisted in his demands
for unconditional surrender Townshend would break off negotiations, destroy his guns and there would be no question of any
payment. Townshend continued that it would be a sorry force
that would fall into Turkish hands. The major-general's doctors
agreed that twenty or even thirty men would die each day and
by the end of the summer at least a quarter of the British force
would be dead. Even if the troops were allowed to return to
India and elsewhere the majority would be unfit for at least
twelve months. In any case they would be on parole not to fight
against Turkey for the remainder of the war. Townshend was,
however, prepared to meet the Turkish general half way. If
tents and food were provided Townshend said he would withdraw all his force from Kut and encamp them on an area of dry

ground near the fort. The sick and wounded, however, would of necessity have to remain in the hospitals. In return the Turkish Commander-in-Chief must allow the *Julnar* to come up to Kut immediately and he must guarantee that the force would be released on parole and allowed to proceed to India as soon as possible. To settle the final details Townshend asked for a safe passage for Beach, Herbert and Lawrence. Halil asked to be excused in perfect French and left the cabin followed by Krazim Bey. Moreland and Shakeshaft waited alone for almost an hour and conferred together in whispers like schoolboys.

Halil Pasha returned and appeared to be in an exuberant mood. He was followed by two orderlies carrying trays of coffee and the inevitable baklava. The British officers gorged themselves while Halil Pasha chatted away. He had the habit of smiling and then suddenly switching it off as if someone had crossed some wires somewhere. He held out a letter to Moreland and flashed a couple of short-circuited smiles at the Englishmen. 'I, like your commanding officer, will take you into my confidence,' he said to their profound surprise. This was Townshend's favourite opener. Moreland tried to take the letter but it was jerked away. They read, with difficulty, the letter swinging from the Turk's fingertips. It was in awful French and was from Enver Pasha.

The Turkish War Minister said that the only condition he was prepared to offer was that Townshend himself could be released on parole in exchange for Kut and all the war material in the defensive area. Townshend must give his word of honour that he would not fight against Turkey or her allies for the duration of the war. He would be allowed to leave Kut with his personal effects. This condition was generous and final. If Townshend refused then Halil Pasha was ordered to break off negotiations and continue the offensive against Kut.

'There is no need to memorise the letter, gentlemen,' said Halil Pasha, 'I have enclosed a copy in my reply to your general.' The smile switched off and he said something that baffled the two British officers. 'Tell him to keep his money. I have lost ten thousand men.'[3] He waved the two officers away.

Moreland and Shakeshaft left the steamer to find that their

launch had been brought upstream. Their escort this time was
three Turkish officers, one of whom was an artilleryman named
Haider Bey, who spoke English with an American accent. He
explained that he was the son of the Turkish ambassador in
Washington and had spent eight years in the United States.
When they arrived at Kut the Turkish officers said that they
had orders to wait for Townshend's reply.

Townshend telegraphed the contents of the two letters to
Lake. Halil Pasha said that he had done all within his power for
the heroic defender of Kut but the matter was now beyond his
control. He said that the Kut garrison was starving, diseased, and
was now incapable of defence, and scurvy was rife. Before food
was allowed to the British force they must march out of camp.
Halil Pasha said that if Townshend handed over his artillery and
rifles he would promise not to use them against the British.
This arrangement would exercise considerable influence towards
the establishment of harmonious relations between Great
Britain and Turkey, a state of affairs undoubtedly desired by
both nations. The Turk demanded a definite reply to his proposals by 7 p.m. that evening. He added that he was leaving for
his headquarters near Maqasis at once. Townshend asked the
Army Commander for orders. He said that his troops were
rapidly coming to the end of their food and that supplies were
urgently required, that the offer of his freedom was unaccept-
able and that he must go into captivity with his troops.

Townshend sent Shakeshaft and Merriman downstream with
the launch and the Turkish officers, with a letter for Halil
Pasha which said that he was waiting for instructions from Lake
but that his final reply would be in the Turkish Commander-in-
Chief's hands the following morning. The launch had just
passed the fort when it developed engine trouble. The Turkish
officers frantically signalled the bank for help and got the shouted
assurance that aid would be on its way shortly. As the launch
drifted downstream the British officers had plenty of time to
examine their surroundings. The second flood was abating now
and the river was dropping down its banks. An appalling stench
came from a large number of bloated dead bodies which were
floating in the reeds on both the right and left banks. The dead

men appeared to be Arabs and Turks. As the water lapped the muddy banks sucking sounds came from the thousands of rat holes. The craft drifted around the bend and there was Fort Maqasis with the *Julnar* off the sandbank now moored inshore near the left bank. She was being unloaded and large quantities of stores were stacked near by. There was no sign of her British crew.

At last the launch drifted ashore and one of the Turkish officers departed with Townshend's letter. After about half an hour had elapsed an enormous Turkish engineer arrived, smiled jovially at the British officers and then began to flail the engine with a spanner. The Englishmen watched aghast at the apparent destruction of their engine, their only means of returning to Kut and possible liberty. The Turkish officers did not seem to notice that anything was amiss and were counting dead bodies. The flies were maddening. The engine at last responded to the treatment and in a few moments Shakeshaft and Merriman were on their way back upstream to report to Townshend.

At 6 p.m. Townshend issued a communiqué to his troops which showed that despite the tone of Halil Pasha's letters he still held hopes of success from the meeting between the Turkish Commander-in-Chief and the three officers from Basra. The communiqué read:

It became clear, that after General Gorringe's second failure on 22 April at Sannaiyat, of which I was informed by the Army Commander by wire, that the Relief Force could not win its way through in anything like time to relieve us, our limit of resistance as regards food being the 29 April. I was then ordered to open negotiations for the surrender of Kut; in the words of the Army Commander's telegram, 'the onus not lying on yourself. You are in a position of having conducted a gallant and successful defence and you will be in a position to get better terms than any emissary of ours. . . . The Admiral [Wemyss], who has been in consultation with the Army Commander, considers that you with your prestige, are likely to get the best terms; we can, of course, supply food as you may arrange.' These considerations alone, namely that I can help my comrades of all ranks to the end, have decided me to over-come my bodily illness and the anguish of mind which I am suffering now, and I have interviewed the Turkish General-in-Chief yesterday, who is full of admiration for 'an heroic defence of five months' as he puts it. Negotiations are still in progress, but I hope to announce your departure for India on parole not to serve against the Turks, since the Turkish com-mander thinks this will be allowed, and has wired to Constan-tinople to ask for this, and that the *Julnar*, which is now lying with food for us at Maqasis, now may be permitted to come to us. Whatever has happened, my comrades, you can only be proud of yourselves. We have done our duty to King and Empire; the whole world knows we have done our duty.[4]

To the communiqué Townshend added two messages he had received from Lake:

The Commander-in-Chief [Beauchamp Duff] desired to express to the troops under Gorringe and Townshend his appreciation of their gallant efforts and their tenacious endur-ance in the face of a brave and determined enemy, and under exceptional physical difficulties. He knows that they will respond to the next call of their leaders in the same spirit, and he looks forward to hearing that success will finally crown their endeavours.'[4]

Special for Townshend: The Commander-in-Chief requires you to convey to Townshend and his brave and devoted troops his appreciation of the manner in which they have undergone the hardships of the siege which he knows has been due to the high spirit of devotion to duty in which they met this call of their Sovereign and Empire.[5]

Instructions to destroy the rifle ammunition were issued; only a few rounds per man were to be retained. The night of 28/29 April was spent dumping the ammunition in the Tigris. It was exhausting work for the weakened men.

The cessation of gunfire had brought respite to the hospitals' operating theatres. During the siege the overworked medical staff had performed thirty-two cranioptomies, forty abdominal sections, thirty-six amputations and six ligations for aneurysm treatment. The result of the cranioptomies had been 'disappointing' but the other surgery had saved 'several' lives, the patients, on the whole, were doing well. There had been thirty cases of tetanus from which only four recovered. Several such cases were treated with injections of carbolic acid but none survived. There were only three instances of gas gangrene from which two had died and the third recovered. The Kut medical authorities attributed their success in a large number of cases of serious wounding to the proximity of the hospital to the firing line and other scenes of wounding. The most serious complications in the latter stages of the siege were caused by the steadily diminishing rations, lack of invalid foods, the outbreak of scurvy among the Indians, and the presence of beri-beri among the British. Of the 2,446 cases of wounded treated in the hospitals (not including those from Ctesiphon and the retreat) 488 had died and the remainder had been returned 'fit for duty'. Many of the latter were poor in health and crippled in some way.[6]

The breakdown of the figures for the 1,746 deaths at Kut since the commencement of the siege were as follows:

	Killed	Died of Wounds	Died of Disease
British Officers	9	10	4
British Other Ranks	84	105	58
Indian Officers	8	7	5
Indian Other Ranks	369	279	531
Camp Followers	67	88	123
TOTAL	537	488	721

Two hundred and forty-seven Arabs had been killed and 633 wounded inside the town.[7]

The official history, referring to the refusal of the Indians to eat horseflesh, says:

The question of the Indians eating meat has always been a difficult one in the Indian Army and an emergency such as this was unprecedented. It was the common impression among the British officers among the Indian units before the (1914–18) war that, if it was absolutely essential, their men would be generally prepared to eat what was necessary and that they would be absolved by their religious leaders of any religious misdemeanour entailed by them acting on the justification of emergency. Anyone, however, with the experience of the power and influence which caste, religion and tradition exercised in India, will understand the difficulties and dangers in issuing such an order if there was any chance of it not being universally obeyed. Many Indians told Townshend of the social disabilities they would be bound to incur in India if they did as he wished, and they did not believe that anything could be done to insure them against these. There is evidence to show that many Indian officers did what they could to persuade their men to carry out Townshend's wishes in the matter; but although some men had begun to eat horseflesh at the beginning of April the majority held aloof. It is noteworthy to consider the opinion of Generals Delamain and Melliss, the two senior Indian army officers in Kut. Melliss was in favour, at an early date, of issuing a definite order to Indian troops that they must eat horseflesh, but Townshend considered this a too drastic measure. While Delamain considers that had a warning been issued officially at an early stage that the garrison were in for a long siege there would have been no difficulty in getting the Indians to do what was required. Both these generals are of the opinion that the communiqués issued strengthened the men in their refusal as after each failure these statements held hopes of early relief and they felt they only had to abstain from meat a little longer to save themselves from embarrassment and trouble when they returned home.[8]

XIV
INTERLUDE NEAR MAQASIS

Those still capable or sufficiently interested took their last look around Kut. It was now common knowledge, repatriation or not, that the garrison would have to march out of the defensive area. It was a hot, steamy afternoon and this threw into marked relief the nauseating conditions at the river front. The Indians and Arabs still lay amongst the rubbish heaped against the protective walls. Attempts to stop the Arabs using this place as a repository for filth and garbage had proved futile.

The *Sumana* and the launches were surrounded by sunken *mahailas*. A small steel barge had been left high and dry on the shelving bank by the sudden drop in the river level. The masts of two *mahailas* stuck out high at midstream and there was another raked at an extreme angle near the mouth of the Shatt al Hai. These craft had been sunk by British artillery when they had mysteriously broken loose and threatened to drift across to the Turkish bank. Another sunken *mahaila* lay close to the river front by the bazaars. Upstream was the enormous double-decked barge, nicknamed the *Lusitania*, which had done service as a floating hospital ward when the wounded from Ctesiphon had arrived in the town. Now the barge was fast aground on the sloping bank and partially submerged. All the white mud walls along the river front were pitted with bullet marks and the foreshore was a mass of shell craters. The walls of the river front bazaar and the *serai* facing the river were in ruins. At least fifty per cent of the Arab houses in the town had been reduced to heaps of rubble.

After issuing what proved to be his final communiqué Townshend telegraphed Lake and suggested that Beach, Herbert and Lawrence should offer Halil Pasha two million pounds sterling plus an exchange of an equal number of Turkish prisoners for the Kut garrison (permission to make the exchange had been received from London after Townshend had despatched his letter on the morning of the 28th). Lake replied that he had wired to London for permission to offer the increased sum of money although the Turkish Commander-in-Chief's attitude did not hold out much promise for the success of this method. Beach, Herbert and Lawrence would go out the following day, attempt to gain an audience with Halil Pasha and start negotiations on those lines. If Townshend heard nothing to the contrary or it was confirmed that these negotiations had proved unfavourable he was to destroy his guns, stores, wireless equipment and sink the *mahailas* in the fairway of the river—and then surrender. He would then inform Halil Pasha that Lake was prepared to take over the Kut sick and wounded and warn him that he would bear a heavy responsibility if he failed to agree to this as he was obviously incapable of giving them adequate medical treatment or transport. Halil Pasha should also be made aware that he was honour bound to provide for and protect the civilian population of Kut who had been involved in the siege through no fault of their own.

At 6 a.m. on the morning of 29 April Major Gilchrist, Captains Moreland and Shakeshaft, accompanied by Lieutenant Merriman and Captain Winfield-Smith, departed by launch for Halil Pasha's headquarters. Townshend's letter simply said that hunger had forced him to comply with the Turk's wishes as he was unable to hold out any longer without food. He said that the negotiation with Beach, Herbert and Lawrence whom he would be meeting that day might gain parole for his troops but could not, at that stage, affect the surrender in any way. He asked that food for his troops should be supplied immediately from the *Julnar* and begged the Turkish Commander-in-Chief to treat his force generously. Townshend suggested that he should send his senior medical officer into Kut so that he could see the state of the garrison. After an inspection this officer would definitely agree that the exchange of the sick and wounded for an equivalent number of Turks would be the best course.

As the launch pulled away from the bank the final destruction began. It was a morning never to be forgotten by those in Kut.

The day had dawned fine and clear and the spirits of the garrison had risen at the prospects that by evening they might have begun their journey to India. And then the blow fell. Townshend published the full text of his final letter to Halil Pasha in the form of a communiqué.

Your Excellency. Hunger forces me to lay down our arms, and I am ready to surrender to you my brave soldiers who have done their duty, as you have affirmed when you said 'Your gallant troops will be our most sincere and precious guests'. Be generous then; you have seen them in the Battle of Ctesiphon; you have seen them during the retirement, and you have seen them during the Siege of Kut for the last five months, in which time I have played the strategic role of blocking your counter-offensive and allowed time for our reinforcements to arrive in Iraq. You have seen how they have done their duty, and I am certain that the military history of this war will affirm this in a decisive manner. I send two of my officers, Captain Moreland and Major Gilchrist, to arrange details. I am ready to put Kut in your hands at once and go into your camp as soon as you can arrange details, but I pray you to expedite the arrival of food. I propose that your Chief Medical Officer should visit my hospitals with my P.M.O. He will be able to see for himself the state of many of my troops—there are some without arms and legs, some with scurvy. I do not suppose you wish to take these into captivity. and in fact the better course would be to let the wounded and sick go to India. The Chief of the Imperial General Staff, London, wires me that the exchange of prisoners of war is permitted. An equal number of Turks in Egypt and India would be liberated in exchange for the same number of my combatants. Accept my highest regards.

A final ray of hope was added.

I would add to the above that there is strong ground for hoping that the Turks will eventually agree to all being exchanged. I have received notice from the Turkish Commander-in-Chief to say I can start for Constantinople; having arrived there, I shall petition to be allowed to go to London on parole, and see the Secretary of State for War and get you exchanged at once. In this way I hope to be of great assistance to you all. I thank you from the bottom of my heart for your devotion and your discipline and bravery and may we all meet soon in better times.

Then followed hastily prepared orders for proceeding aboard the hoped-for ships that were to take the garrison into captivity. British and Indian troops should take with them their blankets, greatcoats, waterproof sheets, waterbottles and haversacks. All tarpaulins should be kept to provide shelter from the sun. A few picks and shovels were required for digging latrines. Food, it was hoped, would be provided at the new camp.

The orders warned:

All ranks must thoroughly understand that it is absolutely necessary for their own well-being to treat the Turkish soldiers with all due courtesy and adopt a conciliatory attitude towards them. Failure to do this may have far-reaching effects as to the ultimate disposal of this force.[1]

It took barely an hour to destroy all the artillery at Kut. The value of the thirty-eight field-guns and the four howitzers thus disposed of was put at £100,000. The troops smashed their rifles to pieces against walls or beat them out of recognition with sledge-hammers. Machine-guns received similar treatment and the remains of the small arms were thrown into the river. The two remaining motor launches (one was downstream with Townshend's messengers) were sunk with dynamite charges. All saddlery and harness was heaped into piles and burnt. Then began the distressing business of killing the chargers and all the remaining transport animals. Of the 18,000 transport mules that had arrived with Townshend's force in December only twenty-six had survived. These were held in a kind of abhorrence. When fodder had become scarce the mules had been fed on the finely chopped flesh of other slaughtered mules. The meat was mixed with bran and was, until it gave out, flavoured with salt. The mules had existed on this peculiar mixture until the grass began to grow after rains. The Indians reserved a particular loathing for these 'cannibal mules' as they were called.

The five British officers arrived at Halil Pasha's camp, Gilchrist handed Townshend's letter to an aide-de-camp and then they waited outside the Turkish Commander-in-Chief's tent. An hour later they were invited to enter and met Halil Pasha and Nizam Bey. Gilchrist was handed the formal Turkish agreement to the surrender of Kut. Halil Pasha said that matters were now settled and that at 1 p.m. Nizam Bey and a regiment of three battalions would march into Kut. Orders for the regiment to move off had already been given. Nizam Bey and the medical officer requested by Townshend would accompany the British officers for a part of their return journey. Halil Pasha waved his hand to signify that the meeting was at an end but Gilchrist seized the opportunity to ask that he be allowed to take some of the *Julnar*'s stores back to Kut. Halil Pasha abruptly dismissed this request and said that provisions would only be provided when the British troops had quitted Kut and not before. He said that he was already being generous in supplying two ships to take the garrison to Shumran.

The five officers with Nizam Bey and the doctor motored upstream until they overtook a column of marching infantry. Nizam Bey then indicated that he wished to join his troops. He landed, accompanied by the medical officer. The launch then proceeded to the fort where Colonel Brown was warned to be ready to admit the Turkish troops at 1 p.m. and then the party continued to Kut and reported to Townshend.

At 11.40 a.m. Townshend telegraphed Lake that he had destroyed his guns as he was unable to hold out any longer. He said that he had informed Halil Pasha that he was ready to surrender. The major-general explained that he would be unable to block the river by sinking his river craft in the channel as he only had the *Sumana* and the launches, which would be inadequate for the purpose. The *mahailas* belonged to the Arabs and he thought that this would only create needless hardship if the craft were confiscated. He also added that even if he was able to block the channel this would prevent the British food ships getting up to Shumran.

At 12.42 p.m. Townshend signalled that a Turkish regiment was marching towards Kut and these troops would take over from the British guards. He said that his troops would commence to embark for Shumran at 2 p.m.

Shortly before 1 p.m. Lieutenant Green finished strapping gun-cotton charges to his wireless equipment. He struck a match and then paused and shook it out again. He switched on the set and tapped out the Relief Force call sign; there was silence; he repeated the signal. An answer crackled in his headphones. Green thought for a second, tapped out 'Goodbye', switched off the set and lit the fuses. He left the wireless shack, slamming the door behind him. There was a muffled explosion and the windows and door blew out, but Green did not bother to look back.

Downstream three British officers waited in no-man's-land between the British and Turkish trenches. It was an ill-assorted trio; a soldier, a member of parliament, and a dreamer. Colonel Beach, a regular officer, was none too keen on the task he had been asked to perform; to bribe the Turks to allow the garrison of Kut to go free. He mused that the going rate had risen. It used to be thirty pieces of silver, now it was two million. Captain Herbert was convinced that their task was a hopeless one and the day before had told the Army Commander so. He said it was quite clear that the Turks would procrastinate. They would do this out of habit but in the end they would insist on unconditional surrender. Captain Lawrence shivered despite the intense heat of the sun. He was recovering from a bout of malaria. He had already received a rough tonguing from a few senior officers of the Indian Army over this expedition and anyway, it was too late for him to do anything. The Arabs of the Nefje and Kerbela, far in the rear of Halil Pasha's army, were in revolt against him. The Arabs, ostensibly under his command, were openly disloyal and even the Turkish Commander-in-Chief made no pretence that the situation was otherwise. If only Britain had adopted a fair attitude to the tribes of the Euphrates and the Hai it would have been different. The makings of the explosion were there. Britain only had to supply the match but she had not bothered. If the Arabs had been befriended by the British, enough local tribesmen would have joined in and hammered the extended Turkish lines of communication between Baghdad and Kut. A few weeks of that and the Turks would have been forced to raise the siege of Kut, or themselves suffer the fate of the garrison. But now it was too late. The British-Indian Army, as reminiscent of bulldogs and oaktrees as ever, had remained an alien force in Mesopotamia. Far from adopting a conciliatory attitude they even believed the myth, a totally untrue one, that the Turks had suggested an armistice be arranged between the two rival forces; they would both set about the Arabs, annihilate them, and then get back to some serious fighting.

These three men waited 200 yards inside no-man's-land under a white flag. It was a terrible place. Muddy and corrupted but still recognisable fragments of human bodies littered the flat plain. Huge black beetles crawled over and fed on these remains and the ground and air seethed with flies. Herbert described the airborne flies as a 'shimmering fire'. They inhaled them through nose and mouth. They rolled into little crushed balls as the men wiped perspiration from their faces. The smell was indescribable.

The small party had to wait for two hours in the heat but now there were signs of movement from the enemy trenches. Two Turkish officers and five N.C.O.'s approached. Herbert explained that he had a letter for Halil Pasha. The Turks suggested that they were prepared to deliver the letter but the English officer insisted that it must be handed to the Turkish general personally. A private was sent to seek permission for the British officers to enter the Turkish lines. An aimless conversation then ensued.

A Turk from Crete said that he had joined the army straight from school and in the five years since he calculated that he had taken part in 200 attacks. 'That is,' he said, 'against regular troops, not brigands.'[2] He displayed his medals and noticing the lack of decorations on Herbert's and Lawrence's chests told them not to worry as they would no doubt have plenty of opportunity of remedying this failing in the near future. Herbert realised that what he had feared was coming to pass. The Turkish officers were just killing time. Any reference to the delivery of the letter was ignored and the conversation sidetracked into another channel. The pointless discussion continued for another two hours. Even Lawrence was showing signs of wilting under the strain.

The British officers raised the subject of the letter once more.

Lower Mesopotamia

The Turks sighed and asked them if they had liked Basra. Then they asked for the letter to be handed over. The British officers would receive a reply very shortly they said. Herbert refused and explained that he had orders to deliver the letter personally and surely the Turkish officers must realise that orders were orders. The Turks agreed. Beach, in desperation, suggested that the letter would be surrendered if their commanding officer would give his personal guarantee that the three officers would meet Halil Pasha. One of the Turks said he would see what he could do and strode away towards the trenches.

The man from Crete sent for some oranges and water bottles. The bottles were soon empty and Lawrence, after receiving permission, dawdled over to the river bank to refill them. Lying along the banks at the water's edge were dozens of decomposing bodies of Turkish soldiers; some looked as if they had died of cholera, others bore unmistakable signs of gun-shot wounds. He returned without filling the bottles.

At last came word that Halil Pasha would see the deputation. The three officers were blindfolded and led into the enemy trenches, constantly bumping against men and corners. After about half an hour their blindfolds were removed. They found themselves in a tent. Before them was a large, fat, fierce-looking staff officer who introduced himself as Bekire Sami Bey. Herbert said that Turk looked like an athletic Old King Cole. He was alternately jolly and fierce and after plying them with coffee and yoghurt begged to be allowed to order them some food. The offer was refused.

Speaking understandable English Sami Bey launched into an appraisal of the current situation. He said that it was all Sir Edward Grey's fault and became quite nostalgic about the Crimea, when the Turks had been on the same side as the British. Sami Bey said he loved England and demonstrated that he knew the country well. At last the Turk glanced at a pocket watch, stood up and said it was time to meet Halil Pasha. Herbert showed his ball of soggy handerkerchief and asked whether it was necessary to be blindfolded again. Sami Bey roared with laughter; 'You have chosen soldiering, a hard profession. You have got to wear that for miles and you will have to ride across ditches.' He shook hands and patted each on the shoulder. Their eyes were rebound and in this precarious state they were led outside and helped on to horses. This manœuvre was additionally complicated by the flies which made their mounts skittish. As they were led off Sami Bey could be heard alternately roaring with laughter and shouting. He called after the British officers; 'Ha, ha, this is perfectly monstrous. He'll be off. Ha, ha, ha.'[3]

After they had been riding for about ten minutes Lawrence complained that a twisted knee was giving him trouble and that he preferred to walk. He was left behind with an escort while Beach and Herbert rode ahead. One of their guards asked if the British officers ever had difficulty changing paper money in Mesopotamia. They did not know what to make of this until the questioner continued that he always had difficulty changing Turkish scrip until recently. 'Now the Arabs accept it quite readily. Tell me gentlemen, to what do you attribute this change of heart?' he asked.

They arrived at a Turkish camp and were unblindfolded. Before them was a single bell tent surrounded by picketed horses. There was a constant coming and going of despatch riders on motorcycles. They were ushered into the tent and were introduced to Halil Pasha and his chief staff officer Krazim Bey. The general seemed pleased to see them.

After quickly examining the proffered letter the Turkish Commander-in-Chief opened the discussion. He spoke in French and asked Herbert if he had met him before; at a dance at the British Embassy in Constantinople, perhaps? Herbert agreed that this was so. The Turk asked if there was any possibility of exchanging some English ladies, now interned at Baghdad, with some Turkish officials and their wives who had been overtaken when the British force had entered Amara. Herbert said he would see what could be done but changed the subject to that of the *Julnar*. Had there been any survivors? Halil Pasha seemed put out. He said that there had been only two killed aboard the steamer but these unfortunately had been 'both the captains'. Herbert was about to press him for details but Halil Pasha suddenly asked about the money. Beach, who spoke neither

French nor Turkish, and was using Herbert as translator, half-heartedly offered the two million pounds but he was interrupted. The Turk rejected the offer out of hand and said he wanted to hear no more. A surprising statement since he had raised the matter. There was a silence.

Herbert mentioned the Arab population of Kut. He said that Townshend was concerned about their welfare after Kut had been occupied. He added that he wanted to know what was going to happen to Townshend himself. Herbert said that surely Halil Pasha must feel for Townshend, whose lifelong study of soldiery had been brought to naught because of the siege. Halil replied: 'There is no need to worry about Townshend, he's all right.'[5] He paused. 'As for the Arabs, I cannot see that they are any concern of yours or your government. They are Turkish subjects and therefore their fate is irrelevant to this discussion.' Herbert pressed for some assurance that the Arabs would not be persecuted. Halil Pasha categorically refused to give any such undertaking but said it was not his intention to exact retribution.

During this conversation Lawrence had arrived. He seated himself and without any preamble asked about the British sick and wounded at Kut. Halil Pasha, after enquiring Lawrence's name, said he would willingly exchange these for Turkish soldiers now in British prisoner-of-war camps but he insisted that they must be well and unwounded. He would exchange Englishmen for Turks and Indians for Arabs. He said he had a poor opinion of both the latter. Upon reflection for a second or so Halil changed his mind. No Arabs would be acceptable as part of the exchange. Herbert argued that this was unfair because the Arabs had fought well but this only seemed to amuse the Turkish general. He said that unfortunately his experience had been to the contrary. One in ten of his Turkish troops had proved to be a coward but only one Arab in a hundred was brave. He continued: 'You can send them back to me if you like but I have already condemned them to death. I should like to have them to hang.'[6]

An officer entered the tent hurriedly and conversed in under-tones with the Turkish Commander-in-Chief. The silent Krazim

Bey joined in. Halil Pasha turned back to the British officers; his jaw working wildly. He shouted: 'Townshend is destroying his guns.'[7] Calm soon returned and he told Herbert that he would require ships to transport the British and Indian prisoners-of-war to Baghdad. Beach told Herbert in English that this was impossible but instructed him to tell Halil Pasha that this matter must be referred to Lake. Herbert complied but Halil Pasha, who had understood every word, was allowing his attention to wander. He was obviously deeply upset over the destruction of the British artillery and kept muttering how disappointed he was with Townshend.

Beach, through Herbert, told Halil Pasha that the British would willingly pay for the maintenance of the citizens of Kut but this offer was brushed aside. 'I repeat that the Arabs are no concern of yours. You have your empire and we have ours— there is no difference between us.' Herbert retorted angrily: 'No difference? Only about 800,000 Armenians.' This remark made not the slightest impression on the Turk. He returned to the subject of the ships. He said that it was important that food for the Kut garrison was sent upstream as soon as possible. Herbert, after a hurried consultation with Beach, said that this would be arranged. He would inform the Turkish authorities when the ships were ready so that any mines could be cleared from the river. The Turk laughed and said he had forgotten about the mines and thanked Herbert for reminding him about them. Halil Pasha now appeared to have lost all interest in the meeting and began to blink his eyes sleepily. He looked at his watch and grinned, 'At this moment, gentlemen, my army is entering Kut.'[8]

Thus ended the last bid to save the garrison of Kut. Halil Pasha was feted throughout the Turkish Empire. He earned himself the title of Halil Kut Pasha. A new thoroughfare was hacked through the city of Baghdad and named after him. Elsewhere he was soon forgotten. One of the young officers, shivering with fever, who had sat opposite him in the tent was, a year after, to earn a similar sobriquet and become a legend in his own lifetime. Halil al Kut later could not even recall meeting Lawrence of Arabia.

XV

THE ROAD TO BAGHDAD

Townshend ordered Captain Shakeshaft to go to the middle line to meet Colonel Nizam Bey. The British officer thought it might be appreciated to meet the Turkish officer on foot although a horse had been spared for his use. As he walked through the town the Arabs were singing and dancing and he wondered if this was because the siege had ended or that the Turks were coming.

At 1 p.m. precisely Nizam Bey, wearing a large pince-nez and riding a grey, crossed the British line with his troops. Shakeshaft greeted him and noted that the Turk was immaculately dressed and wore an 'enverri'—the peculiar sort of head-dress said to have been invented by the Turkish Minister of War. Nizam Bey seemed to be put out that he was being met by a junior officer and adopted an arrogant manner. In French he demanded to be taken to the Mayor of Kut and when Shakeshaft informed him that there was no such person, this annoyed Nizam Bey even more. He then ordered Shakeshaft to take him to Townshend's headquarters and set off at such a pace that the British officer, weakened by the rigours of the siege had to request him to slow down.

As they proceeded towards the town Nizam Bey asked how many guns there were in Kut. Shakeshaft quickly said there had been about forty. The Turk asked what he meant by that remark and the panting Shakeshaft pointed to the wrecks of ordnance. Nizam Bey exploded into a string of Turkish which he then translated into French for Shakeshaft's benefit. The enemy troops halted outside the town and Nizam Bey and an escort proceeded into the town.

Townshend was too sick to meet the Turkish colonel and the job devolved on General Delamain as his second-in-command.

With Colonel Taylor, the military governor of Kut, he waited outside Divisional Headquarters. They saluted Nizam Bey and proffered their swords but the Turk, while not actually refusing them, indicated that he had more important matters on his mind. The officers then had a brief discussion concerning how the change of authority should be made. As the officers talked the Arabs went through the motions of hysterical delight. The men danced frantically, sang and called on heaven to witness their devotion to the Turks; the women emitted a continuous wail. On several occasions Arabs darted forward and attempted to kiss the highly polished boots of the Turkish officers but they were rewarded with kicks in the face.

The discussion over, Shakeshaft was ordered to escort Nizam Bey back to his waiting regiment. Two of the enemy battalions were marched away to occupy the British trenches and the fort. The remaining battalion fixed bayonets and with colours flying and to the clamour of kettle drums and cymbals set off into Kut with Nizam at their head. Shakeshaft was not invited.

Major Barber, hearing the approaching rataplan, strolled from his office in the bazaar hospital towards Divisional Head-quarters. The drums echoed and re-echoed from the mud-walled houses along Spink Road. Barber saw the Turkish officer, tall on his grey, pass, followed by a column of thickset, dirty, dusty and tired-looking infantry. The common Turkish soldiery wore uniforms of an almost infinite pattern and variety. The pre-dominant colour of the tunics was a yellowish-grey but there was also British khaki and bluish-grey, obviously hailing from Germany. Their puttees clung loosely around their legs like ivy and, in some cases, even dragged on the ground behind them. A few wore boots, some wore shoes and others wore neither, having only rags wrapped round their feet. The men carried large heavy packs, each with a rolled greatcoat around it. On waistbelts hung a large number of bulky pouches of ammunition. Here and there, dangling amongst spherical hand-grenades, were personal belongings and loot. Very few had water-bottles. All wore the hybrid cap-helmet, 'enverri' which had a flap down the back to protect the neck from the sun. Most of the officers wore the same head-dress but usually of a superior quality. Some wore a high astrakhan cap with stripes radiating from the crown—gold for combatants and silver for non-combatants. All commissioned ranks had binoculars dangling from their necks, either very short swords or ones of normal length which looked light and extremely fragile, and small automatic pistols in holsters. The infantry looked a genial lot. As they marched, or rather shambled along the road, they threw sheepish grins at the watching British soldiers, almost as if they half expected them to raise a cheer. 'Christ', muttered a British private, '. . . beaten by the Ragged School.' Barber, however, thought the enemy troops looked like brigands out of a melodrama.[1]

The column came to an untidy halt outside Divisional Headquarters and at a command, scattered into long lines. Sentries were ordered off to various stations; the remainder piled arms and removed their packs. Nizam Bey disappeared inside the building to take over his office as military governor of Kut.

Barber walked back along the river bank towards the hospital. A motor launch flying a white flag was scudding across to Woolpress village; a Turkish barge, loaded with troops, was crawling down the river bank, pulled by sweating Arabs. The soldiers, with the air of conquerors, occasionally threw service biscuits to the cheering Arabs on the bank. Barber passed some Turkish soldiers straggling along the river front, but apart from staring at him they did nothing.

The medical officer was surprised to find everything quiet and orderly at the hospital but as he approached his office he was greeted by a distressed Indian servant crying: 'Master, there are soldiers in your room stealing your things.' Barber ran upstairs and found three hefty, ragged Turks trying on his uniforms and bashing open his boxes with rifle butts. The British officer expostulated but the looting continued. One, however, ceased his hammering and stared with interest at the revolver at Barber's wasit. The struggle for possession of the small arm developed into a wordless tug-o'-war. A bayonet, thrust under Barber's nose, decided the matter.

Barber ran downstairs to see if he could find a Turkish officer but as he entered the hospital he found further commotion. Turkish soldiers were robbing the patients of blankets, boots and valuables. Fortunately, outside the hospital was a yuzbashi who immediately stopped the looting but he did not order the men to return what they had already stolen. He did, however, post a sentry to prevent a recurrence. Barber mentioned the matter of his revolver but the Turk simply informed him that he should have handed it in anyway. Barber said later that considering the poor equipment and uniforms of the Turkish soldiers the looting was light. There were a few other instances where men were robbed of their valuables but a request via a British officer to a Turkish officer usually remedied the matter. In one such case a Turkish soldier was shot by his officer with no further ado. The officers seemed to have the power of life and death over their men who meekly submitted to blows and kicks.

By the late afternoon Kut was full of Turks, either resting in groups or prowling along the roads and alleys, singly or in pairs, looking for something of value.

Because of Nizam Bey's temporary rejection of Delamain's and Taylor's swords there was a growing rumour that all British officers were to be allowed to retain them. It came as a shock, therefore, when the officers were ordered to report to Divisional Headquarters and hand them in. As the officers arrived at the building they noticed a guard outside Townshend's house next door. It was said that ill-health was confining the major-general to his bed.

Nizam Bey, now in full command of the situation, seemed relaxed and had lost his erstwhile overbearing manner. As the swords were presented, he greeted the officers cordially and shook each by the hand. This treatment created another rumour that the swords would be returned later but this proved to be unfounded.

Orders were issued that the British garrison was to commence to move up to Shumran as soon as possible. At first the steamer *Busrah*—gaily decked with bunting—arrived, and then the *Burhanieh*. The relays began. The first group moved upstream in the afternoon. A second echelon was scheduled to make the trip that evening. A third party was to leave the following morning.

Meanwhile Kut had become *en fête*. Most houses flaunted

bunting and the red and white star and crescent flags. The
streets were thronged with wandering Turks and Arabs. The
former seemed keen on noting where their shells had fallen.
Patrols of mounted Arabs, covered with pistols, curved daggers
and other trappings, galloped through the town. The sight of
these cut-throats seemed to worry everyone—Briton, Indian,
Turk and town Arab alike.

The morning of the 30th was hot and steamy. The situation at
the hospital was acute; the promised rations had not arrived.
During the morning the *Firefly* had come downstream and
moored. She was smart with new paint and her Turkish sailors
in their neat white uniforms trimmed with red and blue moved
about briskly. A curious crowd collected, mostly Arabs but
with a few of the remaining British officers from the hospitals.
To the latter's surprise Halil Pasha and a cluster of officers
appeared from the direction of Divisional Headquarters. How
he had entered Kut was not known to the medical staff but it
was presumed, rightly, that the *Firefly* had brought him. With
the Turkish commander-in-chief was Delamain and three
British staff officers. With set faces and self-conscious mien the
party boarded the steamer and walked up the small companion-
way to the bridge where they seated themselves in chairs. A
word of command, the ring of the engine-room telegraph, and
the warps were cast off. The *Firefly* began to move upstream.
Townshend remained in his house under guard.

Turkish doctors began to examine the British and Indian
wounded in the hospitals to decide if they were sick enough for
repatriation and exchange for Turkish prisoners-of-war. Barber
found the work hot and laborious; the faces of the soldiers as
they waited to hear their fate were heartbreaking.

The Turks also began measures against all they suspected of
being traitors and defectors. An Arab named Mahommed Sedi,
who had long been known to the British as a pro-Turk, but had
been tolerated at Kut because he was a friend of the powerful
Wali of Pusht-i-Kuh, prosecuted his role of chief informer with
vigour. A Jewish trader named Sassoon who had assisted the
British force by indicating where the Arab population had
hidden food was pursued on to the roof of a house. The merchant

K

had been in hiding since 23 April but had been ferreted out. In desperation he threw himself from the roof but as it was only thirty feet from the ground he merely succeeded in breaking a leg. He was flogged where he lay and then hanged on one of the four contraptions already erected for the purpose on the river front. These were merely tripods constructed of eight-foot poles. The condemned man was jerked up in the air until his toes were just grazing the ground and allowed to choke to death. The old sheikh of Kut, his son and nephew were dragged to the butchery where their right hands were severed with a cleaver and then taken to the river bank where they were similarly hanged. A further row of tripods was erected and these were filled before nightfall. About 250 Arabs, found guilty of various crimes, were marched off to the *serai* where they were shot in parties of six to ten.

At the temporary prisoner-of-war camp at Shumran the conditions were bad. The first group of prisoners to arrive had found that the 'camp' was a stretch of dry ground near the river. Most of the men were without tents and therefore exposed to the full force of the sun. No food had been provided other than Turkish service biscuits. These were five inches in diameter by three-quarters of an inch thick, of a brown rock-like substance interspersed with bits of husk and a considerable quantity of earth. Everyone received a ration of two and a half biscuits. Many had not eaten since dawn the previous day and they attacked the biscuits furiously. One procedure was to pound them into small pieces which were then soaked in river water until a sort of porridge was obtained. Others who could wait boiled the water first. The first method was responsible for an outbreak of cholera which claimed about a hundred lives while the troops were at Shumran. Turkish soldiers walked among the hungry men trying to sell onions, dates, chapaties and bread but very few had money and they had to barter their clothes and boots for food.

At dusk on the 30th the second party of British troops arrived, exhausted after the six or seven miles march from Kut. After the first group the shipment by river had been discontinued. Further groups arrived during the night. Melliss, who was sick himself, marched out of the Turkish hospital and joined his starving men by the river. He protested, pleaded and cajoled the Turks to have pity on the men but his efforts were in vain. Although the Turks listened to Melliss with patience they did nothing. Melliss, ill and tired out, found Turkish apathy too much for him and suffered a severe collapse.

The tentless, starving and now dying troops continually gazed downstream looking for the Relief Force food ships. One steamer came up on 2 May but passed straight on to the Turkish military camp. It was not until the next day that a small ration of food was issued.

The survivors of the *Julnar*, who were among the prisoners, began to ask what had happened to Lieutenant-Commander Cowley. The elderly man had been separated from the crew shortly after the steamer had struck her colours. The Turks at first explained that they had found Cowley dead when they had boarded the *Julnar*. The survivors said this was not possible as when they had last seen him he had been alive. The Turks reconsidered and then said that the old pilot had been shot while trying to escape. They stuck to this version after the other survivors pointed out that Cowley had been wounded in the groin thus rendering a dash for freedom highly improbable. The Turks also had difficulty remembering what had been done with the naval officer's body.

The ever scandal-mongering Arabs, however, were in no doubt as to Cowley's fate. They said that he had been executed for the reason which the pilot had openly joked about and secretly feared: that the Turks considered him to be an Ottoman subject and bore him a deep grudge because of his local knowledge which had been of immense assistance to the Mesopotamia Expedition. According to the official history enquiries made after the cessation of hostilities produced a certain amount of hearsay evidence that supported the Arab story. Both Cowley and the *Julnar*'s captain, Lieutenant Firman, were posthumously awarded the Victoria Cross.

On 2 May 1916 Sir Percy Lake received a letter from Halil Pasha informing him of the number of sick British and Indian troops of the Kut garrison that he was prepared to exchange for Turkish prisoners-of-war. No Arabs would be acceptable and he even particularised which units the Turks were to come from. He also informed the Army Commander that he could not transport the Kut prisoners from Shumran to Baghdad because he had insufficient fuel and requested that Lake provide 2,000 tons of coal. Lake replied that although he could send vessels to bring the sick and wounded back to Basra who would be exchanged as desired, he was unable to supply coal or vessels to transport the British and Indian troops to Baghdad. He reminded Halil Pasha that he had himself given assurances to Townshend that if Kut was surrendered he would feed, clothe and pay the garrison and transport it to Baghdad. Lake felt that as his force was already suffering from a shortage of river transport he would not be justified in jeopardising the situation.

Of the 1,450 sick and wounded at Kut, 1,136 were exchanged and sent downstream. Some three months later a further batch of 345 were sent down from Baghdad for similar exchange.

On the evening of 3 May a small Thorneycroft launch was observed making its way upstream from Kut towards Shumran. The prisoners-of-war at the camp on the bank of the Tigris recognised the small figures in the stern. It was General Townshend; with him were Colonel Parr and Captain Moreland. The troops rapidly lined the bank, some running, some limping, others being carried. As the launch passed slowly upstream cheer after cheer came from the scarecrows on the bank. Two days later on 5 May, the British and Indian officers were separated from their men. At 3.30 p.m. that afternoon the long march into captivity began.

At the time of the surrender the strength at Kut amounted to 13,309, of whom 3,248 were Indian non-combatant camp followers so a total of about 12,000 British and Indian soldiers were taken into captivity, where over 4,000 of them died. Of the British rank and file 1,700, or seventy per cent, died or were never heard of again. Of the Indian rank and file about 1,300 are known to have died in captivity. Exact statistics are not available as to the number of Indians that survived. Even as late as January 1924 Indian ex-prisoners were turning up at their native villages.

During the four months that relief attempts were made, over

23,000 officers and men of the Relief Force were killed or wounded. King George V sent a personal message to Sir Percy Lake's force, which was published as a communiqué to the troops. It read:

> Although your brave troops had not the satisfaction of relieving their beleaguered comrades in Kut, they have under the able leadership of yourself and subordinate commanders fought with great gallantry and determination under most trying conditions. The achievement of relief was denied you by floods and bad weather and not by the enemy you have resolutely pressed back. I have watched your efforts with admiration and am satisfied that you have done all that was humanly possible and will continue to do so in further encounters with the enemy. George R.I.[2]

The news that Kut and its garrison had surrendered was greeted in Great Britain with bewilderment which turned inevitably into anger. Although attacks which failed could be readily enhanced with palliatives such as 'heroic' and 'gallant' a surrender could not. There was a loud outcry in the Press and Parliament which resulted in the publishing, in the form of a White Paper, the telegrams between Mesopotamia, Indian Army headquarters at Simla, Whitehall and the India Office in London. There was one notable omission: Townshend's appreciation to Nixon which clearly stated the incapacity of the 6th Division for the advance. Unfortunately for Nixon, that this telegram existed was almost common knowledge. A *Times* leader, demanding that the whole story be told, invited Nixon to explain why this particular telegram had not been published with the rest and why its contents had not been translated to London.

The death of Kitchener when the cruiser *Hampshire* was sunk off the Orkneys failed to distract those calling for a full investigation into the events that led up to the fall of Kut. In Parliament on Thursday, 12 June 1916, Captain Aubrey Herbert, M.P. who was, of course, well informed on the matter, asked the Prime Minister, Asquith, if he would allocate a date for the discussion of the Mesopotamian campaign. Asquith said that he did not think that the moment was opportune. Another member persisted. Sir Edward Carson said that Mesopotamia, and what was going on there, was causing the very gravest anxiety among 'a very considerable proportion of the people'. He said that he would put the same question again early the following week and if he did not get a satisfactory answer he would move the adjournment of the House. There were loud cheers. The following day *The Times* wanted to know at what stage Nixon had left the battle of Ctesiphon; what part Duff had played in the decision to advance on Baghdad and why Aylmer, the then commander of the Relief Force, had delayed before Dujaila.

At last the Government gave way and the result was the Mesopotamia Commission which was appointed in August 1916 and reported on 26 June the following year. It was described as 'the most distressing document ever submitted to Parliament'. The Commission had the advantage of an earlier report, that of the Vincent–Bingley Committee which had already investigated the medical arrangements in Mesopotamia, as a result of the strange rumours of shortages which had reached the ears of the Government of India. This report had yet to be published.

The 188-page report of the Mesopotamia Commission found that the division of responsibility between the India Office and the Indian Government was unworkable. It said that the Secretary of State for India (Austen Chamberlain) who controlled the policy did not have cognisance of the capacity of the expedition to carry out the policy and the Indian Government, who managed the expedition, did not accompany developments of policy with the necessary preparation. The report said that the scope of the expedition was never clearly defined and that the Commander-in-Chief (Sir Beauchamp Duff) should have visited Mesopotamia.

The Commission found that the weightiest share of responsibility lay with Nixon whose 'confident optimism' was a main cause of the decision to advance on Baghdad. Other persons responsible were: in India: Hardinge and Duff; in England; Sir Edmund Barrow (Military Secretary of The India Office) who had written military appreciations when it clearly was not his province to do so, Chamberlain and the entire War Committee of the Cabinet. The Commission detected the breakdown of river transport and deficiency of medical supplies, river hospital steamers, medical personnel and land ambulances.

The report, however, was accompanied by a detraction by Commander Josiah Wedgwood, D.S.O., M.P., who although a member of the Commission disagreed with its findings. He even described Nixon's part in the advance as 'an honest error'.[3]

Two days of Parliamentary debate followed the publishing of the report, at the commencement of which Chamberlain honourably offered his resignation from the India Office, which was accepted. It was presumed that the Government would introduce a Bill to set up a tribunal at which the persons censured by the report could answer, but the Leader of the House, Bonar Law refused. He said that in coming to this decision the Government had been influenced by the undesirability of diverting the thoughts of the Legislature and the Executive at that crucial time from the prosecution of the war.

Hardinge did, however, take the opportunity of his maiden speech in the House of Lords to answer his accusers. He said that India's war effort which was unexampled could not have failed to hamper that country's contribution elsewhere. He cited India's internal and frontier struggles and her reduced military budget as inhibiting to this effort. He categorically denied that the Indian Government was responsible and said that it was fully opposed to the advance on Baghdad. The inadequacy of the river transport had only revealed itself when it was too late to do anything about it. Hardinge said he had been completely deceived by the misleading reports received from the fighting front but the moment the truth had dawned on him he had made every effort to remedy the situation. Concluding, the ex-Viceroy, now Permanent Under-Secretary of State for Foreign Affairs, pointed out his thirty-seven years of honourable service. Hardinge offered his resignation three times but it was refused. Sir John Biles, the India Office's part-time consultant naval architect, on the other hand, wrote to *The Times* describing the Mesopotamia Commission as incompetent.

The year 1916 had been extremely fertile in supplying reasons for official committees and commissions. In addition to the Mesopotamia Commission others were delving into Gallipoli and allegations of corruption in the supply of aircraft to the Royal Flying Corps. It was in this atmosphere of charges and counter-charges that the feelings of outrage at the handling of affairs in Mesopotamia turned from anger to sadness. After all it was only a minor theatre of war.

Kut was finally recaptured from the Turks in February 1917, six months after Sir Stanley Maude had taken command in Mesopotamia, displacing the raj of antique Indian Army commanders. Maude, a veteran of Gallipoli and France, was the antithesis of those who had preceded him. A brother officer declared that Maude was a happy admixture of strategical and tactical genius with a capacity for staff work and the internal administration of the army. His only weakness was a failure to delegate responsibility and he wore himself out by his meticulous handling of detail which could have been passed on to his subordinates. Under his aegis the port of Basra was entirely transformed and an efficient system of transport, both land and river, was achieved. He preceded every military action with adequate preparation and organisation.

Maude first drove the Turks from the right bank of the Tigris opposite Kut and then crossed above the town. This strategy caused the enemy to abandon Sannaiyat. The Turks lost three-quarters of their force before making a final unsuccessful stand before Baghdad, ironically enough at Diyala, at Ctesiphon, the scene of Townshend's disaster. Baghdad fell in March 1917. The exhausted Army Commander died of cholera seven months later.

Townshend was awarded the K.C.B. in October 1917, whilst still a prisoner-of-war. He returned to England a year later to not a little criticism that he had spent his captivity in comparative luxury while his troops had died of hunger and other privations. He became Member of Parliament for the Wrekin division of Shropshire in 1920. He tried to engage in the post-war settlement wrangles between Great Britain and Turkey but his services were curtly declined by the Government. Apparently ignoring this setback he visited Kemal Pasha in Ankora where he was well received. He returned to England strongly advocating the Turkish cause but again was snubbed. He died in Paris on 18 May 1924 after a period of failing health.

APPENDICES

A

Food rations issued to British Troops during the siege

	Jan 21	Jan 22	Jan 23	Jan 26	Jan 31	Feb 3	Feb 8	Feb 15	Feb 23	Mar 5	Mar 8	Mar 10	Mar 12	Mar 27	Apr 12	Apr 16	Apr 22	Apr 23	Apr 26
	oz	oz	oz	oz	oz	oz	oz	oz	oz	oz	oz	oz	oz	oz	oz	oz	oz	oz	oz
Bread	16	12	12	12	12	12	12	12	12	12	12	10	10	8	6	5	4	6*	4†
Meat	16	16	16	16	20	20	20	20	20	20	20	20	20	20	16	16	16	6	16
Bacon or	3	3	3	2	2	2	1	1	1	Nil	Nil	Nil	Nil	Nil	Nil	Nil	Nil	Nil	Nil
Cheese or	4	4	4	2	2	2	1	1	1	Nil	Nil	Nil	Nil	Nil	Nil	Nil	Nil	Nil	Nil
Jam or	4	4	4	4	2	2	2	1½	1	1	1	1	Nil	Nil	Nil	Nil	Nil	Nil	Nil
Butter	3	3	3	2	2	2	1	1	1	Nil	Nil	Nil	Nil	Nil	Nil	Nil	Nil	Nil	Nil
Potatoes and other Vegetables	Nil	Nil	Nil	Nil	Nil	Nil	Nil	Nil	Nil	Nil	Nil	Nil	Nil	Nil	Nil	Nil	Nil	Nil	Nil
Sugar	2½	2½	½	½	½	½	Nil	Nil	Nil	Nil	Nil	Nil	Nil	Nil	Nil	Nil	Nil	Nil	Nil
Dates	4	4	4	4	4	4	4	4	4	4	Nil	Nil	Nil	Nil	Nil	Nil	Nil	Nil	Nil
Tea	1	½	½	½	½	½	⅓	⅓	⅓	⅓	Nil	Nil	Nil	Nil	Nil	Nil	Nil	Nil	Nil

* Issue of the Reserve ration on 23 April 1916 accounts for the rise in the bread allocation.

† The 4-oz. bread ration issued from 26 April until the end of the siege came from supplies dropped by aeroplane. On 26 April there was a small issue of saccharine and chocolate.

Food rations issued to Indian Troops during the siege

	Normal Ration	Jan 21	Feb 24	Mar 8	Mar 18	Apr 11	Apr 16	Apr 22-29
	oz	oz	oz	oz	oz	oz	oz	oz
Rice or } Atta	1½	Nil	Nil	Nil	Nil	Nil	Nil	Nil
Barley meal	1½	1½	4	Nil	Nil	Nil	Nil	4
Barley, to parch	Nil	Nil	10	10	10	5	4	Nil
Meat	Nil	Nil*	Nil	4	4	4	4	Nil
Vegetables	Variable	Nil	Nil	Nil	Nil	12	9	9
Sugar	2	2	2	⅓	Nil	Nil	Nil	Nil
Ghee (clarified batter)	2	2	½	Nil	Nil	Nil	Nil	1
Dhal (lentils)	4	Nil	Nil	Nil	Nil	Nil	Nil†	Nil

*From 21 January 12 ounces of horseflesh was available to those who would eat it. Before this date meat was not issued to Indians.

† Approximate date on which dhal ration failed.

B

Composition on 14 November 1915 of Major-General Townshend's Column advancing on Baghdad

CAVALRY
Headquarters 6th Cavalry Brigade
'S' Battery R.H.A.
7th Lancers (4 squadrons)
16th Cavalry (3 squadrons)
33rd Cavalry (3 squadrons)
One squadron 23rd Cavalry (Divisional Cavalry)
Total: 11 squadrons and 6 guns

ARTILLERY
10th Brigade R.F.A.:
1st/5th Hampshire Howitzer Battery
86th Heavy Battery R.G.A. (one section in barges)
104th Heavy Battery R.G.A. (less one section at Amara)
One post gun, Volunteer Artillery Battery
Total: 29 guns (of which 3 guns were left with the garrison at
Aziziya

INFANTRY
16th Brigade:
2nd Dorsetshire Regiment
66th Punjabis
104th Rifles
117th Mahrattas

17th Brigade:
43rd Light Infantry
22nd Punjabis
103rd Mahrattas
119th Infantry

18th Brigade:
2nd/7th Gurkhas
24th Punjabis

76th Punjabis

Total: 16 battalions (of which half 24th Punjabis were to be left at Aziziya as garrison)

DIVISIONAL TROOPS
Maxim Battery
17th Field Company, Sappers and Miners
22nd Field Company, Sappers and Miners
Bridging Train
Searchlight Section
Divisional Ammunition Column
34th Divisional Signal Company
One Brigade Section Army Corps Signal Company:
  One section Army Corps Signal Company
  One waggon wireless station
Two pack wireless stations
Field ambulances
Clearing hospitals (on the *Bloss Lynch* and *Mosul*)

AIR SERVICE
Five aeroplanes, Royal Flying Corps (two more arrived on 17 November)

C

Order of Battle of the Force, under Major-General Townshend, besieged at Kut

HEADQUARTERS, 6TH DIVISION
G.S.O.1 Lieutenant-Colonel V. W. Evans, R.E.
A.Q.M.G. Lieutenant-Colonel W. W. Chitty

16th Infantry Brigade (Major-General W. S. Delamain):
2nd Dorsetshire Regiment (Major G. M. Herbert)
66th Punjabis (Lieutenant A. Moore)
104th Rifles (Captain C. M. S. Manners)
117th Mahrattas (Major McV. Crichton)

17th Infantry Brigade (Brigadier-General F. A. Hoghton):
43rd Light Infantry (Lieutenant-Colonel E. A. E. Lethbridge, D.S.O.)
22nd Punjabis (Captain A. O. Sutherland)
103rd Mahrattas (Lieutenant-Colonel W. H. Brown)
119th Infantry (Captain F. I. O. Brickman)

18th Infantry Brigade (Brigadier-General W. G. Hamilton):
2nd Norfolk Regiment (Major F. C. Lodge)
7th Rajputs (Lieutenant-Colonel H. O. Parr)
110th Mahrattas (Major H. C. Hill)
120th Infantry (Major P. F. Pocock)

30th Infantry Brigade (Major-General Sir Charles Melliss, V.C.):
Half 2nd Queen's Own Royal West Kent Regiment (Major J. W. Nelson)
One company 1st/4th Hampshire Regiment (Major F. L. Footner)
24th Punjabis (Lieutenant-Colonel H. A. V. Cummins)
76th Punjabis (Captain E. Milford)
2nd/7th Gurkhas (Lieutenant-Colonel W. B. Powell)
Half 67th Punjabis (Major C. E. S. Cox)

PIONEERS
48th Pioneers (Colonel A. J. N. Harward)

CAVALRY
One squadron, 23rd Cavalry (Captain C. H. K. Kirkwood)
One squadron, 7th Lancers (Lieutenant F. T. Drake-Brock-man)

ROYAL ENGINEERS (Lieutenant-Colonel F. A. Wilson):
Bridging Train (Captain E. W. C. Sandes)
17th Company Sappers and Miners (Lieutenant K. B. S. Crawford)
22nd Company, Sappers and Miners (Lieutenant A. B. Mathews)
Sirmur Company, Imperial Service Sappers (Captain C. E. Colbeck)
Engineer Field Park (Captain H. W. Tomlinson)

ARTILLERY
10th Brigade R.F.A. (Lieutenant-Colonel H. N. St. J. Maule):
63rd Battery (Major H. Broke-Smith) ⎫
76th Battery (Major O. S. Lloyd) ⎬ 18 guns
82nd Battery (Major E. Corbould) ⎭
1st/5th Hampshire Howitzer Battery (Major H. G. Thomson) 4 guns
86th Heavy Battery, R.G.A. (Lieutenant-Colonel M. H. Courtenay) 4 guns
One section 104th Heavy Battery, R.G.A. (Major W. C. R. Farmar) 2 guns
Volunteer Artillery Battery (Major A. J. Anderson) 4 guns
One spare 18-pounder
One section 'S' Battery R.H.A. 2 guns
6th Divisional Ammunition Column (Captain E. T. Martin)

MISCELLANEOUS
Maxim Battery (Captain C. H. Stockley) 6 machine-guns
Detachment, Army Signal Company (Major F. Booth)
34th Divisional Signal Company (Captain H. S. Cardew)

One Brigade Section, 12th Divisional Signal Company
Wireless Section (two waggon and one pack sets)
A few details Royal Flying Corps (Captain S. C. Winfield-Smith)
Supply and Transport Personnel, including details of the Jaipur Transport Corps and of the 13th, 21st, 26th and 30th Mule Corps (Lieutenant-Colonel A. S. R. Annesley)
No. 32 Field Post Office
Three chaplains: Rev. H. Spooner (Church of England)
                    Rev. T. Mullen (Roman Catholic)
                    Rev. A. Y. Wright (Wesleyan)

MEDICAL UNITS (Colonel P. Hehir, I.M.S.)
    No. 2 Field Ambulance
    No. 4 Field Ambulance
    No. 106 Field Ambulance
    No. 157 Indian Stationary Ambulance
    No. 9 Indian General Hospital
    Half No. 3 British General Hospital
    Officers' Hospital
    One section Veterinary Field Hospital (Captain H. Stephenson)

NAVAL DETACHMENT
    H.M.S. *Sumana* (Gunboat) one 12-pounder and two 3-pounders which were moved ashore in March 1916 (Lieutenant L. C. P. Tudway, R.N.)
    Four steam launches (3 destroyed during the destruction of the bridge on 9–10 December 1915)
    Two motor launches
    Six barges
    Four 4·7-inch guns in horse-boats
    One 12-pounder intended for the captured H.M.S. *Firefly* (mounted ashore on the town river front at beginning of January 1916)

D

Reorganisation of Tigris Corps on 15 January 1916

3RD DIVISION (Major-General H. d'V. Keary)

7th Brigade:
1st/1st Gurkhas
1st/9th Gurkhas
93rd Infantry

9th Brigade:
1st/4th Hampshire Regiment (less one company)
107th Pioneers
2nd Rajputs (less half a battalion)
62nd Punjabis

28th Brigade:
2nd Liecestershire Regiment
51st Sikhs
53rd Sikhs
56th Rifles

Divisional Troops:
One battery, 9th Brigade R.F.A.
61st Howitzer Battery
23rd Mountain Battery (less one section)
Cavalry Brigade (less two squadrons)
Administrative units
Field Ambulances

7TH DIVISION (Major-General Sir George Younghusband)

19th Brigade:
72nd Highlanders
28th Punjabis
92nd Punjabis
125th Rifles

21st Brigade:
73rd Royal Highlanders
6th Jats
9th Bhopal Infantry
41st Dogras

35th Brigade:
1st/5th The Buffs
97th Infantry
37th Dogras
102nd Grenadiers

Divisional Troops:
9th Brigade, R.F.A. (less one battery)
1st/1st Sussex Battery, R.F.A.
72nd Heavy Battery, R.G.A.
128th Pioneers
Two squadrons cavalry
Administrative units
Field Ambulances

Corps Troops:
13th Company, Sappers and Miners
Bridging Train
7th Battery, R.G.A.
Air Service

E

Order of Battle and Distribution of the British Forces in Mesopotamia on 27 February 1916 (excluding the garrison of Kut al Amara)

3RD DIVISION (Major-General H. d'V. Keary)
7th Infantry Brigade (Major-General R. G. Egerton):
1st Connaught Rangers (including drafts for the 2nd Royal West Kents at Kut)
27th Punjabis
89th Punjabis
128th Pioneers

8th Infantry Brigade (Lieutenant-Colonel F. P. S. Dunsford, 2nd Rajputs):
1st Manchester Regiment
2nd Rajputs
47th Sikhs
59th Rifles

9th Infantry Brigade (Brigadier-General L. W. Y. Campbell, 89th Rajputs):
1st Highland Light Infantry
1st/1st Gurkhas
1st/9th Gurkhas
93rd Infantry
4th Brigade, R.F.A. (7th, 14th and 66th Batteries)
20th Field Company, Sappers and Miners
21st Field Company, Sappers and Miners
34th Sikh Pioneers
One squadron 16th Cavalry
No. 3 Divisional Signal Company
Mobile Veterinary Section

7TH DIVISION (Major-General Sir George Younghusband)
19th Infantry Brigade (Brigadier-General E. C. Peebles):
Composite Highland battalion (2nd Black Watch and 1st Seaforth Highlanders)

28th Punjabis
92nd Punjabis
125th Rifles

21st Infantry Brigade (Brigadier-General C. E. Norie):
Composite English battalion (2nd Norfolks and 2nd Dorsetshire Regiment)
6th Jats
9th Bhopal Infantry
Composite Mahratta battalion (drafts for Mahratta battalions
at Kut)

28th Infantry Brigade (Major-General G. V. Kemball):
2nd Leicestershire Regiment
2nd/43rd Light Infantry
51st Sikhs
53rd Sikhs
56th Sikhs
9th Brigade R.F.A. (19th, 20th, and 28th Batteries) 18 guns
3rd Field Company, Sappers and Miners
107th Pioneers
One squadron 16th Cavalry
No. 7 Divisional Signal Company
Mobile Veterinary Section

Cavalry Brigade (Brigadier-General R. C. Stephen):
14th Hussars
4th Cavalry
7th Lancers (three squadrons strong)
33rd Cavalry (less one squadron)
'S' Battery, R.H.A. 4 guns

CORPS TROOPS
38th Infantry Brigade (Brigadier-General G. B. H. Rice):
Composite Territorial battalion (1st/5th The Buffs and 1st/4th
Hampshire Regiment)
Composite Dogra battalion (37th and 41st Dogras)
97th Infantry

36th Infantry Brigade (Brigadier-General G. Christian):
1st/6th Devonshire Regiment
26th Punjabis
62nd Punjabis
82nd Punjabis
12th Company, Sappers and Miners (less one section)
13th Company, Sappers and Miners
Field Troop, Sappers and Miners
13th Brigade, R.F.A. (2nd, 8th and 44th Batteries) 18 guns
60th and 61st Howitzer Batteries twelve 4·5-inch howitzers
23rd Mountain Battery (less one section)—four 10-pounders
Home Counties Brigade, R.F.A. (less one battery):
  1st/1st Sussex Battery } eighteen 15-pounders
  1st/3rd Sussex Battery
One section 104th Heavy Battery, R.G.A. (two 4-inch guns)
7th Divisional Ammunition Column

SIGNAL UNITS
Wireless, one waggon and two pack stations
No. 1 Army Corps Signal Company
No. 12 Divisional Signal Company (less two brigade sections)
No. 33 Divisional Signal Company (less two brigade sections)

MEDICAL UNITS
No. 18 Cavalry Field Ambulance (two sections)
No. 131 Indian Cavalry Field Ambulance
No. 3 Combined Field Ambulance (two sections)
No. 1 Field Ambulance (less headquarters)
No. 20 Combined Field Ambulance
No. 7 British Field Ambulance
No. 8 British Field Ambulance
No. 19 British Field Ambulance
No. 20 British Field Ambulance
No. 21 Combined Field Ambulance
Nos. 111, 112, 113, 128, 129, 130 Indian Field Ambulances
No. 19 Combined Clearing Hospital
No. 4 Sanitary Section

Various Administrative Units

AIR SERVICE
One flight R.N.A.S. (only one aeroplane serviceable)
'B' Flight, No. 30 Squadron Royal Flying Corps (three serviceable aeroplanes)

EN ROUTE TO JOIN THE TIGRIS CORPS
37th Infantry Brigade (Brigadier-General F. J. Fowler):
1st/4th Somerset Light Infantry
1st/2nd Gurkhas

F   TURKISH PAMPHLET FOUND AT KUT DURING THE SIEGE

'Oh Dear Indian Brethren.

You understand the fact well that God has created this war for setting India free from the hands of the cruel English. This is the reason why all the Rajahs and Nawabs, with the help of brave Indian soldiers, are at present creating disturbances in all parts of India and forcing the English out of the country. Consequently not one Englishman is to be seen in the North West Frontier of Indian districts of Saad, Chakdara, Kohmond and Kohet. Brave Indians have killed several of their officers at Singapore, Secunderabad and Meerut cantonments. Many of the Indian soldiers have on several occasions joined our allies the Turks, Germans and Austrians, of which you must have heard. Oh heroes our friends the Turks, Germans and Austrians are merely fighting for the freedom of our country from the English and you, being Indian, are fighting against them and causing delay. On seeing your degraded position one feels blood in the eyes that you have not got tired of their disgraceful conduct and hatred for you. You should remember how cruelly Maharajah Ranjit Singh of the Punjab and Sultan Tipu were treated by the British Government, and now, when our beloved country is being released from their cruel clutches, you should no further delay the freedom of your country and try and restore happiness to the souls of your forefathers as you come from the same heroic generation to which the brave soldiers of the Dardanelles and Egypt belong. You must have heard about the recent fighting in the Dardanelles when Lord Hamilton was wounded and the cowardly Lord Kitchener ran away at night taking only the British soldiers with him and leaving the Indians behind. The Indian soldiers on seeing this murdered all their British officers and joined the Turks. Nearly everywhere we are finding that our Indian soldiers are leaving the British. Is it not a pity that you still go on assisting them? Just consider that we have left our homes and are fighting for only fifteen or twenty rupees; a subaltern of only twenty or twenty-five years old is drawing a handsome amount as salary from Indian resources while our old

Risaldar [native cavalry commander] and Subadar majors are paid nothing like him—and even a British soldier does not salute them. Is that all the respect and share of wealth we should get for the sake of which we should let them enjoy our country? For instance, see how many of you Indian soldiers were killed during the battle of Ctesiphon and there is nobody to look after the families of the dead and wounded. Brothers, just compare the pay that a British soldier draws with that which you get. Brethren, hurry up. The British Kingdom is now going to ruin. Bulgaria gave them several defeats; Ireland and the Transvaal have left them but you will already know this. H.M. the Sultan's brave Turkish forces which were engaged on the Bulgar frontier before are now coming over to this side in large numbers for the purpose of setting Indians at liberty. We were forced by the British to leave our beloved country and to live in America, but on hearing the news that our country was being freed from English hands, we came over here via Germany—and found our Indian brethren fighting against our friends the Turks. Brethren, what is done, is done, and now you should murder all your officers and come over and join H.M. Sultan's Army like our brave soldiers did in Egypt. All the officers of this force and Arabs have received orders from H.M. Sultan that any Indian soldier, irrespective of any caste, Sikh, Rajput, Mahratta, Gurkha, Pathan, Shiah or Syed, who comes to join the Turks should be granted handsome pay and land for cultivation if he would like to settle in the Sultan's territory. So you must not miss the chance of murdering your officers and joining the Turks to help them to restore your freedom.

G

SIXTEENTH ANNIVERSARY DINNER
RELIEF OF LADYSMITH
TO BE HELD AT THE OPTIMUS HOTEL, KUT
FEBRUARY 28TH AT 8 P.M.

MENU

Hors d'oeuvres

OLIVES   ALL NATIONS

Soup

CHEVAL   D'ARTILLERIE

Fish

SOLE   TRENCH SABOT

Entrée

CUTLETS   JAIPUR PONY SUPERB

Joint

HORSE LOIN   SHELL TRIMMINGS
MULE SADDLE   BHOOSA SAUCE
                           VEGETABLE AU COTTON

Sweets

WINDY LIZZIE PUDDING FLATULENT FANNY SAUCE

Savoury

WHIZZ BANG WITH STARLING ON TOAST

Dessert

LIQUORICE ROOT   MAHAILA SQUARES
CORACLE CHUNKS   BOMB SHELLS

Coffee

S & T SPECIAL AND ARABIAN

Wines

LIQUORICE, TIGRIS WATER, DATE JUICE, ETC.

Cigars   RELIEF SPECIAL
Cigarettes   KUT FAVOURITES

GOD SAVE THE KING EMPEROR

By kind permission of Fritz and Franz the Kut Orchestra will render the following programme during dinner

PART I

1.	Overture	'Here we are again'	Aylmer
2.	Waltz	'Tantalising Aeroplanes'	Turco
3.	Selection	'Shelling Recollections'	Windy Lizzie
4.	Song	'I'm a Long Way from Kut 'Al Amara'	'J.N.'
5.	Fantasie	'The Whizz Bang Glide'	Woolpress Bill
6.	Waltz	'Those Tingling Geggs'	Observer
7.	Selection	'Bombing Melodies'	Miles Running
8.	Two Step	'Be Quick and Get Under'	A. Dugout

INTERVAL

During the interval the anti-aircraft squadron, ably supported by 13-pounder, will give a short sketch entitled 'Aeroplanes and how to scare 'em'

PART II

1.	March	'Over the Hills Not Far Away'	Percy Lake
2.	Cornet Solo	'I Hear You Calling Me'	Aylmer
3.	Selection	'Odiferous Kut'	A. Smell
4.	Song	'We Don't Want to Lose You But We Think You Ought to Go'	Von der Goltz
5.	Waltz	'Mail Time Dreams'	I.E.F.
6.	Romance	'When Shall We meet Again'	Weston-Kee-Craw
7.	Gallop	'The Gee-Hee's Lament'	Stewpot
8.	Regimental Marches	R.F.C. Mechanical Transport Maxim Gun Battery	

H DEFINITION OF TERMS 'WHIZZ-BANG' AND 'WINDY LIZZIE'

The term 'whizz-bang' was World War One trench argot for a shell fired from a gun with a high muzzle velocity and low trajectory such as a field-gun, the expression deriving from the noise it made in flight and the consequent explosion. On the other hand a 'Windy Lizzie' was a low-velocity shell lobbed high in the air by the howitzers, also onomatopoeic. This term seems to have been favoured in Mesopotamia while 'Jack Johnson' (after the then heavy-weight boxing champion) was preferred on the Western Front. It was said that the shell that fell into neither of these acoustic categories and made no noise at all was the one that was going to kill you ('got your name on it') but obviously this theory lacks verification.

BIBLIOGRAPHY

Anonymous: *History of 30 Squadron Royal Air Force*, printed privately, undated

Anonymous: *Short History of the 17th and 22nd Field Companies Sappers and Miners in Mesopotamia 1914–1918*, printed privately, 1918

Anonymous: *Straight Tips for 'Mesopot'*, Thacker, Bombay 1917

Anonymous: *The Devonshire Regiment*, Simpkin, Marshall 1926

Anonymous: *With a Highland Regiment in Mesopotamia*, Times Press, Bombay 1918

Barber, C. H.: *Besieged in Kut and After*, Blackwood 1917

Bishop, H. C. W.: *A Kut Prisoner*, Bodley Head 1920

Blackledge W. J.: *The Legion of Marching Madmen*, Sampson Low 1936

Buchanan, Sir George: *The Tragedy of Mesopotamia*, Blackwood 1938

Candler, E.: *The Long Road to Baghdad* (2 vols), Cassell 1919

Cox, C.: *The Navy in Mesopotamia*, Constable 1917

Cusack-Smith, Sir Berry: *Territorials in Mhow and Mesopotamia* (typescript), c. 1920

Erdman, H.: *Im Heiligen Kreig nach Persien*, Ullstein, Berlin 1918

Ferryman, A. F. Mockler: *The Oxfordshire and Buckinghamshire Light Infantry* (vols xxiv–xxviii), Eyre and Spottiswood 1915–1920

Hall, L. J. (compiler): *Inland Water Transport in Mesopotamia*, Constable 1921

Herbert, A.: *Mons, Anzac and Kut*, Hutchinson 1919

Kearsley, A.: *A Study of the Strategy and Tactics of the Mesopotamia Campaign 1914–1917*, Gale and Polden undated

Kiesling, Hans von: *Mit Feldmarschall von der Goltz Pasha im Mesopotamien und Persien*, Dieterich, Leipzig 1922

Lawrence, T. E.: *Seven Pillars of Wisdom*, Jonathan Cape 1935

Moukbil Bey: *La Campagne de l'Iraq*, Istanbul 1919

Neville, J. E. H.: *History of 43rd and 52nd Light Infantry in the Great War*, Gale and Polden 1938

Nunn, W.: *Tigris Gunboats*, Melrose 1932

Sandes, E. W. C.: *In Kut and Captivity*, Murray 1919

Sandes, E. W. C.: *The Indian Sappers and Miners*, Institute of Royal Engineers, Chatham 1948

Townshend, Sir Charles V. F.: *My Campaign in Mesopotamia*, Butterworth 1920

Wilson, Sir Arnold T.: *Loyalties, Mesopotamia*, Oxford University Press 1930

Official Publications and Documents used as Sources

Mesopotamia Commission, Report of, H.M.S.O. 1917

Mesopotamia, The Campaign in, vols. 1–4, H.M.S.O. 1927–1933

Mesopotamia, Despatches, H.M.S.O. 1917

Mesopotamia, Communiqués to Troops (Townshend), Unpublished, in Imperial War Museum, London.

Historical Record of 110th Mahratta Light Infantry during the Great War, Government of India Press 1927

Orders of 48th Pioneers, Unpublished fragment in Imperial War Museum, London

War Diaries, Unpublished in Imperial War Museum, London

SOURCES

The following abbreviations are used:
Barber: *Besieged in Kut and After* by C. H. Barber
Bishop: *A Kut Prisoner* by H. C. W. Bishop
Buchanan: *The Tragedy of Mesopotamia* by Sir George Buchanan
Candler: *The Long Road to Baghdad* by E. Candler
Lawrence: *Seven Pillars of Wisdom* by T. E. Lawrence
Moukbil Bey: *La Campagne de l'Iraq* by Moukbil Bey
Neville: *History of the 43rd and 52nd Light Infantry* by H. E. H. Neville
Sandes: *In Kut and Captivity* by E. W. C. Sandes
Townshend: *My Campaign in Mesopotamia* by Sir Charles V. F. Townshend

1 THE ROAD TO NOWHERE
1 Mesopotamia Commission's Report
2 Ibid.

2 CTESIPHON
1 Townshend
2 *The Campaign in Mesopotamia*, Vol. 2
3 Ibid.
4 Townshend
5 Bishop
6 Neville
7 Moukbil Bey
8 Ibid.
9 Ibid.
10 Townshend
11 Ibid.
12 Ibid.
13 *The Campaign in Mesopotamia*, Vol. 2
14 Ibid.

3 THE AFFAIR AT UMM AT TUBAL
1 Townshend
2 Ibid.
3 Ibid.
4 Moukbil Bey
5 Ibid.
6 *The Campaign in Mesopotamia*, Vol. 2

4 KUT AL AMARA
1 Barber
2 Ibid.
3 Ibid.
4 Townshend
5 Ibid.
6 Ibid.
7 Ibid.
8 Ibid.
9 Ibid.
10 Bishop
11 Townshend
12 Sandes

5 THE HOLD TIGHTENS
1 Townshend
2 Ibid.
3 Ibid.
4 Sandes
5 Barber
6 48th Pioneers' Orders
7 Ibid.
8 Townshend
9 Ibid.

10 Ibid.
11 Sandes
12 Townshend
13 48th Pioneers' Orders
14 Ibid.

6 THE ASSAULT
1 Moukbil Bey
2 Townshend
3 48th Pioneers' Orders
4 Ibid.
5 Ibid.
6 Bishop
7 Townshend
8 48th Pioneers' Orders

7 MUD AND MUDDLE
1 Buchanan
2 Ibid.
3 Ibid.
4 Townshend
5 Candler, Vol. 1
6 Barber
7 *The Campaign in Mesopotamia,*
Vol. 2
8 Townshend
9 Ibid.
10 Ibid.
11 Ibid.
12 *The Campaign in Mesopotamia,*
Vol. 2
13 48th Pioneers' Orders
14 Townshend
15 Ibid.
16 Ibid.
17 Ibid.
18 Ibid.
19 Ibid.
20 48th Pioneers' Orders
21 Sandes
22 Barber

8 HANNA
1 *The Campaign in Mesopotamia,*
Vol. 2
2 Ibid.
3 Townshend
4 Ibid.
5 Ibid.
6 Townshend
7 *The Campaign in Mesopotamia,*
Vol. 2
8 Townshend

9 48th Pioneers' Orders
10 Sandes
11 48th Pioneers' Orders
12 Townshend
13 Ibid.
14 Ibid.
15 Ibid.
16 48th Pioneers' Orders
17 Ibid.
18 Ibid.
19 Ibid.
20 Townshend
21 Ibid.
22 Ibid.
23 Ibid.
24 Sandes
25 Townshend
26 Ibid.

9 DUJAILA
1 Barber
2 Townshend
3 Ibid.
4 Ibid.
5 Ibid.
6 Ibid.
7 Ibid.
8 48th Pioneers' Orders
9 Townshend
10 Ibid.
11 48th Pioneers' Orders
12 Townshend

10 SANNAIYAT
1 Neville
2 Townshend
3 Ibid.
4 Ibid.
5 Ibid.
6 *The Campaign in Mesopotamia,*
Vol. 2
7 Townshend
8 Ibid.
9 Candler, Vol. 1
10 Townshend
11 48th Pioneers' Orders
12 Ibid.
13 Ibid.
14 Townshend

11 AIR DROP
1 Mesopotamia Commission's
Report

2 Barber
3 Townshend
4 Ibid.
5 48th Pioneers' Orders
6 Neville
7 48th Pioneers' Orders
8 Townshend

12 JULNAR
1 Townshend

13 NEGOTIATIONS FOR SURRENDER
1 Townshend
2 Lawrence
3 Sandes
4 48th Pioneers' Orders
5 Ibid.
6 *The Campaign in Mesopotamia*, Vol. 2

7 Ibid.
8 Ibid.

14 INTERLUDE NEAR MAQASIS
1 48th Pioneers' Orders
2 Herbert
3 Ibid.
4 Ibid.
5 Ibid.
6 Ibid.
7 Ibid.
8 Ibid.

15 THE ROAD TO BAGHDAD
1 Barber
2 *The Campaign in Mesopotamia*, Vol. 2
3 Mesopotamia Commission's Report

INDEX